Skating on Skim Ice

Skating on Skim Ice

The Life and Times of Richard Andrew Gartee

Richard Gartee

Lake and Emerald Publications

Books by Richard Gartee

—Fiction—

Orgone Gizmo

Atlantis Dying

Atlantis Obsession

Lancelot's Grail

Lancelot's Disciple

Ragtime Dudes at the World's Fair

Ragtime Dudes in a Thin Place

Ragtime Dudes Meet a Paris Flapper

—Poetry—

Mountain Breathing

Watching Waves

Canyon Falls

Arbor Encore

—Non-Fiction—

Quest for Lancelot's Arthur

Skating on Skim Ice

The Hippodrome Theatre First Fifty Years

A complete list of currently available titles by the author can be found at www.gartee.com

Published by Lake & Emerald Publications, LLC
www.lepublications.com

ISBN 978-0-9906768-2-9
Third Edition
Library of Congress Control Number: 2018908181

Cover photo: Shutterstock. Back cover photo: Florence Gartee. Unless otherwise credited, interior photographs are public domain or author's family archives.

Typesetting services by BOOKOW.COM

for Ida Helen Rathke Gartee Schroeder
1905 – 1982

Dick Gartee and his children: Richard Gartee and Sharyl Beal.

FOREWORD

My father, Richard Andrew Gartee, known to friends and relatives as Dick Gartee, was born in the Roaring Twenties, survived the Great Depression of the thirties, enlisted in World War II in the forties, and raised a family and learned engineering in the Fabulous Fifties. He watched men walk on the moon in the sixties, constructed factories in the seventies, designed robotics for manufacturers in the eighties, and served as a hospital chaplain in the twenty-first century.

Young adults in the current century cannot even conceive facets of everyday life that were ordinary to him. Dad is among the dwindling few of his generation still alive. The stories my sister and I grew up hearing him tell about his life informed our understanding of the radical paradigm shift he had seen occur in nearly every aspect of our society: economics, agriculture, transportation, education, manufacturing, and communications, to name a few. He not just witnessed, but he also actively participated in significant decades of change as the twentieth century unfolded.

Author Amor Towles writes, "A new generation owes a measure of thanks to every member of the previous generation. Our elders planted fields and fought in wars; they advanced the arts and sciences, and generally made sacrifices on our behalf. So by their efforts, however humble, they have earned a measure of our gratitude and respect."

The generations alive today, including mine, do not plant small farms. Wars seem endless, without defined enemy or purposeful resolution. And too few of us know anything about the sacrifices made by preceding generations or the humility with which they viewed their achievements.

With these ideas in mind, I thought it important to write my father's experiences before they were lost. His stories are more than one man's trials and joys. They are representative of, and similar to, those of his peers, and they give context to periods that altered America forever. Without stories like his, the transformative decades of the last century are just subheads in a history book.

Although this is a biography, not an autobiography, I elected to write it in first person to allow Dad's voice and vernacular to show through as if he were telling the reader the stories he told me. I consider myself fortunate that he was available to review and correct my manuscript, but any factual errors that remain are strictly my own.

CONTENTS

Chapter 1
New Year's 2000

New Year's Day 2000, the first day of a new century, the beginning of the next millennium. The twentieth century was over. Sunrise through our kitchen window filled the room with pale light. I started whistling a happy tune that dated back to my boyhood during the Great Depression.

I turned on the coffeemaker and it worked. Thank God! We still had electricity. For months, news stories had fretted about a problem they called "Y2K," warning us that electric power grids and all manner of services managed by computers would fail January 1. Because early computers didn't have much memory, programs stored dates with two-digit years—for example, "98" instead of "1998." Once we reached the year 2000, the computer wouldn't know if "00" meant 1900 or 2000. A hundred-year date error would cause big problems in nearly every computer system, the news had warned. Programmers for computer companies, utilities, government agencies, and businesses scrambled to update their systems. It must have worked.

I watched my coffee drip into the pot, reassured that we had not been thrown back into the Dark Ages as doomsayers had predicted. I poured a cup, sat down at the table, and waited for my wife to join me for breakfast. Taking a sip, I shook my head in wonder that I was still alive. In nine months, I'd celebrate my seventy-fifth birthday. When I was growing up, the oldest people around me seldom lived past seventy. I'd outlived my predecessors.

When I was a boy, the year 2000 seemed impossibly far in the future. Yet here it was. I'd seen rockets launch and men walk on the moon.

Astronaut Buzz Aldrin walks on the surface of the moon, July 1969. Photo by Neil Armstrong, courtesy of NASA.

Amazing stuff, because when I was a child, there were as many horse carriages as there were automobiles. In the rural communities where I grew up, a lot of people didn't have cars. If they were going somewhere far, a friend or relative who owned a car drove them.

That morning, I drank hot coffee in a well-lit kitchen. Y2K hadn't crashed the nation's power grid. But during my childhood, a lot of farms didn't have electricity; people used oil lamps, kerosene lanterns, or candles. And I'm not describing colonial times or pioneer days. I mean the twentieth century.

Many things we take for granted today were different when I was a boy. For example, grocery stores sold very few prepackaged goods. Flour, sugar, salt, cornmeal, and other staples were kept in big barrels. The grocer would place a paper bag on a scale and, using a scoop, fill it until it weighed the amount the customer had requested. Peanut butter came in a stoneware crock, and the oil would separate and rise to the top. The grocer stirred it with a big paddle until it was mixed and then filled a carton and weighed it. The carton was white cardboard with a wire handle, the type Chinese takeout comes in today.

Boys wore knickers, pants that came just below the knee. I was probably ten or eleven before I got out of knickers. Mine were heavy corduroy and sometimes too hot, but I didn't mind if I could wear my high-top boots. These boots came almost up to my knee and had a pocket on one side with a jackknife inside. Oh, that was big stuff, don't you know?

Back then, haircuts were done with hand clippers. If the guy moved the clippers too quickly, it would pull your hair instead of cutting it. My dad cut my hair for a long time, and when the clippers pulled, I'd instinctively yank away. He'd cuff me and say, "Sit still—can't cut your hair if you wiggle." Dad didn't have to put up with that, though. He went to a barber and paid a quarter for a haircut. Barbers began to use electric clippers right after I started going, and I was glad of it.

Home entertainment and newscasts came via the radio during my childhood. Television stations didn't start broadcasting until after World War II. Our radio was a Crosley table-top model with a big speaker on top. It was staticky, and to get a good signal, we'd have to turn the antenna in the direction of whichever station we wanted to hear. The type of programs we listened to every night aren't broadcast on radio anymore —mysteries, comedies, Westerns, and dramas. Compelling stories with acted dialog and sound effects, but we had to visualize the action in our imaginations. In order to actually see the scenes, we had to go to the movies.

Back then, a night at the movies was really a full night's entertainment. Theaters showed "double features," two full-length movies preceded by a cartoon, a newsreel, and a serial, all for the price of one ticket. The majority of feature films were in black and white, and that remained true up through the 1950s.

For most people, travel of any distance was by train. Even small towns had spur lines and depots. The alternative was the bus. Cross-country trips by automobile were possible, but not popular. Although a portion of the Pennsylvania Turnpike opened in 1940, the freeways and interstate highways we have today weren't built until the 1950s.

Commercial air travel had yet to take off. A few airlines formed in the late 1920s and early 1930s, but the Great Depression, followed by World War II, stalled their development. It wasn't until the 1950s that air travel as we know it today came to be. In contrast, personal flight was popular. There were grass airfields on farms everywhere, and even moderate-size cities, like Monroe, Michigan, had three airfields. A small single-engine plane could be purchased for little more than the price of a new car; flying lessons and a pilot's license were easy to get.

In my kitchen on New Year's Day, I poured another cup of coffee and slid a pan of sweet rolls into the oven. The aroma of warm cinnamon would soon wake my sleeping wife. She'd come into the kitchen and say, "What are you doing up so early?"

I'd explain that I'd been thinking about the different eras in which we had lived. I'd say, "Things we experienced in our life seem incomprehensible to kids born after 1940."

"Even more so for our grandkids, born in the '70s, '80s, and '90s," she might add.

Those are whole other eras, I thought as I imagined this conversation. We were the last generation of single-income families with stay-at-home moms. Today, both parents have careers.

Since that New Year's morning in 2000, almost two decades have passed. Technology today is as different from 1980s technology as 1950s technology was from technology in the 1920s, and I've seen it all. Think of me as a time traveler who has gone ninety-three years into the future—one day at a time.

The past? I can fly back decades at the speed of thought . . . usually.

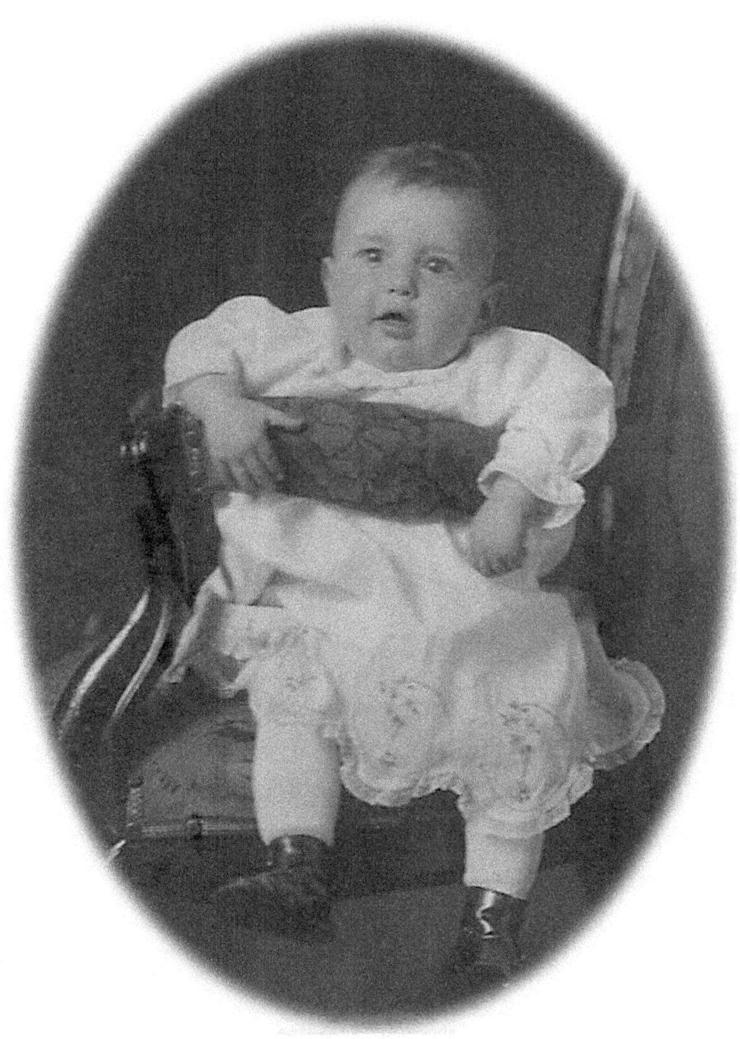

Dick Gartee's baby photograph, age unknown.

Chapter 2
Born on the River Raisin

Mother gave birth to me in a small house on the banks of the River Raisin in Monroe, Michigan. In the 1780s, the river was named *La Rivière aux Raisins* by French settlers because wild grapes grew along its banks. Their settlement, Frenchtown, is now part of Monroe.

River Raisin is 139 miles long, running through six counties of southeastern Michigan and emptying into Lake Erie at Monroe. Along its course are the small towns and villages where I lived and worked during the first half of my life: Monroe, Petersburg, Deerfield, Dundee, and Tecumseh. When I was a boy, my friends and I swam the river in summer and ice-skated on it in winter.

The river has been an important resource for rural industry since the mid-1800s. Dams were built to power gristmills, sawmills, and, later, factories. The largest dam is in Dundee, where I attended high school. My friends and I used to jump off the Dundee Dam and swim in its deep spillway. The dam powered a gristmill until 1910 when it was converted to produce hydroelectric power. In 1934, Henry Ford bought the mill and made it into a factory that produced welding tips used at his auto plants. Today it is a museum.

River Raisin was used by many other industries as well, particularly paper manufacturing, which required the plentiful supply of water the river provided. Across the street from where I was born were three paper companies: Monroe Paper Company, Consolidated Papers, and the River Raisin Paper Company. These were major employers in Monroe, occupying both sides of the intersection of Elm Avenue and North Dixie Highway. My dad worked for them, and so did several of my uncles. Other uncles worked for the railroad, which delivered pulp wood and coal to feed the paper mills.

My father worked for the River Raisin Paper Company, and my parents lived in a house owned by the company. Our house faced North Elm Street and our backyard faced the river. Dad only had to cross the street to go to work.

Although I was too young to know it at the time, about two blocks southeast of my birthplace was the site of the Battle of Frenchtown, a significant massacre that became the rallying cause to drive the British from Michigan during the War of 1812. Today, the site is a national park. When I was a boy, it was a factory.

The three paper mills are gone now.

I don't know how long my parents lived in the company house prior to my birth, but they stayed there until I was three. Then Dad got a sales route selling Watkins products and Eureka vacuum sweepers and moved us to Onsted, Michigan. I remember very little about the Onsted house except it had large columns on the front porch.

Dad didn't make a go of it as a salesman, so he returned to factory work. He and Mom bought a home in Ida, Michigan with the help of my grandfather, Andrew Gartee, who cosigned the mortgage.

Most houses at that time didn't have running water. One of my uncles had a hand pump on his kitchen sink, but everyone else I knew had a hand pump outside and carried in their water. The pump in our yard was a little taller than I was as a boy. It had a long handle you lifted up and pulled down to draw water up from the well. The water would gush out a spout into a bucket for as long as you kept pumping.

Although we got our drinking and cooking water from the outside pump, our new house had a galvanized tank on the second floor that filled itself from a pipe outside when it rained—a kind of indoor cistern. Another pipe inside the house connected the tank to a kitchen faucet.

The water was just unfiltered rain, but it was suitable for washing dishes or a boy's dirty face.

Another labor-saving feature of the new house was a built-in water reservoir on the wood-fired kitchen stove. This provided Mom with ready hot water anytime she cooked. But like most houses then, we had an outhouse instead of an indoor toilet. There was also a barn, and we kept chickens.

My earliest recollection of chickens wasn't favorable. We had a big old rooster, meaner than the devil, and I was just a little guy. If that bugger was in the yard when I went to the outhouse, he would chase me. A couple of times, he got me down and pecked the heck out of me. Dad finally put him in the stew pot.

Dad must have started making pretty good money after we moved to Ida because he and mom saved enough to buy a brand-new Pontiac. But they didn't have it long. Before I tell you what happened to it, let me give a little of my dad's history.

Years before Dad met Mom, he lived for a time in Casper, Wyoming with his brother Ira and Ira's wife. At age seventeen, Dad had left home and driven to Wyoming with Ira's brother-in-law, George Collins, in George's Model-T Ford. Wyoming was still rugged then, only a state for twenty-eight years. In places, the terrain was so steep the car couldn't go forward. Since the Model-T's reverse gear delivered more power to the wheels than its forward gears did, they'd turn the car around and back up the mountains.

Dad found work in Wyoming driving wagon teams of six horses. This really built up his muscles. I remember him showing me the furrows that had been worn in his leather gauntlets where the reins wrapped around them and pulled on his arms. He stayed in Casper for about three years and became a muscular, powerful man who probably weighed 240 pounds. His hands were half again the size of most men's.

By the time he returned to Michigan and met my mother, Congress had passed a constitutional amendment prohibiting the sale of alcohol.

Prohibition lasted from 1919 to 1933. The Monroe County Sheriff's approach to enforcing Prohibition was to hire Dad and his friend, Grant Gody, to clear out speakeasies where bootleggers were selling illegal booze. Grant was about the same size as Dad. The sheriff would send the two of them in to throw everybody out and hold the proprietor until the sheriff came to make the arrest.

Being of good size and having experience rousting bootleggers made Dad overconfident. The night thieves came to steal his and Mom's new Pontiac, he grabbed his shotgun and started for the door. Mother, fearing the thieves had guns and would shoot him, pleaded, "Don't go. Don't go."

Dad wasn't about to let anybody steal their car. They'd only bought it a month before. He ignored Mom's cries and charged out into the yard with his shotgun, but the men got away. The wrecked car was found three days later, totaled, beyond repair. My parents had no car insurance and lost the money they'd paid for it—their whole savings.

John Henry Rathke family. Top row: Elsie, John (Dick's grandfather), Bertha (Dick's grandmother), Hermina (Min); little boy in center row: Herman; bottom row: Edward (Ed), Martin (Brick), Ida, Henry (Hank), Fred.

CHAPTER 3
CRASH OF 1929

The stock market crashed a month after my fourth birthday, plunging the economy into what came to be known as the Great Depression. When it began, I was too little to know anything was happening. Neither my parents nor any of their siblings owned businesses, or stocks, or investments. They were ordinary workers who had followed the trend of their times—leaving the farms they'd been raised on for jobs in factories or on the railroad.

My mother and her siblings were first generation Americans. Her parents, John Rathke and Bertha Howe, came from Germany as babies when their families immigrated in 1871. They married in 1893 and had eight children, all born in the United States. My mother was the second youngest.

Her father owned a farm outside Dundee, Michigan. A railroad track ran along the edge of his property, and he got a contract pumping water to refill the coal-fired steam locomotives. It supplemented his income, but he was mainly a farmer. He sent his kids to a German-Lutheran school, but none of them could remember a word of German later in life.

The Rathke children were Elsie, Fred, Hermina (called Min), Ed, Henry (called Hank), Martin (called Brick), Ida (my mother), and Herman. Both of her parents died when Mom was seventeen. The older children were married by then, making her and Herman the last two still living at home. The Rathke farm was sold and mother moved in with her sister and brother-in-law, Min and Russ Murdoch, who lived near Monroe.

My dad also came from a large family, four boys and five girls. Unfortunately, four of the girls died in infancy, and the fifth died at age thirty. The boys all lived into their seventies. My dad was the youngest. His legal name was Carey, but soon after he was born, Teddy Roosevelt became president and the family nicknamed him Ted. The name stuck, and he was called Ted Gartee for the rest of his life. His brothers were George, Ira, and Walt.

Andrew Gartee family. Top row: Walter (Walt), George, Edith Pearl, Ira; bottom row: Andrew (Dick's grandfather), Carey (Dick's father, also known as Ted), Mary Elizabeth (Dick's grandmother).

The Gartees arrived in America eighty years before the Rathkes, settling in Pennsylvania in the late 1700s. Throughout the 1800s, subsequent generations migrated into the Midwest territories of Ohio, Indiana, and

Michigan. By the time I was born, my grandfather and great-uncles were living in southeast Michigan and in northern Ohio near the Michigan border.

Although the Great Depression started in 1929, it didn't impact our families initially. Dad and my uncles still had jobs, and Uncle George owned a farm. Grandpa Gartee was a housepainter and had developed a special gritty soap to take paint off your hands. He sold it in cans and peddled it all over.

I'm sure my family talked about the economy, and I know President Hoover gave speeches about it on the radio. I was a small child then, so the following are not facts I was aware of at the time. They are things I came to understand as I grew older.

Unemployment had doubled by March 1930, and banks were failing at an alarming rate. By December of that year, the number of failed banks was twice that of the previous year. I don't know if my aunts or uncles lost money in the banks, but my parents' savings had already vanished with the stolen car. People stopped putting money in the bank and withdrew their deposits. Banks stopped loaning money, and businesses everywhere were closing. Companies that had capital and didn't need to borrow money held on to it, slowed production, and laid off workers. There were "runs" on banks where depositors, fearing their bank might be in trouble, would rush the bank demanding their money. Remember the scene in the perennial Christmas movie *It's a Wonderful Life* when Jimmy Stewart returns to find his bank full of people clamoring for their money? Scenes like that happened repeatedly over the next few years.

Herbert Hoover had won the 1928 presidential election on the promise of "a chicken in every pot," but by November 1932 people didn't have either the chicken or a pot to put it in, and he was handily defeated by Franklin Roosevelt.

In February 1933, fearing the largest bank in Detroit was about to go under, the Governor of Michigan closed all the banks in our state for two weeks. Governors in New York and Illinois followed suit, and by March, banks in thirty-eight states were on "bank holiday."

Eight days after his inauguration, President Roosevelt came on the radio and said, "I want to talk for a few minutes with the people of the United States about banking." Roosevelt thanked the public for its "fortitude and good temper" during the banking holiday and said the banks would reopen the next day. Throughout the Depression and into World War II, Roosevelt continued to have calming, thoughtful radio chats with the American public.

However, I've gotten ahead of my story. Back in 1930, the Depression was on but my dad still had his job and our house in Ida, Michigan.

What I actually remember about those years are family gatherings. We'd have the main holidays—Thanksgiving, Christmas, and New Year's—at our house. The adults would shove all the furniture against the walls, roll up the parlor carpet, and square-dance. It takes eight people to square-dance, so there would be at least eight adults, usually Uncle Herm and Aunt Edie, Mom and Dad, Uncle Ed and Aunt Loi, and a couple more of Mom's family, plus all their kids. Uncle Ed would call the square dances and play the mouth organ. Dad would hum on a comb.

Wedding receptions were held at a hall like the Odd Fellows. They'd serve draft beer and dance to music from a guy playing a fiddle and maybe another playing a guitar. There would also be a caller. They'd square-dance, then round dance. I didn't care which. I danced as soon as I got big enough—not very well, but I danced. Uncle Brick's wife, Aunt Alice, was a tall, heavyset woman, yet light on her feet. She could dance. If you had her for a partner, you could just float across the floor.

At Christmas, Uncle Ed would dress up as Santa and pass out gifts. We kids weren't fooled. We knew it was Ed, but it was fun. The Rathkes celebrated Christmas together for a few years, but then it got to where some of the men would be half-drunk and the women would squabble over who brought what food and who hadn't brought enough. Eventually, they ended big Christmas get-togethers, visiting each other's houses during the holiday season instead. We'd go to Aunt Elsie's, then Uncle Herman's, then Uncle Fred's, continuing until we either got to everyone or they made it to our house.

Even though they argued like brothers and sisters will, Mom's family members were always visiting one another, often to play cards. In this era before television, card games were a principal form of entertainment—better than sitting around listening to radio programs because you could converse while you played.

Aunt Elsie didn't play cards, and Uncle Brad didn't care a lot for cards, but the rest of our family played euchre, a popular card game in Michigan. I learned it at a young age, and whenever someone got up from the table to get something, I'd slip into the empty seat and play that person's hand.

Euchre is a fast-paced game played by two teams, each with two members. The game uses a twenty-four card deck that consists of nines through aces in each suit. Each player is dealt five cards, and the top card of the remaining deck is turned up. This is a trump game. Play begins clockwise from the dealer, and each player has an opportunity to say whether the suit of the exposed card will be trump. If a player "orders" the card to be trump, the dealer picks it up and discards a card in exchange. The team that orders trump must win at least three tricks or they are "euchred" and the opposing team scores two points.

When it came to euchre, Mother's brothers were fierce competitors, yelling at each other if someone misplayed or should have trumped a trick and didn't. If one team got euchred, the other might gleefully rub it in. But whatever was said was forgotten by the next hand, and no one held grudges. However, that was not true of my father's family—the Gartee brothers didn't get along.

I remember family dinners at Grandpa and Grandma Gartee's house in Petersburg as being just awful. Uncle Walt, Dad, Uncle Ira, and sometimes Uncle George would be there. Uncle Walt and Dad would get into heated arguments with one of them threatening to knock the other one on his ass—nasty, nasty rows ensued just about every time they were together. Walt had probably been jealous of Dad since childhood because, as the "baby" of the family, Dad had been favored. Dad's animosity stemmed from his belief that Walt was taking advantage of Grandpa because Walt and his children lived in Grandpa's house without paying.

Uncle George was the oldest and got along with his brothers, but Grandma had him prior to marrying Grandpa, who adopted George. Adoption made him a Gartee, but sometimes one brother would say something like, "George isn't a real Gartee." That would set Dad off and they'd be up in arms. Grandpa always treated George like his son, but he'd never step in when his boys were squabbling at the dinner table. I much preferred visiting my mother's family.

We remained in Ida, Michigan until I was in the fourth grade. I went to Ida High School, which included first through twelfth grades. It was close to our house, and I just walked across a field to get there.

Next door to us was a slaughterhouse owned by Charlie Mathew. He butchered hogs. I used to go over to Mathew's slaughterhouse every chance I'd get because he liked me, and while I talked to him, he'd shave off a little piece of smoked ham, hand it to me on his knife, and say, "Try this. You think this is ready to eat yet, Dick?"

Oh, it'd be so good. And he made really good cracklings, the crisp pork skin remaining after fat has been rendered. Charlie got all the lard he could possibly get out of them with a big press. He squeezed them down until nothing more came out. He'd give me fresh cracklings, not a lot, but I'd get some off him. He also made a smoked sausage cured all the way through so you could eat it without cooking. He'd give me a hunk of that to try. So I'd hang out over there every chance I got.

Throughout the 1930s, most farmers didn't have tractors; they farmed with horses. They needed to get to the feed stores and grist mill, but they farmed all day, including Saturday. On Sunday, stores were closed. So small villages kept stores open one night a week for farmers to shop. Villages that were close together chose different nights, Deerfield on Tuesday, Ida on Wednesday, and Petersburg on Thursday. To draw people in, the villages would show free movies. First there'd be a cartoon, and then there would be a serial like *Tarzan and Jane*. Serials were short chapters of an epic that ended each week in a cliff-hanger. You had to come back the next week to see what happened to the hero. This was followed by a regular Hollywood movie, maybe a Western or a mystery or a drama.

Aunt Elsie's husband, Brad Munson, was the custodian for Dundee schools. During the Depression, he'd take the school projector to Deerfield and Petersburg to show movies. If I spent the night with Aunt Elsie and Uncle Brad, I could go with him and see a different movie because he didn't show the same one as they did in Ida. That meant I'd sometimes get to see movies two or three times a week. He got the movies through the mail in big containers containing several reels.

The main feature always had an intermission while the projectionist changed reels for the second half. During intermission, everybody would go downtown and buy one last thing before the stores closed. The kids would go for ice cream if they had any money. You could buy a Popsicle or Fudgsicle for five cents. Sometimes, when you'd eaten it, you'd see the word "free" on the stick. When that happened, you could turn it in and get another one for free. It was a good deal because you got a "free" stick pretty often.

On Friday nights, Jim Malone's, a tavern in downtown Ida, served a fish sandwich, a dill pickle, and potato chips for thirty-five cents. The place filled up on Fridays because it was a meal for a modest price. Dad liked it because he could get a pitcher of beer for a quarter. A bottle of soda pop cost a nickel. Mom and I would each get a soda, which left him with the whole pitcher of beer. Some Fridays, Uncle Russ and Aunt Min would drive over and join us at Malone's. Uncle Russ liked to drink beer as much as Dad did.

One Saturday night, we were getting ready to go out. Since we didn't have an indoor bathroom, we would set up a washtub in the kitchen to take our baths. Everyone had to stay out of the kitchen until the person bathing was finished. Mom and Dad were having their baths and I was in the dining room, dressed and waiting on them. On the table was a cake Mom had made.

Now, in those days there were no box mixes. All cakes were made from scratch. If you got the ratio of flour or liquid or shortening wrong, or the oven temperature wasn't right, the cake would "fall," meaning the batter would rise and then collapse. The cake would come out lopsided or sunken in the center.

The cake I was eying had fallen in the center, but we couldn't afford to waste it. Mom frosted it anyway. She was always short on powdered sugar, so she made the icing thin. Because the cake had a dip, the icing collected in the center.

I yelled, "Hey, Mom, can I have a piece of cake?"

She thought a minute before replying, "Okay, one piece."

I cut out the center, right where all the icing was. Made sense to me; "one piece" was what she'd said.

Chapter 4
Times Get Hard

When I was six or seven, I developed yellow-jaundice. I was very sick, and the treatment included total bed rest. Keeping me in bed was no little chore. I had a youth bed with sides on it. I'd climb out and my parents would put me back in. Then I'd climb out again.

Sometime after I recovered from jaundice, the Great Depression really hit. Uncle Herman was without a job, and he and Aunt Edie didn't have a place to live. Our house was two stories with bedrooms upstairs and downstairs. They moved into our upstairs. They only lived with us for a couple of years. Mom and Aunt Edie had gotten along before, but living together was a different matter. I think Aunt Edie resented having to live in someone else's house.

Maybe as a kid I hadn't realized how bad the Great Depression had gotten until Uncle Herm and Aunt Edie moved in, but then Dad got laid off, too. There wasn't a job to be had anywhere.

Mother bought flour, made bread, and sold it for five or ten cents a loaf—delivered to your door. She replaced her wood-burning cookstove with a kerosene stove to gain better control of the oven temperature. The house, though, continued to be heated with wood. On weekends, Dad and Uncle Herm went to local farmers who needed downed trees cleared. They cut up the fallen trees, split the logs, and chopped it into the firewood we burned for heat. If there was extra wood, they'd sell it.

For my part, I raised rabbits. When they were grown, Dad would kill them and Mom would cook them. Rabbits are good to eat and cost us little to raise. I'd take my wagon and a big burlap sack six blocks to a guy who had alfalfa hay. For a nickel, he'd let me go up in his haymow and take all the chaff I could sweep up. I'd fill my bag until it bulged, tie it shut, drop it into my wagon below, climb down the ladder, and pull my wagon home. This would be enough hay to feed my rabbits for a month.

Dad got a job on a farm five miles away. Every morning he'd walk there, work a ten- or twelve-hour day, and walk back home. He earned five dollars a week—a dollar a day, plus a sack of food: vegetables, butter, or milk. The groceries helped, but walking five miles after a full day's work, you don't carry much.

At the end of our street, was a large pasture. Mother and I would go there in spring and dig fresh dandelions. Then she'd fix dandelion greens for us to eat. In summer, she and I walked the railroad track out to see Leona Cooper, Mom's first cousin on her mother's side. We'd have lunch there and walk back. Asparagus grew wild in the ditches, and Mom would harvest that, too.

When hunting season came, Dad, Uncle Herman, Uncle Hank, and Uncle Russ hunted pheasants, rabbits, and quail. If Uncle Russ shot more than they could eat, Aunt Min would cold-pack the extra for later. (Cold-packing is a canning method for preserving raw foods in glass jars.)

During the Depression, few people had money for new clothing. If our clothes got torn, Mom stitched or patched them. She always said, "It's no disgrace to wear something mended as long as it's clean and ironed." There was no reason to feel ashamed; my friends, and even their parents, were in the same situation. Everything was repaired for as long as could be. You didn't throw something away and buy a new one. These days, my great-granddaughters buy ripped jeans with ragged knees—and pay extra for the privilege. My mother would have never let me out of the house with a tear in my pants.

* * *

I was ready to start fourth grade when my parents lost their house. Grandpa Gartee, who had cosigned the mortgage, didn't have enough money to take over the payments, so the bank foreclosed. After that, we rented a house from Frank King. It was located on South Custer Road, five miles from Ida. It was the first place I ever lived in that had an indoor bathroom. Our previous houses in Onsted and Ida had outhouses.

Sometime after we moved to South Custer Road, Dad caught on at Woodall, a company in Monroe that made auto interior parts for Chrysler and other car manufacturers. It wasn't much of a job at first. He'd go in, work for maybe two hours, and then they'd tell the men to clock out and wait. He'd sit on a bench until there was more work to do, then clock back in. His whole day would go like that, working an hour or two at a time. But it was a job.

He stuck with Woodall until times got better, and then he became a full-time employee. Dad stayed with the company until he retired thirty years later.

Pictured left to right: Dick Gartee, John King, Jason King.

Chapter 5
Life on South Custer Road

I transferred from Ida High School, where each grade had its own classroom, to King School, a one-room schoolhouse that was next door to our new place on South Custer Road. My teacher, Miss Anna Haystead, had grown up with and gone to school with my dad.

In those days, a teacher had to sweep out her own school, clean her own blackboards, tend her own fire, and carry in water from an outside pump. Most of the time, we boys would clean off the blackboard, carry in wood or coal to be used in the stove the next day, and take out the ashes. Our teachers had their hands full with twenty-five children ranging from grades one through eight, all together in a single room.

The fourth grade consisted of two girls, plus John King and me. There were four kids in the eighth grade, three or four in the seventh grade, two students in sixth, two more in the fifth, and eight or nine spread across the grades below me.

It sounds like a heck of a way to get an education, but you learned a lot because you would hear the older kids reciting, spelling, and doing their math, and you couldn't help but pick up a little of it. By the time you reached the next grade, the lessons were already familiar.

John King had three brothers, Jason King and Tom and Jack Woodruff, and a sister, Lorraine King. They lived diagonally across the road from us. John and I became best friends and remained so for life.

Although the Depression years were hard, my friends and I still had fun. We liked to play baseball and competed against Bridge School, a two-room school a few miles away on Ida-Maybee Road. That was how I met Cal Zorn, another friend I had for life. When we were grown and I was living in Tecumseh, Cal became the city manager of Tecumseh. He held the position until he retired.

Mr. Upjohn, who was Dad's boss in Monroe, had a nice Irish terrier, but his son had severe asthma and was allergic to her. Upjohn knew I didn't have a dog and asked Dad if I'd like to have her. Dad said, "I'm sure he would."

I named her Ginger, and we bonded at once. Wherever you saw me, you saw her. Since we lived next to the school, Ginger would come over whenever we were out in the schoolyard. When we played baseball, she'd want to play with us, but we'd chase her away: "Get out of here, Ginger. We got a ball game going."

She'd sit at the edge of the field and watch. Pretty soon, somebody would miss the ball. She would have it in a snap, and home she'd go with the whole school chasing after her, yelling, "Ginger, bring that ball here."

Dick, age eleven, with his Irish terrier, Ginger.

North Custer Road and South Custer Road ran parallel on either side of the River Raisin. We now lived just a hop, skip, and a jump from the river, and it was a boy's paradise. Although I never took swimming lessons, I'd swim and dive in the deeper pools during the summer. I taught myself to swim—just got in and paddled around until I got better.

Behind John King's house, a big rock stuck up out of the river. We'd get on top of it and dive in, but you had to dive shallow because the base of the rock extended out into the riverbed. One day, I dove a little too deep and hit my head on the bottom ledge of that rock. It knocked me cuckoo. We could have swum further upriver, where the water was deeper, but the bottom there was silt and we didn't like it.

In the winter, the River Raisin would freeze. We'd skate on it and play hockey. Sometimes we'd skate the river all the way from the King house to Monroe, five miles there and five miles back. Just for something to do.

"Hey, let's skate to Monroe."

"Okay, let's go."

Aunt Min and Uncle Russ lived on the river, too, about a half-mile from King School. There was a steep hill next to their house. In winter, when snow covered the hill, you could slide down it and go way out onto the ice. One year, after a good snowfall, the whole school went sledding there. I had a big Red Flyer sled, about five feet long, with steel runners and a wooden crossbar you held onto and turned to steer. I got a running start, plopped face-down on that thing, and started downhill when *whomp*, something fell right on top of me. It was Miss Haystead! She was on my back, holding my hands onto the steering bar. We flew down the hill and out onto the ice, laughing all the while.

When we boys played hockey, we had to use a tin can. No one had money to spare for a puck. Then Christmas came. I asked for a hockey puck, and somehow my parents got the money together. I opened my present and there was this official hockey puck—made of solid rubber, just like the professionals used. Oh, it was nice!

One day, we were playing hockey where the river was about eight feet deep. It was frozen solid where we were playing, but if you got further out, the ice was thin, what we called "skim ice." Well, someone hit my puck out onto the skim ice.

We tried lying down to reach the puck with a hockey stick. We tried holding someone's feet so they could edge out further. Still, we weren't able to reach it. Someone else got back and took a run at it but couldn't get out far enough.

I was one of the fastest skaters among us, also the smallest and lightest. I said, "Let me get a good start. I'll go fast as I can, bat it back, and let my momentum carry me onward because trying to skate might break the skim ice."

Sounds foolish, but it was the only hockey puck among all the boys, and it was valuable to us. So, I did it. Skated out and hit the puck. It came back. Then *whoosh*, I plunged into eight feet of frigid water. I tried pulling myself out, but the edges of the ice kept breaking off and making the hole larger.

John, Jason, and the other boys playing hockey with us lay on the ice and stretched out their hockey sticks. I finally got to where the ice quit breaking off, and they pulled me out. My skates quickly turned into two balls of ice. I couldn't get them off with the laces frozen, but I discovered I could ride my bike with my skates on. I had to, I didn't have a choice—our house was a mile away, and my pants were starting to freeze stiff.

Mom gave me hell for the five minutes it took to draw a hot bath. Then she put me in the tub to thaw. Thank God we now had a house with indoor plumbing. When I was warmed, I put on my pajamas and she sent me to bed. I didn't see any reason for her to get excited about it. I thought, *So I fell through the ice. I got out, didn't I?* But she said, "You're going to drown one of these days."

Later that same winter, we were playing hockey on the river and Ginger was sitting on the riverbank, watching, waiting. Somebody made a bad shot, the puck came close enough for her to get it, and home she ran with the puck in her mouth.

Home was a mile from where we were playing hockey and she had a head start. By the time we got our skates off, put our shoes on, and rode our bikes there, we couldn't find a trace of it. We looked through the snow for dog tracks and looked for any sign of where she might have dug to bury it. I looked the next day and the day after, but the puck wasn't to be found.

Spring came. Mom had a big flower bed, and it was my job to spade it. I was out there spading away and what did I turn up? My hockey puck. I don't know how Ginger buried it in the frozen ground or how she did it without leaving marks where she'd dug, but there it was. I kept that puck well into adulthood, eventually giving it to one of my grandsons.

Another winter memory from those years was Dad towing me around Lake Erie on my sled. The Great Lake froze over in winter. Dad used a rope to tether my sled to the car bumper and drove out onto the ice with me sliding across Lake Erie behind him.

CHAPTER 6
A PIG FOR A BIKE

Twice I've mentioned riding home on my bicycle, and you might wonder —if I couldn't afford to lose a hockey puck, how did I get a bike?

Dad's brother, Uncle George, owned a farm in Deerfield, Michigan. His sow farrowed a litter with too many piglets for her to nurse. Uncle George gave me the runt and said, "It's just going to die. If you want to take it home and see if you can raise it, it's yours."

I named him Pork and bottle-fed him until he could eat solid food. Pork liked to be clean, and I'd brush him. He was all white, and he did not like mud. Unlike other pigs, he'd walk around a mud hole and lie where it was dry. Raising him, I realized that not all pigs wanted to wallow in mud. They do it to get cool. But Pork didn't need mud. His pen was shady, and since he was the only pig there, he didn't have to compete for shade.

A little peach tree, six or seven feet tall, shaded his pen. Its lower branches were two or three feet off the ground. Pork ate the low branches off the tree, and then one day I looked out the window and caught him sitting up on his hind legs to eat the higher ones. I thought, *Well, he likes the peach leaves, so he might like beet tops.* Thereafter, whenever Mom sent me out to dig beets, I'd cut off the tops and call him: "Hey, Pork." I'd hold the tops up, beyond his reach, and he'd sit up like a dog begging for a treat.

When Pork grew to weigh three hundred pounds, I told my folks I was going to sell him.

"How much do you want for him?" Dad said.

"Ten cents a pound," I said. I'd already done the math in my head. Gecko-Martin's hardware store in Monroe had a beautiful red bicycle with wide chrome fenders and big whitewall balloon tires. I'd gone there two or three times to look over that bike. I had negotiated and the store agreed to take thirty bucks for it.

I collected my thirty dollars from Dad, bought my bike, and showed it to my friends at school. Everyone admired it.

One day, Helen Aper, a girl whose father owned an orchard up the road, said, "Dick, you'll ride me home, won't you?"

I wasn't all that big, and Helen was a fairly grown-up girl, a head taller than I was. Peddling with her on my bike all the way from King School to her farm was the hardest, longest ride ever.

Dad and Uncle Russ took Pork over to Charlie Mathew's slaughterhouse in Ida. They'd had more than a few beers before they went there. Charlie said he would butcher the hog, but they'd have to do the killing. So, they discussed the situation and decided Charlie would chase the pig out the door, Uncle Russ would shoot him, and Dad would cut his throat to bleed him.

In front of the slaughterhouse was a mud puddle. As I said, Pork disliked mud, and maybe he sensed what they had in mind. When Mr. Mathew chased him out, Pork put his head down and dumped my dad on his ass in the middle of the puddle. Then Pork raced all over the field.

Mr. Mathew said they couldn't kill him that day because his blood had gotten too hot with adrenaline. So they had to go back to do it the next day.

Now, both Dad and Uncle Russ like to drink, and when Dad was drinking, he could get a temper. One night, a while after I got my bicycle, he drove into the garage drunk and hit the bike, breaking its pedal. He came in the house, hauled me out of bed, and spanked me, telling me it was my fault for putting my bike where he would hit it. I wasn't to blame, though. I'd parked it right where I was supposed to and he'd only run into it because he was soused.

* * *

Besides raising a pig, I tried many other money-making endeavors throughout my boyhood.

Dad grew cucumbers one year, and I asked if I could plant some extra. When mine came on the vines and reached finger-length, I harvested them because the ladies liked that size to make sweet pickles called gherkins. I filled a ten-pound bag and Dad took it to a lady. She gave me a lousy quarter for the whole ten pounds. I quit the pickle business right then.

John King's grandma raised red and black raspberries, strawberries, and currants. I picked her berries for four cents a quart, but not her currants. Currants are tiny, about the size of a green pea. I could pick and pick and never get a quart. Nope, didn't want any part of picking currants.

John's uncle, George King, had corn planted in long, long rows. The crop wasn't full height yet, but it was too tall to cultivate and he wanted the weeds out. He paid a nickel a row to hoe his corn, but to do a good job took a couple of hours per row. I'd no more than reach the end of one row and hoe a second one back and it was noon. We'd go up to the house for lunch, then come back and work the rest of the afternoon. I'd get four rows of corn hoed and make twenty cents. I only did that one year.

The next year I picked tomatoes for a nickel a hamper. Tomatoes back then grew big. I could set a hamper between two vines and fill it half full off one vine, turn around, and fill it the rest of the way from the second vine. I'd set it out in the path, get another hamper, and fill that one. Someone else came along with a horse and cart, loaded up the hampers, and hauled them to the canning companies. I could make money picking tomatoes.

There were three canning companies in Dundee, and one summer I worked for VanDeVenter's Canning. They cooked the tomatoes in a big vat. They'd put me in the vat between batches to scrub it out because I was small. The man in charge of the vat would run water in there; I'd roll up my pants, get in barefoot, and scour the residue off the sides. Then I'd get out and he'd rinse it. If I had missed anywhere, I'd get back in and clean it again. But that man chewed tobacco, and one time while he had a big batch cooking, I saw him spit right in it.

For a time, I mowed a one-acre cemetery across the road from King School with an old-fashioned reel mower. This type of mower doesn't have a motor. I had to push it to make the cutting blades turn. I also trimmed the grass around every tombstone with hand clippers. The job paid three dollars a week.

One year, I helped a farmer who lived near the Kings to thresh. I drove the man's team through the field while men pitched wheat bales onto the wagon. I worried because the wagon wobbled badly when the stackers made the load uneven, and I feared I would tip it. I was small and the horses were big. I decided that job was not for me.

For three summers, I stayed at Uncle George's house during harvest. He owned a threshing rig and we'd take it from farm to farm. My job was to bag the wheat. I'd stand in the grain wagon holding a bag under a chute, and I'd fill it until it was as heavy as I could drag. When the bag was full, I'd turn a lever, like a damper in a chimney, and it would stop the flow. I'd tie the bag, drag it to the side, and then get another bag and fill that one. When we finished, Uncle George would move the tractor and threshing machine to the next farm and get it set up for the following morning. I'd drive a horse-drawn wagon over and pick him up. Then we'd go home and do chores.

The farm women would throw big feeds for the threshers. Boy, I liked that. Every woman made her special pie recipe—apple or peach. The last day of threshing, they always had beer for the men and ice cream for the women and us younger boys.

Chapter 7
King School Years

Sadly, during the summer between my fourth- and fifth-grade years, Miss Haystead's appendix burst, and she died. When school started in the fall, we had a new teacher, Mrs. Lipp. Her husband was a pharmacist in Monroe. John King and I told Mrs. Lipp we fifth graders wanted to study history. She pointed to the sole bookcase that was the King School library, and said, "If you can find four books plus one for me in there, I'll teach it."

So we found five world history books and she taught us. I continued to study history in the sixth and seventh grades and began civics in the eighth. By the time I left King School, I'd had four years of history. When I took history in high school, I'd open the book, read the title at the top of the page to see what the teacher would discuss that day, close my book, answer her questions, take a test, and make an A.

I enjoyed King School. Once a week, we had music class. The teacher played piano and we sang songs from an old paperback song book. She'd ask the class what we wanted to sing, and the kids always chose "Loch Lomond." I'm sure you've heard the song, probably sung it in school yourself:

> O ye'll tak' the high road, and I'll tak' the low road,
>
> And I'll be in Scotland before ye,
>
> But me and my true love will never meet again,
>
> On the bonnie, bonnie banks o' Loch Lomond.

When we had a school program, every kid got to be in it. Talent didn't matter. If you couldn't sing, you might recite a poem instead. Everybody got a part, and all the parents applauded each kid's performance. For stage curtains, we stretched a wire across the room and Mrs. Lipp hung sheets on it—all dyed the same color. Two kids would pull the sheets open and closed between acts.

One year, a magician performed at our school. He brought me onstage, tied me up, ran his rope around me, and put my coat on me with an end of the rope coming out of each sleeve. He'd have to cut me in half to get that rope out. Holding the ends of the rope, he counted, "One, two, three." Then he pulled, and out came the rope. There I stood holding my arms out. Nobody knew how he did it, including me. I thought that guy was wonderful.

On my tenth birthday, Mother invited the whole school to our house for ice cream and cake to celebrate. Mrs. Lipp dismissed class early so kids who had farm chores could go to the party and still get home on time.

The kids crowded around our dining room table. We barely fit, even with the table leaves in. Scrunched together or standing up, everyone found a place at the table. Then Mom came out of the kitchen carrying the saddest cake you ever saw. It had fallen, leaving one side taller than the other. As usual, Mom was short on powdered sugar so she'd thinned the icing to make enough to cover the cake, and it ran. One side of the cake had a lot of icing and the other side had hardly any.

The promise of cake excited my classmates, but I looked at it and thought, *Oh God, Mom, you bake better cakes than this. Why would you bring out this cake in front of my friends?*

A bakery in Toledo, Sherlock's, delivered in our area. Sherlock's sold a fifteen-inch cake that was professionally decorated with colored icing. I had really set my heart on a cake from Sherlock's, but Mom had brought out this embarrassment instead. I was looking for a way to crawl under the table when she said, "Wait, I forgot something." She went into the kitchen and returned with a cake from Sherlock's. It had ten burning candles and "Happy Birthday Dick" written on it in icing.

The school system held district spelling bees at Bridge School because it had two rooms and ours only had one. In seventh grade, I was a finalist in the district bee. Martha Long, the preacher's daughter, and I were the final two. She was smart as a whip. We'd already gone through the main word list and a supplementary list. We were on the second supplementary list when I lost because Dr. Kelly's daughter mispronounced the word "prescription." I made her pronounce it again. She pronounced it "per-scription" a second time. I figured a doctor's daughter must know, so I spelled it "p-e-r . . ." and it wiped me out of the contest.

Bridge School in Raisinville Township, where the school district held spelling bees because Bridge had two schoolrooms and King School had only one.

King School always had a picnic at the end of the school year. Every family brought a dish to pass, and we'd have a ball game against anybody in the community who wanted to play. We put the taller boys in the outfield and pitcher positions to catch fly balls. The year I was twelve, I was the catcher. Russell Stokes was pitching.

Walter Gerwick, a farmer we nicknamed Cap, was playing on the opposing team. His nephew, Bob, played second base for us. Bob had graduated eighth grade that year and was going on to high school. He was bigger than the other eighth graders and weighed about 170 pounds.

Cap got a hit and stood on first base taunting us. "I'm going to steal on you guys."

I called a time-out and we met at the pitcher's mound for a little conference. I told Stokes, "If Cap threatens to steal second, you pitch out and I'll catch it in a position to throw to Bob. We'll get Cap out."

We resumed play and Cap edged off first, still taunting us. So I signaled Stokes for the pitchout. He threw and Cap took off for second. I stepped out, caught it, and made a perfect throw to second base. Bob caught the ball and Cap slid into base feet first, knocking Bob's legs out from under him. Bob landed on Cap, breaking Cap's ankle.

We stopped the game and took Cap to the doctor. He came back home on crutches. Cap had eight milk cows, and in those days there weren't any milking machines. You milked by hand. I felt bad because I felt I'd instigated it, so I went to Cap's and asked him how he intended to milk. He said, "I don't know."

"Well," I said, "I'll do it for you." I milked his cows morning and evening until Cap could get around.

CHAPTER 8
MY WORLD COLLAPSES

I completed eighth grade at King School. The economy had improved and we moved from South Custer Road to a house on Detroit Avenue in Monroe. I had just started my freshman year at Monroe High School when, on my thirteenth birthday, my world collapsed.

One of my aunts had given me a quarter for my birthday, and I knew of an ice cream shop on Monroe Street that sold big double-dip cones for a nickel. I asked Mom if I could ride my bike there. She said, "Sure."

I bought my ice cream cone, but it was difficult to ride with the cone in my hand and I didn't want it to melt. So I was standing with my bike at the intersection, licking away, when Dad and Dorothy Schultz, our neighbor from South Custer Road, went winging by in a car. I thought nothing of it.

I finished my ice cream and rode home. "Hi, Mom," I said. "Seen Dad."

"You did?" He'd told her he'd be working late, but I didn't know. "Where did you see him?"

"Oh, he and Dorothy Schultz were in a car going out Monroe Street toward Toledo."

Now, I never heard the scrap between them when Dad got home, so I don't know what was said, but when I came home from school the next day, Mom had his clothes packed and told me Dad wouldn't be living with us anymore. For years I felt guilty and believed that I shouldn't have told on Dad, that I was somehow responsible for their divorce. It doesn't make sense, but sometimes that's the way kids think.

Without Dad, Mom and I couldn't afford to stay in the Detroit Avenue house. She found us an apartment for ten bucks a month. It wasn't much of an apartment.

Mom picked up all the work she could while hunting for a steady job to latch on to. Dad was supposed to pay fifteen dollars a week child support, but he only paid it when he felt like it. When he didn't, she'd have to go to the courthouse and complain. They'd call Dad in and he'd pay thirty or forty-five dollars to cover his back payments. He'd pay regular for the next couple of weeks and then stop. We'd have no money again, and Mom would have to decide whether to make rent, pay the light bill, or buy groceries.

My mom could really iron shirts—make one look like it just came out of the package. She found steady work in the home of a lawyer in Monroe keeping house and ironing his shirts. He gave her room and board and ten bucks a week, but there was no place for me. So I moved in with John King's family.

The Kings' farm was not in the Monroe school district. I would have to pay tuition to continue at Monroe High, but Dundee High School was free because I lived with the Kings, so I changed schools. I didn't mind transferring to Dundee High because my friends from King School went there and so did the guys from Bridge School who I'd played in baseball. There were also kids at Dundee that I knew from the church Mom and I attended while we lived on South Custer Road.

However, Dundee didn't have school busses. We had to get there on our own. John, his brothers, and I carpooled with the Sorter boys. I didn't have a car, but I could help drive. The King boys and I would drive one week and the Sorters the next.

In Michigan, if you lived in the country more than a certain distance from school and passed a driving test, you could get your driver's license at age thirteen. I had no problem passing the test. I'd been driving since I was eleven. Mom had taught me while we were living on South Custer Road. The Kings had a mile-long lane back to their woods, where we had planted a garden. Mom would let me drive us there to get vegetables and then drive us back to the house. All cars back then had manual transmissions, so I learned to shift gears. When Mom went to Monroe to get groceries, I'd badger her to let me drive. Sometimes she'd let me drive toward town, and sometimes I'd get to drive home.

I wasn't the first person Mom taught to drive. She had also tried to teach her father-in-law, my Grandpa Gartee. He'd bought a brand-new, four-door Model T and was sobbing one day that none of his boys would teach him how to drive it. They claimed they couldn't do anything with him. So Mom said, "Well, come on, I'll show you how to drive." We got in the car. Grandpa drove, Mom rode in the passenger seat, and I sat in the backseat.

In Petersburg, where Grandpa lived, there was a railroad track. The highway had an "S" curve so it crossed the track and then, a little further down the road, doubled back and crossed the track again. Mom told Grandpa, "Turn here." He did.

"Now, turn and go across the railroad track." He did.

"Turn again, to the left," she said, but he didn't turn.

He drove straight across the road, through a shallow ditch, and out into a field—with her yelling, "Stop! Stop!" I was laughing the whole time.

Mother finally got him to stop. She got out, walked around to the driver's side, and said, "You slide over. I'll get us out of here." She drove us back to his house and said, "I'm not going to teach you anymore."

I don't know who taught him after that, but he eventually drove.

* * *

After living about four weeks with John King's family, I moved into Dundee and lived with Uncle Brad and Aunt Elsie. Uncle Brad was still custodian at the Dundee schools, and when I lived with them, he got me a job mowing the football field. The school had a big riding mower, and I liked that. He paid me a dollar or two to do it, and he mowed around the school buildings himself.

I remember Aunt Elsie loved marmalade on her toast in the morning. I never cared for it because I didn't like the peel in it. But it was sweet, so I'd eat a little. Also, I ate whatever she put in front of me.

Later in the semester, I moved in with Uncle Herm and Aunt Edie for the rest of my freshman year. Because I stayed with family I didn't realize it at the time, but in retrospect, it must have been difficult on me to be constantly shuttled from one place to the other.

While we were living apart, Mom worried about where I was, what I was eating, who I would stay with next. At the end of my freshman year, she decided she had to move to Dundee because she couldn't make a go of it in Monroe and couldn't go on shuffling me from aunt to uncle. She got a job taking care of Mr. Peters, an old man who lived up the road from Uncle Brad and Aunt Elsie. We got room and board, and Mom earned the ridiculously low wage of five dollars a week. But we had a roof over our heads and the Peterses were feeding her and me, so she was happy for that. But it was a terrible job.

Mr. Peters had had a stroke. His wife was a slender, little woman, no bigger than a minute—she probably didn't weigh ninety pounds. She couldn't lift him; he was dead weight. So Mom and I had to lift him out of bed, put him on and off the chamber pot. Then I had to take that pot to the outhouse, empty it, rinse it, and bring it back to his room. Meanwhile, Mom washed his bottom, and when I returned we'd lift him back into bed. I was only thirteen.

Mother had saved a little money while working for the lawyer. She didn't have much, but enough for us to quit Mr. Peters and rent an apartment in Dundee for fifteen dollars a month. Her next job was cleaning the bank after hours. She'd dust the entire bank and then scrub the tile floors on her hands and knees every night. For all that work, they paid her fifteen dollars a week.

At the same time, I got a job at a bakery owned by Norm Rauch. He paid me twelve bucks a week in summer and six bucks a week during the school year. My summer hours were from midnight to nine o'clock in the morning. When I started, he first taught me how to bake bread. He'd throw a huge batch of dough on the table and have me cut off pieces, weigh them on the scales, and add a little pinch or take off a little pinch until they equaled one pound. Then he'd have me pull the balls of dough and shape them to fill the bread pans. Next, he taught me to mix cakes, then how to mix the cookies. Then I learned the fried goods. How to roll the dough, cut out donuts, and fry them. After they cooled, I'd sugar or ice them, or fill them with jelly.

About three o'clock in the morning, Norm would go to the restaurant across the street and get something to eat while I mixed the cookies. When he came back, I'd have the cookies done and be ready for the cakes. By the time I got the cakes finished, it'd be seven o'clock and I'd begin to clean up.

I also had to make deliveries to the stores—take the fresh bread over, stock it on the shelves, and bring back stale bread. Our competitors were the big commercial companies that brought out truckloads of bread. Their drivers would push our bread over and scrunch it to the back to give theirs the prominent shelf space. So, I tried to get to the stores right after they left. I'd scoot their loaves out of the way and put mine up front. I'd only bring six or eight loaves, and I wanted them to sell. I didn't want to have to take them back to the bakery the next day.

When school was in session, I started at four in the morning and worked until nine o'clock. I arranged my class schedule so study hall was first. I'd skip that, get to school by nine thirty, and be on time for my second class. Since I didn't go to study hall, I had to do all my studying the night before. On Fridays, I worked from nine at night until nine Saturday morning.

At the end of the block the bakery was on, the intersecting street came up a steep hill. The town had constructed concrete steps in the sidewalk down to the crosswalk at the intersection. One night, I was working at the bakery when my boss and I heard a huge crash. We ran outside to see what had happened.

A semi-truck with a cab, a trailer, and a second trailer behind was hauling huge rolls of paper from Consolidated Papers. Each roll weighed twenty tons. The driver had cut the corner too close. His wheels rode up the incline where the steps were, and it lifted the truck into the air just as a local man, Ed Rod, turned the corner in his Model-T Ford. The truck had landed on top of Ed's Ford, burying it.

By the time Norm and I got from the bakery to the scene of the accident, the driver was out of his truck but the Model T was completely hidden. The truck driver called out, "Anybody alive down there?"

Ed said, "Yeah, but I wish you'd give me a hand and get me out of here."

The truck driver almost fainted.

My junior year in high school, I quit the bakery job with its awful hours and got a job at a hardware store. The work was easy. It mostly involved dusting everything and restocking inventory. The store had an old hand-operated elevator you moved by pulling a rope hand-over-hand. When shipments arrived, I'd use the elevator to take extra stock upstairs and unload it until we needed it.

Prepackaging nuts, bolts, washers, nails, and other hardware items in plastic bags is a relatively new concept. In the old days, hardware stores kept these goods in bins. Customers scooped the quantity they wanted into a paper bag and were charged by the pound. When a bin of screws or nails ran low, I'd go up to the second floor, get a box of the item, bring it down, and refill the bin.

We'd occasionally have an order to deliver, and the store owner let me drive his car. That was the best part of the job for me because Mom had no car, so I didn't get to drive often.

Mom and I depended on each other. In my mother's eyes, I could commit no sin. I walked about four feet off the ground. From my perspective, her willingness to tackle almost any kind of job to support us was her strongest quality.

Although she was a divorced parent, Mom never said anything bad to me about my dad, even when we had to skimp along on her fifteen dollars and my six dollars a week because he'd skipped paying child support again. Dad, on the other hand, would make nasty innuendos against

Mom if he was drunk. But his unkind remarks only made me think less of him and respect her more.

Old Mill dam in Dundee, Michigan, where Dick and his high school friends swam during the summer.

Chapter 9
High School Years

I said earlier a kid could get a good education at a one-room school, in part because you heard the upper grades' lessons several times before you reached that grade. But that only applied to academic classes. When I graduated eighth grade and went to a city high school, I quickly realized that one-room schools were deficient in arts, music, and sports programs.

Yes, we'd played baseball at King School, and I was good at it, but I'd never seen a basketball court, never played football or tennis. Many of my high school classmates had been playing these and other sports since grade school.

In basketball, the guys who made the varsity team had already played together for three or four years. I, on the other hand, had never seen a basketball game before. King School didn't even have a basket. But I didn't let that deter me. I tried out for the junior varsity team. Unfortunately, I didn't know what to do. The first time they threw me the ball, no one was open, so I walked with it to find an opening. The referee blew his whistle and tried to take the ball from me. I wouldn't give it up. That ended my basketball career.

A similar situation occurred with band: the other kids had learned how to play cornet, trombone, clarinet, or flute in previous years. King School had a piano, but only the teacher was allowed to play it. From day one, the Dundee High band director was looking for freshmen who knew how to play. I joined the band, but the only thing I could play was drums, and not very well. Eventually, the teacher took me off drums and put me on cymbals.

I was equal to or ahead of other kids in my academic subjects. But for music and extracurricular activities, I would have needed several years' experience before high school to fit in.

Baseball was another matter. As a freshman, I tried out for baseball. To make the team, I had to compete against a senior named Mathis. Because he was bigger, he hit better and threw farther than I did, but I could outrun him. I whipped his butt in tryouts—I got the center field job and he didn't. The coach recognized that if he put me in center field, I'd cover left field all the way to right field.

I became good friends with our team pitcher, Bill Kuhlman. His family lived diagonally across the street from Uncle Brad. One game, Bill was pitching, and a kid named Siler was in the outfield. A good hitter from the opposing team was coming up to bat and the coach sent me in to replace Siler at center field.

The batter got a hit off of Bill, and as soon as I heard the crack, I knew it was gone. The field wasn't fenced—if a ball got beyond us, it'd be a home run. I spun around and took off at a dead run with my glove hand outstretched. The ball fell right into the pocket of my glove. I held it up. The player was out, the game over. Bill cheered from the mound, "Way to go, Siler! Way to go!"

For years afterwards, I teased Bill about calling me Siler, even after we were in the service.

We had two semi-professional ball teams out of Dundee, a semi-pro baseball team and a semi-pro fast pitch softball team. My sophomore year, I made both teams. That was pretty heady stuff for a kid. I was fifteen years old, and here I was playing semi-pro ball with grown men.

We played night games in Temperance, Michigan, because they had one of the few stadiums with lights. Elsewhere, we had to schedule games during daylight hours. Everybody on the team liked the opportunity to play under the lights.

Although it may sound like all I did outside of school was work, I squeezed in some fun, too. After all, I didn't have to be at the bakery until midnight.

I learned to play tennis, and in summer we swam. The River Raisin flows through downtown Dundee. The river is dammed by a mill and a hydroelectric dam, which, at that time, was owned by Ford. Just below the dam was a very deep pool we called the mill wash. We'd jump off the dam into the mill wash, come to the surface, and swim around. We also swam at a more remote spot upriver, where a lot of us boys would skinny-dip. One day while we were swimming there, one of us spotted the doctor's daughter watching us through a pair of binoculars.

Life at home was just Mom and I, so we had to entertain each other. We played card games and Chinese checkers, listened to radio shows, and confided in one another.

One of our favorite programs was *Lux Radio Theater*. The announcer would say, "The house lights are dimming, and now . . ." Then they'd go into a dramatic play. The show lasted for an hour. My other favorites were *The Lone Ranger*, *The Air Adventures of Jimmie Allen*, and comedies like *Jack Benny*, and *Fibber McGee and Molly*.

When we needed more than our own company, we'd play euchre with Uncle Herm and Aunt Edie. Their house was only a few blocks from our apartment house, and Mom and I walked over there at least once a week.

Most of our family members played cards when they socialized. If we visited Uncle Russ and Aunt Min, we played cards. If we were at Uncle Hank's, we played cards. If any of Mom's family came to Uncle Herman's, we might go over there and join them in a card game. Even years later, after I married and had kids, my wife and I continued to play cards with my aunts and uncles.

Since I was an only child, Mom had to be not only my mother but also my sister, brother, and friend. And just the way brothers and sisters will aggravate each other, I found I could tease her and get away with it.

One night, Mom was cooking supper. I'd been picking on her for about an hour. I'd untie her apron; she'd retie it and give me hell. I'd do it again. Finally, I snuck up behind her and tied her apron strings in seven knots.

When dinner was cooked, she drained the potatoes and dumped them into a bowl without mashing them. Sometimes she'd serve them like that and we'd mash them on our plates with our forks, adding a little butter or gravy.

Mom started to take her apron off and discovered what I'd done. Then I came over and poked her in her ribs with my fingers because she was ticklish as a goose. That got her upset. She told me to quit it. But I laughed at her and kept at it. Finally, she'd had enough. She took one of the hot potatoes from the bowl and threw it at me. I ducked, and it hit the wall. She started throwing potatoes at me with both hands. I'd duck, and she kept missing. By the time she ran out of potatoes, the wall we'd freshly painted when we moved into the apartment was a mess.

"You clean that up," she said.

"No," I said. "I didn't do that. You threw the potatoes, you clean it up."

That pissed her off. She cleaned the wall, but she kept saying, "Damn kid, smart-ass kid, I ought to cuff him up."

But she couldn't catch me to cuff me.

Another time, I teased and pestered her until I got her to the point where she didn't have any patience left. She grabbed the yardstick and hit me with it, and it broke. I cracked up laughing. Then she grabbed the vacuum cleaner hose and tried to spank me with it. The hose was so long and unwieldy she could hardly swing it; it wound itself around me and did nothing.

Yes, I knew how to get her goat. But she loved me dearly. Then, one day when I was fifteen, I nearly frightened her to death.

After I learned to play tennis, Harold Pilbeam and I were playing doubles one summer day with his sister Juanita and Loretta Sharp. It was hot, and we were wringing wet with sweat. Harold had his dad's car and he said, "Let's take a ride to cool off."

We got in the car, guys in front, and girls in the back. Harold was driving. We rode out into the country until we came to where an old railroad had once been. The railroad company had taken up the rails and removed the ties, leaving the gravel bed.

"This goes all the way through," Harold said. "I'm going to cut across here and we'll come back into town that way. If I don't, we'll have to go four or five miles further to the crossroad." Nobody argued.

So Harold took the shortcut, but he could only go about fifteen miles an hour because there were humps every two feet where the railroad ties had been removed.

Unseen by us was a place where the railroad workers had removed a huge culvert and left a deep chasm. The car went up a little rise, and all of a sudden plunged straight down, hood first. Cars then didn't have seatbelts or safety glass. My head smashed through the windshield.

I was sticking through the glass up to my neck and bleeding like a stuck hog. I said, "We got to get help."

"I'll go," Harold said. He took off running, and his adrenaline kicked in. I could see him jumping woven-wire fences as if they were high-hurdles.

Loretta had struck her chin, and it knocked her goofy. She began a little sing-song, "We were playing tennis, we were playing tennis."

Juanita was trying to find out if there was anything wrong with Loretta —then she looked at me. Two arteries in my head were lacerated, and my hand was cut. I was bleeding profusely. I still don't know how I survived.

Finally, Harold reached someplace to call the ambulance, which in those days was literally a hearse. They rushed out, picked me up, and drove me to Dr. Pensotti's office because Dundee didn't have a hospital and they needed a doctor to stop the bleeding.

The doctor examined me, asked how long ago it happened. I told him and he said, "He doesn't have enough time left for us to get him to the hospital in Monroe. I'm going to have to sew him up right here. Dick, there isn't time to administer an anesthetic. This is going to hurt."

I thought, *How bad could it be? I'm already hurt.* So I said, "Do what you gotta do."

He turned to someone in the room and said, "Go get me three *big* men."

Dundee was a small town. A crowd would gather whenever anything happened, and a group of people now stood outside the doctor's office. Whoever he sent outside returned with three big farmers. The doctor had one man lie across my body, weighing me down, and he had another man hold my arms down. To the third man, holding my head, he said, "Don't let his head move no matter what."

Dr. Pensotti stitched my arteries and then put stitches in my temples, under my chin, and in my hand, all without anesthetic. He cleaned me up so I looked halfway presentable and then sat me up. "How do you feel? Can you walk?"

"I don't know. I haven't tried."

"Well, just sit there a minute." After a while he said, "You think you can get home?"

Home was five or six houses up the street. I said, "I think so."

He helped me stand. "You all right?"

"Yeah, I'm all right." What made me think I was all right? Just something a fifteen-year-old kid would say. I was actually thinking, *Just let me go.*

I went to the door and saw Mom coming down the middle of the street, crying like a baby. Dr. Pensotti brought Mom inside and said, "You think you can get him home?"

"Yes," she said.

So she and someone, I don't recall who, got on either side of me and walked me home. We lived in an upstairs apartment. They got me up the stairs, and she put me to bed. The next morning I was up, but I looked like a mess. For years, the scars from that accident were real dark red.

Chapter 10
War

On December 7, 1941, Mother and I were riding to Monroe with Uncle Herm and Aunt Edie. We were going to play cards at Uncle Hank's. It was about three o'clock in the afternoon and we were on South Custer Road. As we rounded a curve in the road, a gigantic plane flew over us very, very low, possibly only five hundred feet off the ground, heading toward Selfridge Airfield in Detroit. Well, it looked gigantic to us. It was probably a DC-3, but we'd never seen a plane that big.

"Look at that big plane!" Uncle Herm said, looking up instead of at the road and steering us right toward a ditch. Aunt Edie yelled, and he swung back onto the pavement.

When we got to Uncle Hank's, we started telling about what we'd seen. The radio was on, but we were trying to talk over it to tell everyone about this big plane.

"Don't you know?" Uncle Hank said. "We're at war. We've been attacked by the Japanese."

We huddled around the radio listening for more news, but there wasn't a lot known yet, just that bombs had been dropped on Pearl Harbor and ships had been sunk. President Roosevelt gave a speech on the radio telling us we'd been attacked by the Japanese, but we were not to worry. Everything was going to take time. The Japanese had done damage to our navy, but we had ships on the way. The next day, the president and Congress declared war, and I recall Roosevelt talking to the nation a couple more times in the first weeks of the war.

As 1942 got underway, the country began to gear up for the war effort. Industry switched from making consumer goods to manufacturing armaments, ammunition, boots, uniforms—everything for the military. By May, the government began to ration gasoline. Soon there were shortages of many things. On the "home front," we were asked to cut back on meat, sugar, coffee, canned foods, fuel, shoes, and consumer goods so there would be enough for our servicemen. At school we held scrap drives to salvage and collect items from a long list of materials deemed useful for the war effort. These included paper, tires, silk stockings, cooking fat, and all types of metal: aluminum, iron, tin cans, and even toothpaste tubes. Contests were held to meet established quotas, and newspapers reported the results.

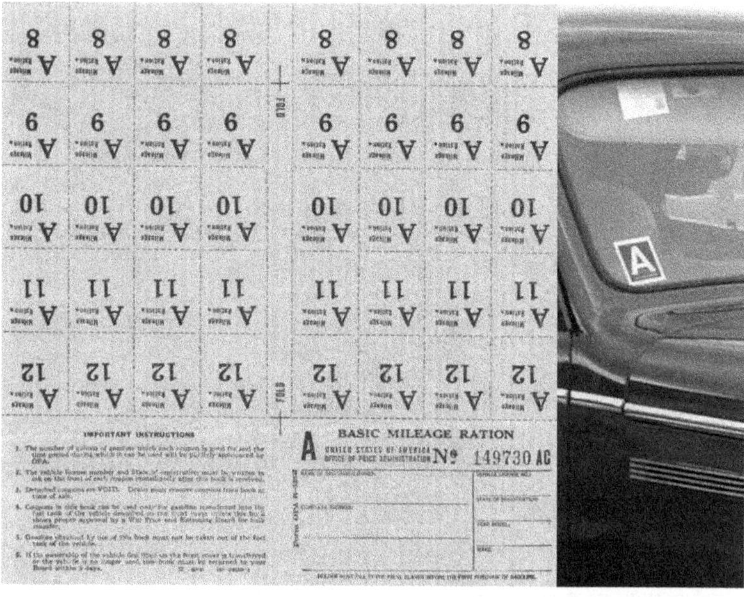

World War II gasoline ration coupons were required to purchase gasoline. The letter on the stamp had to match a decal on the windshield of the vehicle being fueled.

The government issued stamps to ration gasoline. The letter on the stamp had to match a sticker on the car's windshield. "A" stamps allowed the purchase of three to five gallons of gasoline per week for essential activities such as shopping, attending church, and going to the doctor. People who used their cars in their jobs got "B" or "C" stamps, which allowed them to buy more gasoline. "T" stickers permitted truckers to buy all they needed, as did "X" stickers for politicians and others. Initially, gas wasn't what they were rationing at all. At first, the purpose of restricting gasoline was to conserve tires because the Japanese had cut off our supply of rubber. However, by the end of 1942, all types of fuel became rationed. Kerosene, diesel, and fuel oil were necessary to power planes, ships, and tanks.

The military also needed large amounts of food to feed soldiers. In the spring of 1942, sugar was the first food rationed. By late 1942, other foods on the home front were running short. Grocery stores rationed the amount of canned goods they sold to each customer in order to prevent hoarding. Meat was in especially short supply. The government limited the amount shipped to grocers and restaurants and set a "voluntary ration" of two-and-a-half pounds of red meat per adult per week. But stores often didn't even get that much to sell. Later in the war, ration books were issued to cover sugar, coffee, red meat, dairy products, and fats. People could avoid the limits imposed by rationing—and save food for soldiers—by planting "victory gardens" in backyards and empty lots. I'm sure my aunts and uncles did this. Home-canning was encouraged, and women who canned could apply for extra sugar rations based on the amount of food they expected to can.

Even before we entered the war, the government had started gearing up to meet projected demand by European allies for the B-24 Liberator, a bomber airplane. In the autumn of 1940, the United States Air Corps created the Liberator Production Pool Program to build B-24 bombers in five factories run by three different companies. The massive Ford plant at Willow Run would become the largest of the three.

Henry Ford owned vast tracts of farmland in southeastern Michigan on which he grew soybeans to make plastics used in his automobiles. One of these tracts, his Willow Run farm, was ideally situated on the main highways and rail lines that connected Detroit to Chicago, Fort

Worth, and points west. Since the site already belonged to Ford, there would be no delay acquiring land.

Ford broke ground for the plant in March of 1941. At 3.5 million square feet, it was the largest assembly-line plant in the world. Ford was initially assigned to produce knocked-down B-24s and ship the components to companies in Oklahoma and Texas for final assembly. His Willow Run location was not only ideal for a factory but also for an airfield. In October of 1941, Ford got permission to produce fully assembled B-24s and add runways. (After the war, the runways became Willow Run Airport.) The first Ford-built Liberator rolled off the Willow Run line in September of 1942.

Ford's idea of applying his automobile mass-production methods to manufacturing aircraft got off to a rocky start. First, building airplanes required higher precision than cars, and second, there were labor shortages. Once the United States entered the war, men were taken out of the labor pool into military service. Also, the plant was located an hour west of Detroit, and with gas rationing in effect, workers didn't have fuel to commute. Ford solved these problems by hiring women to replace men and providing bus transportation to the plant from communities throughout Lower Michigan.

Mom was among the women hired at the bomber plant. She made good money and she liked the work, especially after all the terrible jobs she'd done during the Depression. At the plant, she worked in the gauge crib. The B-24 was such a big bomber that there were hundreds and hundreds of gauges and tools used to measure the thickness of a plane part or the distance between rivets. It was Mom's job to keep track of the tools. Workers had to have ID tags to get tools. They'd hand her their tags. She would then give them the gauge or tool they needed and hang the tag in its place so she knew who had checked out every tool.

As problems with the plant smoothed, Ford's methods proved out. By the end of the war, Willow Run was rolling a completed B-24 off the assembly line every fifty-eight minutes. My mother played a small part in that.

Mother rode the bus to the bomber plant and back to Dundee each day. Wayne Schroeder was her bus driver. He was a kind soul with a heart of gold, exactly what she needed.

The attack on Pearl Harbor gave rise to a wave of patriotism, and men rushed to enlist. Wayne was no exception. He went to the Army recruiter and said, "I want to sign up."

The recruiter looked at Wayne's hands and said, "We need whole men, not ones who are already half gone."

Wayne had lost fingers from both hands at age four. His father's farm had a horse-drawn elevator that raised bales of hay up to the hayloft by a complex series of ropes and pulleys. Wayne's hands got tangled in the ropes and were dragged into the pulleys. He was left with only a thumb and forefinger on one hand, and a thumb and two fingers on the other, but one of those was paralyzed. Yet he had amazing dexterity. He could catch a fly in midair with either hand.

Still, Wayne knew he could do something to help the war effort. He could drive—trucks, busses, forklifts, anything. So he became a bus driver taking workers to and from the bomber plant. And that was how he met and started dating my mother.

Henry Ford's Willow Run "bomber" plant, where Dick's mother worked.

Chapter 11
Ford's Camp for Boys

In 1942, the summer I was sixteen, I worked at Ford's Camp for Boys.

Henry Ford had long had an interest in plastics developed from agricultural products, especially soybeans. He'd fostered a relationship with George Washington Carver for this purpose. Soy-based paint and plastics were used in Ford automobiles throughout the 1930s. Ford was also keen on the virtues of country living. He brought sixteen-year-old boys out to his farms to learn about farming, nature, and the rural way of life. The camps were intended to teach us self-discipline and the value of hard work.

My first camp was at Willow Run, where the bomber plant was being built. Forty of us lived in ten tents, four guys to a tent. There was also a chapel and a kitchen. We had chapel every morning—attendance was mandatory. We received room and board and two dollars per day. But we didn't get paid for rainy days.

Our job was simply to farm. We tilled and planted the fields and cultivated the soybeans when they were big enough to cultivate. We didn't harvest, though—someone else would do that after we returned to school in the fall. The fields ranged in size from forty to three hundred acres, and it would not be unusual to see a line of fifteen to twenty tractors going across the field. Many times, we would get to the end of a field and standing there would be Mr. Ford himself, dressed in a suit and tie, wearing his white straw boater—a style of summer hat that was flat on top, had a wide brim, and was popular in the 1890s. Mr. Ford still wore one fifty years later.

Whenever Henry Ford went out, he rode in a Ford, but his two bodyguards rode behind him in a Studebaker coupe. I don't know why they weren't in a Ford, too, but that was how we knew Mr. Ford was coming. If we saw a black Ford with a Studebaker following, it was him.

Ford's Camp was a good place to work. Our kitchen served great food. Ford hired real chefs—they could have worked in any fine-dining restaurant. Most of us farmed the fields, but a few of the boys worked in the kitchen. They got the same pay we did, two bucks a day. They cleaned up and washed dishes, or they peeled potatoes and washed vegetables, but the chefs did the actual meal preparation and cooking.

The camp had a bus and a truck to transport us out to the fields. Anyone with a driver's license was allowed to drive either vehicle. I drove both. I look back on it now and think, *God Almighty, a sixteen-year-old driving a busload of people.*

We called the boss Bathtub Jack, a play on the term "bathtub gin," because he drank pretty heavily and you could smell the gin on him. He was a decent guy to work for, though. He was firm but clear on what we needed to do each day.

One Friday, it rained. We didn't get paid for rainy days. So on Saturday, another kid and I went to see Jack. This kid's nickname was "Bug-eye" because his eyes bulged a bit. Bug-eye and I asked if we could do some work to make up for the lost pay.

"Yep," Jack said. "Get push brooms and sweep the driveway all the way to the road and back. I'll pay you a day's wages."

Our camp at Willow Run was on a hilltop. The drive was three-quarters of a mile long and divided at the bottom of the hill into a circular drive that went around the mess hall. The two halves of the circle met on the other side of the mess hall, and the driveway continued to the highway entrance.

Bug-eye and I started sweeping. When we got to where the driveway divided, I said, "Which way you want to go?"

"Let's go this way," he said.

We were sweeping along when Bug-eye saw two cars coming up from the main road. "Put your head down and just keep sweeping," he said. "We'll sweep right up to their bumper."

So we swept like the devil and got almost up to the first car's bumper before we looked up. *Uh-oh,* I thought. *It's Mr. Ford.*

We stepped aside, and he waved at us. We waved at him, and the two cars continued up the hill to the camp. Mr. Ford only stayed up there three or four minutes, but to us it seemed like at least half an hour. When he and his bodyguards came back down, they drove around the opposite side of the circle drive. We never looked up; we were sweeping hell-bent for election.

When we finished, we said to Jack, "Who was that?" We knew it was Mr. Ford.

"What do you mean, 'Who was that?'"

"In those cars that came up here earlier."

"Oh, that was Mr. Ford," Jack said.

We were shuffling around, scuffing the ground. "What did he want?"

Jack eyed us suspiciously. "What did you guys do?"

"Oh, nothing. We were sweeping."

"What did you do?"

We told him and thought for sure we would get canned. Instead, he laughed. "No, Mr. Ford didn't even stop to talk this morning. He just drove up, looked around for a few minutes, and left."

Unfortunately, sometime later, Bug-eye lost an eye. The kitchen boys would snap dish towels at each other. One of them snapped him in the face and it took his eye right out. Oh, the shit hit the fan. All the boys who worked in the kitchen expected to be fired. The camp took care of Bug-eye and got him the best medical care. But they really laid the law down for the rest of the boys.

I got promoted from tractor driver to being field boss over a crew of six to eight guys. The job came with a raise, so now I made $2.50 a day. One of my guys was Stanley Sorter, who I knew from Dundee High.

One day my crew was cultivating a sixty-acre field that had a low spot in it. The previous night we'd had a hard rain, and I could see the low spot had a mud puddle that must have been an acre in size. We were cultivating beans. So I told my crew, "Go down the row, and when you get to the water, raise the cultivator and go around it. I don't want those beans torn up. When you get to the other side of the puddle, get back in your same row, lower the cultivator, and finish out the row."

Well, things were okay for the first hour. Then I looked and there was Sorter, stuck in the middle of the puddle, spinning the tractor's wheels, mud flying, tearing up bean rows. I charged out there and said, "Shut that damn thing off. I don't know how we're going to get you out."

I had a chain on my tractor, and two other guys did, too. We put three chains together to get enough length so we could pull from beyond the puddle. I hooked my tractor to Stan's and said, "Before we start, raise that cultivator." But his cultivator was mired and wouldn't lift out of the mud. He'd buried it trying to go forward. Now, he couldn't go backwards, either. Finally, the guys on the crew had to wade into the water and lift the cultivator out of the mud by hand to break the suction so the tractor's hydraulics could pick it up.

I hooked onto Stanley's tractor and had just got it moving when I saw Mr. Ford leaning on the fence at the far end of the field. I thought, *Man, we're in trouble. If he reports this, we'll get fired.*

I pulled Stanley free, got him in his correct row, and said, "That's Mr. Ford standing down there. Start cultivating and don't make one mistake, 'cause if you do, I'm going to kick your ass."

Our line of tractors moved down the field. When we reached the end of the row, Mr. Ford just waved and smiled. So we turned to our next rows and kept going.

Midway through the summer, Ford was ready to start runway construction for the Willow Run bomber plant right where we were farming. They shut down our camp and moved us to Cherry Hill, near Plymouth, Michigan. From there we farmed Ford's land all the way to Belleville, Michigan, an area of about ten miles.

While we were working a field over by Belleville, I had trouble with another kid on my crew. The field had a drop-off and I told the guy assigned to that part of the field, "When you get over to the side of the hill, don't get the tractor wheels anywhere near the edge."

We started working the field, and then I heard a yell. His wheels had slipped off the edge. The tractor had tipped over and slid downhill on its side. No way to pull him out of that mess. There was nothing to do but wait for the boss. When Bathtub Jack came, I told him, "The guy rolled his tractor. It's down that hill. I warned him to stay away from the edge, but he didn't."

Jack brought in heavy equipment, hooked chains to the tractor, and tipped it upright. He towed it uphill and loaded it onto a truck. I don't know what happened with the tractor, but the kid never returned to work —they canned him.

Chapter 12
Joining the Navy

I'm not blaming my father for my decisions, but the one thing I needed in my life at seventeen was a firm hand. My senior year, I got strong-willed and did whatever I wanted. I'd skip school to go shoot pool and things like that. I wasn't a bad boy, just young and irresponsible. Mother and Wayne married in November of 1942. Wayne was a great guy, but he wasn't a disciplinarian. I needed someone to boot me right in the ass.

I got it in my head I'd get a job that paid enough so I could buy a car. Five of us, Julian Brown, Vern Wakefield, Sheldon Morrin, John King, and I, learned Ford's Willow Run bomber plant needed men. So we decided to quit school and get factory jobs. Well, we got hired as stockmen, but the job only paid a dollar an hour. It'd take a long time to get a car at that rate.

We had to work long, hard hours, and the work wasn't great. We kicked around what we should do next. Julian returned to school and the superintendent let him back in so he could graduate with our class. The rest of us got the idea that, with the war on, we'd enlist.

Sheldon and I went together to several enlistment offices. The Air Corps sounded good to me, but Sheldon wore thick glasses. We knew he'd never get in. So we tried the Marines. They took one look at Sheldon's glasses and told him to take them off and read an eye chart. He flunked the eye test.

We walked to the next building, which was the Navy. There, they separated us into groups and gave us physicals. I passed. When Sheldon came out, I got his attention and gave him a "thumbs-up." He held up his hands and shrugged his shoulders, meaning he didn't know.

The recruiter called my group into a room where we signed our enlistment papers. I was instructed to get a parent's signature and told when to report back. Outside, I met a dejected Sheldon. He'd failed his eye test. Sheldon eventually did get accepted into the United States Naval Construction Battalions, known as the Seabees, and served in the Pacific.

A lot of men had joined the Navy. They couldn't take everyone right away, so I continued working at the bomber plant until my report date.

On July 7, 1943, I stood up, raised my right hand, and said, "I will." Suddenly, at seventeen, I was a sailor in the US Navy.

Next morning at 8:00 a.m., I joined 250 other men and boys at the Federal Building in Detroit. At 10:00 a.m. they put us aboard the train for Chicago. The ride should have taken four or five hours, but we were a troop train with no priority, so we were diverted onto a siding for every freight train.

Excited and tired, we arrived just outside of Chicago at the Great Lakes Training Center at 3:00 the next morning. They marched us to a two-story barracks that held 250 men on each floor, Northerners on the bottom floor and Southerners on the upper. They gave us a mattress, a pillow, and a blanket and then assigned us a bunk. By then, it was 4:00 a.m., and we slept.

Reveille—our wake-up call—sounded at 5:00 a.m. First, we marched to a mess hall for breakfast. Then we marched to another building. We were each handed a box and ordered to strip, fill it with all our personal belongings except for our watches, and write our home address on the label. Naked as jaybirds, we marched to the spot where they gave us a mattress cover and told us to hold it open. As we marched in line, we called out our size and they threw clothes to us, sometimes landing in the mattress cover, sometimes missing. After this, they told us which clothes to put on, and we carried the rest to our barracks. There they instructed us on how to make our beds, how to take care of our clothes, and how to pack our sea bags.

Next, they marched us to a building and gave us a five-dollar bill, called "the flying five" because it was immediately taken back in exchange for chits (vouchers). These were for a haircut, shaving soap, razor and blades, and a jackknife (which I still have). From there, we marched to the barbershop.

They continued to give us instructions until supper, after which we were free until 9:00 p.m. Then lights out, no talking. And we soon found out what no talking meant. The instructor rousted us out of bed and took us to the drill field to stand at attention or march until he thought we had learned to keep quiet. But then some smart-ass would say something and back we'd go to the drill field.

If the Navy did one thing for me, it disciplined me. I quickly learned that you didn't say "I don't want to do that" or "I'm not gonna do this." If they told you to clean the head, you scrubbed toilets. If they told you to stand at attention, you stood at attention.

While we were in boot camp, they took us to Navy Pier in Chicago to practice firing big guns, 20mm and 40mm. They'd have planes fly by that were towing targets for us to shoot. Sometimes a gunner would hit the tow cable instead. That was pretty close to the plane's tail. You didn't want to be the pilot towing targets.

We loaded a drum-shaped magazine on top of the 20mm gun. It held sixty rounds of ammunition, and a spring on the magazine had to be wound to a certain number of pounds of tension so another shell would pop into the breech when the gun fired.

Our trainer was a chief petty officer who had been firing big guns for thirty years. While we were practicing, a 20mm magazine jammed because its spring didn't have the proper tension. Our trainer saw it, grabbed it, and threw it off the pier. It exploded. He lectured us quite sternly about winding the magazine spring. He told us a kid he was training had fired a gun without having proper tension on the magazine and it blew up, severely injuring him.

An Oerlikon 20mm machine gun. The round cylinder on top is the magazine that required tension not to jam.

After nine weeks of boot camp, the Navy sent me and the others in my group home for two weeks' leave. They formed us up, marched us to the train station, and put us on the train to prevent us from missing it. They also gave us specific orders about where and when to report back.

September 22, my leave ended. The Navy took me by train back to Great Lakes and marched me and the other returning men to OGU (Outgoing Unit), where we got our assignments. No one knew who would be going where. I was assigned to gunnery school and was put on a troop train to Gulfport, Mississippi.

I was stationed in Gulfport four weeks. Mom came down by bus and stayed for three or four days in Biloxi, fifteen miles away. It took courage for her to make the trip alone because she'd never traveled further south than Toledo. But she knew that after gunnery school, I'd be sent out on a ship and she'd have no idea where I was or when I would be back. During the war, Navy censors cut any information like that out of our letters home.

Even though I'd been home on leave the previous month, she wanted to spend a few more days with her only son before he shipped out. I had evening hours off, so we could visit, but there wasn't much to do in Gulfport. It was, at that time, a tiny town overrun by the military.

After four weeks of gunnery school, they sent me to Shell Beach, Louisiana, a real crap hole, for three days of gunnery practice aboard a ship. Our first day, I was on deck with the 20mm gun when one of the guys threw a magazine on it. I noticed he didn't have any tension on it. I remembered the incident at Navy Pier and knew the round would explode and probably injure him if I let him fire it. I yelled, "No tension on it," grabbed the magazine, and threw it over the side of the ship. About halfway to the water, it exploded. No one was hurt and it didn't damage the ship. It wasn't something I did because I was braver than anyone else. I just happened to be at the right angle to see it and reacted out of instinct.

While I was stationed at Shell Beach, the Navy took us out for gunnery practice on an old wooden ship infested with crab lice. We didn't learn of the problem until we got back in port. They made everyone strip and looked us over with a flashlight. It made me feel like a hunk of meat hanging on a hook. Out of 160 of us, almost every man had body lice, so they made us shave off our hair.

After they got us deloused, I left there and went to the naval base in New Orleans. When I reported into New Orleans, they already had me assigned to a ship. By five o'clock that night, I was sailing down the Mississippi River and out to sea aboard the *War Admiral.*

Chapter 13
Aboard the War Admiral

I served aboard the *War Admiral* from late October 1943 until May 1944. The ship was an old Danish freighter, the *E. M. Dalgas*, that had been sitting in an American harbor when the Nazis invaded Denmark. The United States took over the ship under the Ship Requisition Act. The Navy mounted a couple of guns on it and renamed it "the War Admiral." Due to a treaty, they couldn't sail it under an American flag, but they could sail it under the Panamanian flag.

The government hired the Danish sailors who had been with the ship and didn't want to go back to their country, which was now under Nazi rule. Our mess crew was from Puerto Rico, and we had crew members from other countries, too. So we had a real multinational crew.

My unit was called the US Navy Armed Guard. We were a twelve- to fourteen-man gunnery crew with one lieutenant in charge. Our job was to protect the old freighter as she carried supplies for the Navy. We were supposed to fight off submarines, surface raiders, and aircraft, but all we had to fight with on that old tub was a single 3-inch 50mm gun on the stern and a couple of 20mm guns amidship.

At this point in the war, Germans were sinking ships right outside the mouth of the Mississippi. My first night out, I caught guard duty. I'd just finished gunnery school, where they'd shown us movies about how to spot the wake of a submarine periscope. But they never told us about phosphorus rays caused by a ship's own stern wake. Well, big long phosphorus streams generated by your own ship look like a periscope wake, too.

The *E. M. Dalgas*, a 1930 Danish freighter requisitioned by the United States and renamed the *War Admiral.* Photo source: ImgEd.

I was standing guard on the stern of the ship when my heart jumped up in my mouth. *God, that's a submarine*, I thought. I called the bridge and said, "Do you see that?"

"Where?"

I told the man on the bridge where to look. But he was at a different angle.

"No, I can't see anything."

Finally, I decided there was only one thing to do: call general quarters, an alarm instructing all hands to their battle stations. I threw the switch and got the whole damn ship up. By the time they got up to me, I had the 3-inch 50mm ready—breech opened, a shell in the gun, breech closed, and ready to fire.

They wanted to know what I saw.

"A submarine." I pointed.

They looked, but all they could see were those phosphorous rays.

"Where?"

"Right out there."

Well, they looked and looked, climbed up to the bridge and searched with binoculars. They finally decided there was no submarine. The officer told me those were phosphorous rays and he gave me a chewing out.

He told me not to be so damn skittish. Then he discovered I had a shell in the gun already. That pissed him off, so he chewed me out some more and took me off that station. From then on, I was on bridge watch.

From New Orleans we sailed to Guantanamo Bay, where we anchored while waiting to join a hundred-ship convoy to Panama. We stayed in Cuba for three days. The officers wouldn't let us go ashore, but we could go swimming. So we jumped off the side of the ship into the water about fifteen or twenty feet below. Later, we discovered that while we were swimming on one side of the ship, men fishing off the other side were attracting sharks all around.

Once the convoy assembled, we left Cuba. The convoy maintained radio silence and ships communicated with lights or signal flags. At night, destroyers would cut across the convoy with sirens blaring, meaning they had gotten a sub warning and were trying to find it on sonar. Our old tub didn't have sonar or radar, and it would only go eleven knots at full speed. German subs were looking for any ship that fell out of convoy or trailed at the end—slower ships were sitting ducks.

As luck would have it, we broke down, and the convoy kept going without us. We fixed the problem and got moving again. We never did catch up with our convoy, but we never got sunk either. Maybe the submarine commanders decided we weren't worth wasting a shell on.

We came into Cristóbal, Colón, which is on the Atlantic side of Panama. Earlier, a hurricane had set bigger ships than ours up on the rocks of the breakwater. But our old clunker just chugged right into port.

I had the opportunity to go through the Panama Canal twice. The first time was just to see it. Our lieutenant got permission for four or five of us to ride with him on a ship crossing to the Pacific. At the other end, we caught a different ship coming back. No one knew where we'd be going when we left Cristóbal, or if we'd get back to Panama, so it seemed worth doing. Going across was interesting, but the ride back was a little boring. After all, it was only the reverse of the trip we'd just taken. But now we could say we'd been through the Canal. At the time, I didn't know I'd return a year later and go through again.

We unloaded our cargo in Panama and left. On our voyage back to New Orleans, we stopped in Puerto Barrios, Guatemala, where we picked up a load of bananas. While in port, we were allowed to go ashore for two or three hours. There wasn't anything to see there, just the port, some shacks where the local people lived, and a marketplace that didn't have much. But we discovered we could buy three- and four-foot-tall stalks of bananas for twenty-five to fifty cents. Every guy who went ashore bought a stalk and brought them back on board. We put them down in the munitions locker, where it was cool. Well, we ate bananas and more bananas for about two weeks.

In January, we delivered supplies to the naval air base at Pensacola, Florida, unloaded cargo, and took on some more. On shore, we wore our heavy dress-blue uniforms and pea coats because it was cold in Florida that week. The men on base wore a variety of uniforms according to their duty, but none of them wore dress uniforms. We'd walk in anywhere and people would say, "Oh, you're off that ship."

After my second trip to Panama, we stopped in Nicaragua to pick up a load of mahogany logs. We weren't allowed ashore in Nicaragua, but I got to know the Nicaraguan stevedores who carried goods aboard. One of them who spoke English told me a blue chambray shirt like we wore in the Navy would cost them eight dollars. A pair of shoes cost them twelve dollars. These prices were way beyond their wages, so none of them wore shoes or shirts. They wore only shorts made from the cheapest type of cloth, and they worked barefoot. Their entire lunch consisted of a plain tortilla, no meat, beans, or anything on it. I felt sorry for the man. I put my leftovers from lunch on a napkin, took it out on deck, called the guy over, and said, "Here, would you like this?"

"Oh, yeah."

Whenever possible, I'd take him a pork chop, a piece of chicken, or whatever. We had more food than we could eat.

I asked him at what age they married and how they supported a wife on such meager means.

He said it was difficult. Wives grew food and prepared it. Made their clothing, plus things they could sell. Sometimes the wives made more money selling things than the men did working.

About marriage, he explained, "We've got a different marriage custom."

"What's that?" I said.

"You have to go see the shaman. He'll marry you, but the first night he must sleep with your bride."

"You're not serious."

He said it was true. I wouldn't like that.

While the ship was underway, we had ridiculous hours. Everyone had to stand watch from first light to sunrise and from sunset until dark because that was when it was most difficult to see subs, which would surface to recharge their batteries. In between, we had our regular watch—four hours on, four hours off.

One night, during our return from Nicaragua, I had guard duty up on the bridge. When my replacement came on to relieve me, I had to get up again in a couple of hours to stand general quarters, so I walked over to the gun tub, threw down a life jacket for a pillow, lay down, and slept.

The guy on duty decided he needed to use the head, but he didn't wake me—he just left his post. The officer came on deck and found me sleeping. He grabbed my hair and pulled me up. I doubled up my fists and almost hit him until I realized it was the officer. I came within an inch of knocking him flat on his ass, which thank God I didn't do or I'd have been court-martialed.

The officer was really pissed at me and wouldn't listen to reason. He said, "I'm sending you to the brig."

I didn't deserve to go to the brig, so I argued with him. The more I argued, the madder he got.

"But I wasn't on duty."

He wouldn't listen to that. When we docked in New Orleans, he put me in the brig and I was in there for five days. I kept telling them, "I'm not lying! I was not on duty." I told them who was.

Someone finally got the officer to talk to the man who was on duty, and he admitted he'd left his watch to go to the head. The Navy later cleared the incident from my record because I raised so much hell about being put in the brig unfairly.

Dick Gartee in "dress blues" Navy uniform.

CHAPTER 14
NEW ORLEANS

When I was released from the brig, I was told, "You don't need to go back to that ship. Obviously, you and that officer are not going to get along and you will only have more problems. How would you like to stay on base? We'll give you a job here."

I had been working toward becoming a gunner's mate third class petty officer. If I stayed on ship and made third class, my pay would go from $66 a month to $78. But I said okay.

They looked over my record and decided I'd be a good fit in disbursements. "How would you like to work in payroll?"

"Fine. I like numbers."

Unlike the Navy today, there wasn't a school or training program at that time. I reported in on Monday, and they sat me down with a person who had been there awhile. "Show Dick how we figure payroll."

He showed me, and within a week I was better at it than many who had been doing it right along. It wasn't difficult for me. It was math, and it was simple. I understood it.

A little while after I'd started in disbursements, I was on my way to the canteen when I ran into Lieutenant Grafrath, a guy I'd gone through gunnery school with. We had become good friends in Gulfport but got separated after school because we were assigned to different ships. He was excited. "Dick, I've got a new ship."

"Wonderful."

"How would you like to go with me?"

I'd only had my position in payroll a few months, and I liked it. I said, "Can I think about it until tomorrow?"

"Yeah, but I've got to know. We're leaving in a day or two. I'd like you to go. I'll make you a gunner's mate third class."

It was tempting because I had wanted to be a gunner's mate third class, plus I'd get more pay. "Let me think about it until morning." So, we agreed to meet at the canteen.

I mulled it over all night and thought, *No, I just got this job and I like what I'm doing. It won't hurt me to know this when I get out of the service. I might find work as a bookkeeper or something.*

When I saw him the next day, I said, "I'd really like to go, and I'd like to serve under you, but I need to explore where the job I have now will take me."

Well, he sailed without me. Six months later, he was back in New Orleans when I ran into him again. "I'm glad you didn't go," he said. "It was a real mess. We never had a chance. The kamikaze came in low, hit our ship, and exploded. Its bombs killed nearly everybody and threw the rest of us in the water. I lost all but twenty-six of my men."

Could have been me, I thought.

There were ten of us working payroll. The New Orleans Naval Base paid all the ships that came in there, so we had a constant flow of personnel who needed to be paid. Heck, the job fit me like a glove because numbers were easy for me. Where most men in our department were doing three payroll records an hour, I would handle eight or ten. Soon I made third class.

Bill Kuhlman, a good friend that I'd played baseball with in Dundee, docked in New Orleans. We'd enlisted in the Navy at different times, so we hadn't been in basic training together or assigned the same ship. While his ship was in port, we had ten days to catch up and carouse around the Big Easy.

One night, he and I came into a place where they had dance music and we spotted two women sitting at a table.

"Let's ask them to dance," Bill said.

"Why, sure."

Bill said, "I want the one on the right."

"That's okay with me."

We approached them and asked, and the women said yes. But when they stood up, the woman Bill had chosen was six foot seven and he was five foot seven, so his nose was about even with her bosom.

Whenever my partner and I danced near Bill and his partner, I'd say to Bill, "Can you breathe in there?"

We'd teased each other about little things like that ever since high school.

While I was in the service, the scars from my high school car accident were red and still looked fresh. With the war on, people would see me and assume I had been injured in battle. I'd be standing at a bar waiting for a beer and someone would and say, "Here, sailor, let me buy you a drink."

"Well thank you, sir." They never asked about my injuries, and I never told them.

* * *

Mom made her second trip south to see me, this time by train. This was undoubtedly the longest train trip she'd ever taken in her life, but rail travel was much easier at that time than it is now. She bought her ticket, got on the train in Michigan, and changed trains in Cincinnati to one that took her straight into New Orleans. She couldn't get lost.

Mom brought along Faith Keck, a girl I'd dated in Michigan. Faith had just finished nursing school.

The morning after they arrived, Mom looked out the window of her hotel at a meat market across the street. A sign in the window advertised "Fresh Horsemeat." She said nothing about it then, but that sign stuck in her mind.

I took her to eat at Antoine's, the best restaurant in New Orleans. "Mom, what would you like, chicken or beef?"

"I don't want any beef," she said.

"Why?"

"It's probably horse meat."

"No, I don't think so."

"Well, they're selling it."

"I know they're selling it, but I don't think they'd serve it to you without telling you it was horse meat."

She wasn't convinced. Even though beef, rationed since the war began, was available here, she wouldn't eat a bite of it the whole time she was in New Orleans.

During the war, a lot of things were rationed. For example, women couldn't buy anything made of silk or nylon; it all went into parachutes and other war materials. To make it appear as if they were wearing hose, women would apply makeup to their legs and sometimes draw a line up their leg like a stocking seam.

Mom and Faith stayed a week or ten days. I took them to St. Louis Cathedral and the zoo, and for a ride on a paddle-wheel riverboat. At night we danced to orchestras. Mom could afford the trip because she was now making more money at the bomber plant than she'd ever made in her life. She and Wayne had bought a gas station in Dundee and he didn't come with her because he had to stay home and run it.

The gas station wasn't a success because Wayne was too trusting. He had a very generous nature. If you said, "Wayne, I need a dollar," he'd give it to you even if that was all he had in his wallet. Gas rationing had started as soon as the war began. You had to have ration stamps to purchase gasoline. Wayne couldn't handle that—he was too good-hearted. Someone would come in and say, "Wayne, I don't have a stamp, but I need gas to get to work today. I gotta work."

He'd look around and there'd be nobody else in the station. "Well, how much gas you need?"

"Four gallons will get me there and back. Tomorrow I'll have stamps."

"Okay, you bring me in a stamp."

At the end of the month, he'd be short of stamps. Mother would go crazy running around to find friends or relatives with extra stamps so they could account to the government for the amount of gasoline they'd sold.

He was the same way with his tools. Back then, gas stations didn't just sell gas and snacks. They serviced and repaired cars, changed oil, put in batteries. He'd buy nice tools to work on cars in his service station. Someone would come in and say, "I need a wrench. Can I borrow one?"

"Yeah, help yourself. Bring it back, though."

"Yeah, I'll bring it back tomorrow." Of course, they never did, and he didn't remember who he'd lent it to.

He was just that way, a very easygoing guy. Schoolkids would come into the station and say, "Wayne, I'm getting a candy bar. I'll pay you tomorrow."

"Okay," he'd say. But they never paid him. Next day they'd do the same thing. God knows how much candy he gave away.

Meanwhile, I was doing well in payroll. It didn't matter what they put in front of me, I mastered it. We had to do monthly reports to BUPERS (Bureau of Naval Personnel). I did those for a couple months, until my supervisor came by one day and said, "You're doing such good work. Why don't you take the test to become second class?"

I took the test and made second class, but I wanted to get on a ship. Be where the action was. It was May of 1945, and I'd been stationed in New Orleans for a year. The war in Europe had just ended, but we were still fighting in the Pacific.

Naval activities and administrative command ashore was divided into eighteen districts or "Coms." I had a friend over at Com 12 headquarters. I told him, "I want to catch a ship. I don't care where it's going. I just want to catch a ship."

He called one day and said, "Dick, there's a brand-new ship coming in. It will be here about five o'clock this afternoon. They're not going to have a layover. They'll only be tied up long enough to drop something off and pick something up. If you want that ship, you've got to tell me right now."

I didn't hesitate. "Yes."

"Go pack your sea bag. Don't worry about your orders. I'll get them typed and sent to your commanding officer. You report aboard ship. They'll have your name and be waiting for you."

USS *Hecuba* departed New Orleans on May 31, 1945, for duty in the Pacific and returned to San Francisco on December 19, 1945.

CHAPTER 15
IN THE PACIFIC

I boarded the USS *Hecuba* and we departed New Orleans on May 31, 1945, for duty in the Pacific Ocean. She had just been commissioned. We were headed for Pearl Harbor. This was my second trip through the Panama Canal, but this time it wasn't for pleasure.

The *Hecuba* was a supply ship named for the Queen of Troy in ancient Greece. She—the ship, not the queen—was 441 feet long and 57 feet wide at the beam with a 28-foot draft. She was better armed than my previous ship, outfitted with eight 20mm guns and two larger-caliber, dual-purpose guns capable of firing at both surface ships and aircraft. Our full crew complement was 195 men.

My job aboard the *Hecuba* was disbursements—same thing I'd been doing on base. There was an officer in charge of disbursements, but he didn't know how to do payroll or the report to the Bureau of Personnel (BUPERS) office in Cleveland, Ohio, which handled all of the Navy's accounting.

"Do you know how to fill out this BUPERS report?" he said.

"Sure."

"Well, you do it."

So I took on the entire payroll. He never even came down to the office to see how it was going. He'd just initial whatever I gave him. It was the same with the report to BUPERS. I'd fill it out, he'd sign it, and I'd send it in.

During the trip to Hawaii, our executive officer served as acting captain. He was a gruff old guy who drank and cussed a lot, a thirty-year man with more stripes on his sleeve than you could count.

We arrived in Hawaii on June 22. Commander Northrup H. Castle took over our ship and became the official captain. Commander Castle was from one of the five families that ran the Hawaiian Islands. The Castles owned the main shipping lines between Hawaii and the mainland United States. He'd had lots of experience sailing big ships, so he got command of the brand-new *Hecuba.*

Castle had a whole different perspective on being captain. He was strict about standing watch and staying alert for threats, but lax about less important things. He didn't get excited about whether a guy was in uniform or, depending upon the occasion, if a seaman didn't happen to salute. If the captain came up on the bridge and the lookout said, "Good Morning, sir," but didn't salute, Castle wouldn't say anything.

He had a relaxed style. Our executive officer, a strict Navy man, would never have been seen on deck without a perfectly pressed khaki uniform. Commander Castle would come out wearing ragged cut-off shorts, bare chested, suntanned brown as a berry.

From Pearl Harbor, we sailed to Eniwetok in the Marshall Islands and waited there a week, just buying time. Pearl Harbor was a busy port, and I think they wanted us out of the way of more important ships.

All we did at Eniwetok was drop anchor in the bay and go over to the island, half the crew one day, half the next. On the island, each man could have two bottles of beer or Coke, whichever he wanted. That's all you got, but you could play baseball or write letters or sit on the beach. When the week was up, we returned to Pearl Harbor. After the war, the government blew up a portion of Eniwetok in the first hydrogen bomb test.

All busy ports require every ship be brought in by a harbor pilot. Pearl Harbor was no exception. They'd run the pilot out to the ship on a little gig and he'd take over and navigate the ship into port. When we returned from Eniwetok, Commander Castle, who had sailed Hawaiian waters all his life, wouldn't let the pilot take over. He wouldn't even let him aboard ship.

The pilot said, "Throw me a line."

Castle said, "Stand clear." The crew was ready to throw the lines, but he told them, "You throw him a line and I'll court-martial you." He would never have done it, but he told them he would.

"He doesn't get no line," Castle said. "I'll take this ship in." Then he took our ship right to the dock as though he were parking a car.

We were sure he was going to get hell for it, but when we were ready to leave, he and his wife rode out together in the pilot's boat as if they were all best friends. She came aboard and spent a few minutes, then they helped her down the ladder into the pilot's boat. She waved goodbye, and the pilot took her back to shore.

While we were in Pearl Harbor, the supply officer and I, along with another man who served as a guard, went ashore to the Federal Reserve Bank in Honolulu and picked up two million dollars. It was my first experience of being inside a Federal Reserve. One-dollar bills were wrapped in packages the length and width of a dollar bill, but ten inches thick. Each package contained four thousand dollars. This was a mind-blowing amount to a kid who, only a few years before, thought a quarter was big money.

I plucked bundles of cash from the shelves like I was picking out boxes of cereal at a grocery store. I counted them as I handed them to the supply officer, and he counted them as he put them into the bag. When I had enough ones, we moved on to fives, tens, and twenties. Maybe we took two-dollar bills, I don't remember, but no denomination larger than a twenty. The money filled eight mail bags, each three feet in circumference and as high as my waist.

We took the money back to the ship, put it in a big locker, and locked it. Then we had a welder come in and weld two big pieces of steel across the door. If our ship sank, no one would get in that locker.

With the money secured, I then had to file a detailed report to BUPERS listing the quantity I had of each denomination. In addition to the $2 million, we already had $280,000 in cash aboard ship to take care of our payroll and expenses.

USS *Hecuba* underway in Pearl Harbor.

We sailed from Hawaii to the Philippines, stopping to offload supplies at an atoll in the Caroline Islands, which are southwest of Guam, before going on to Leyte in the Philippines. Once we got anchored in the Philippines, the welder unwelded the locker where we had stored the millions. We didn't have to take the money ashore, though. It was payroll for the Army, so they came with their own guard crew. We divided it up and they transported it back to shore.

In the Philippines, the airmen would go out on bombing runs. There were markings on their planes to identify them as friend, not foe, so the men on watch wouldn't shoot at them. But the guys on duty were so jumpy they'd see something and shoot at it. You'd hear the guns go *boom, boom.* And as soon as one started, they'd all shoot. Meanwhile, the poor pilot was trying to land. I never saw one of our planes shot down, but they sure shot at them.

After we disbursed the money and unloaded our cargo, we loaded supplies and started for Okinawa. The plan was to form up a huge convoy in Okinawa and from there invade Japan. Although Nazi Germany had been defeated, we didn't feel peace in the Pacific because it was such a bitter war there. Japan was a force to be reckoned with. If it had not been for the atomic bomb, I don't know how many lives would have been lost in an invasion of Japan. The Japanese would never have given up their homeland.

Of course, the invasion never happened because the United States bombed Hiroshima and then Nagasaki. Aboard ship, we heard the news. I don't remember the time of day, but it was probably at the same time President Truman announced it stateside.

Although the war ended with Japan surrendering on August 15, 1945, our ship continued on to Okinawa. On the way there, we got caught in a typhoon. The ship rolled from side to side. Waves broke over the bow and hit the flying bridge, which was thirty-five feet above deck. The deck was twenty-eight feet above the normal water line, so these waves were sixty-five to seventy feet high. By the time we got out of the typhoon, we were almost at Okinawa. There we saw the typhoon had picked up big ships and set them on dry land.

While we were anchored in Okinawa, I went ashore and tried to find my cousin, Wes Murdoch, who was the son of Aunt Min and Uncle Russ. He was stationed there as a mechanic in the Air Corps. I found a guy with a jeep who for some reason didn't have any duty and knew where all the air bases were. He drove me to four or five air fields. We spent the whole day at it but couldn't find Wes.

Finally, the guy said, "I gotta get back, and I don't believe we're going to find your cousin."

"I don't think so either," I said.

Once Wes and I were both back home, I told him I'd tried to find him. He told me the name of the air field he was at, but by then I didn't remember which base was which, I'd been to so many.

With the war over, orders came to disperse all the hardware that we could, such as pipes and pipe fittings. The Navy had too much surplus and didn't know what to do with it. We were told to get rid of everything.

I sat right there in Buckner Bay (Okinawa) and watched men on aircraft carriers push brand-new Pratt & Whitney engines, still in the crates, off the fan tail. They'd been told not to come back with them, to get rid of them at sea.

Enormous numbers of soldiers throughout the Pacific now needed to go home. Although, we were a supply ship, we took a whole Army company (about two hundred men) with us when we left Okinawa. They slept on cots in the cargo holds and did their cooking below or on deck. We furnished them some supplies, but they had most of what they needed, except frozen food, which we supplied from our stores.

On our way back to the States, we hit the damnedest storm. It covered six hundred square miles. We never got out of that storm from the time we left Okinawa until we were four or five days out of San Francisco. The storm was so bad that on deck, a man was likely to be washed overboard. For safety, we ran cables from the bow to amidship and from amidship to the stern, and you weren't allowed to go on deck unless you held the cables. Our mess hall had six-foot-tall coffee urns, and the cooks could fill them only one-quarter full or the storm would splash coffee out the top.

We ate mostly cold rations and sandwiches—very little hot food for the twenty-six days it took us to get out of that storm. The force of the storm was such that even a new ship like ours couldn't make any speed.

Chapter 16
Getting Home

We survived the storm and, after a month at sea, sailed into San Francisco. Commander Castle didn't return with us, and Harold Benthusen, who'd been our executive officer, became ship captain for the journey home. As I said earlier, he was traditional "old Navy." When we came into San Francisco, he lined us up and had us stand at parade rest along both sides of the deck, wearing our dress whites, as the ship sailed under the Golden Gate Bridge. That's the way the old Navy ships came into port, with all the crew members out in full dress uniform. The *Hecuba* was almost tied up before he dismissed us.

In San Francisco, we were to decommission our ship so it could be taken to Bikini Atoll and used in an atomic bomb test. The government wanted to compare how old ships and new ships fared in an atomic blast. The *Hecuba*, only a year old, commissioned just a month before we left New Orleans, was slated to be blown up.

We had about $128,000 left in cash, so an officer and I took our remaining money to the San Francisco Federal Reserve Bank and turned it in. I filed the final reports to BUPERS while the supply officer took care of disposing of any remaining tools and steel in the cargo holds. Since we weren't going be disbursing money any longer, my job was over. My new duty would be to stand watch or something like that.

A new captain, Francis McCann, took command. If I stayed on the *Hecuba* and sailed to Bikini, it would have been hard to catch another ship back. I'd be taken off my ship and put on some island where I'd wait four or five days for a ride back to Pearl Harbor. Once I got to Hawaii, I'd have to get into the numbering system to get a ship back to the mainland. There were a lot of men waiting to come stateside. I could be there three to four months waiting for a chance to go. Even once I got back to the mainland, it might take another month or two to get sent to Chicago, which was my home base. I thought, *Why do I want to go out there? I got enough points to get out right now.*

Points were based on how long you were in service and how much time you'd been overseas. I had the points required to get out, but I had to be discharged at my home base.

My stepfather, Wayne, had had a heart attack. So I finagled a bit to get home.

The yeoman who did the clerical work was a good friend of mine. I asked him how I could get leave to go home. He said, "Emergency leave, that's the easiest to get."

"How long is that?"

"Thirty days."

"Where will I report back to?"

"You can report to the closest naval base."

"The closest base to Dundee is Toledo, Ohio," I said. I knew Toledo was a discharge station. "Well, you better write me up leave papers. I'll try to get the captain to sign them." Emergency leave couldn't be signed by the officer of the deck; it had to be signed by the ship captain.

"Okay, I'll write it for you to report to Toledo, Ohio," the yeoman said.

The captain went ashore most evenings and drank beer until he was soused. He'd come back bouncing off the rails and the sailors would help him aboard ship.

I told the crew of the gig that ferried the captain back and forth that I had emergency leave and asked if they'd run me back in when they brought the captain out. They said sure.

That night, as soon as Commander McCann reached the top of the gangplank, I was waiting with my papers in hand and my sea bag packed.

"Sir, I need to go home on emergency leave. My stepfather has had a heart attack."

"Oh, hell, Dick, I'm sorry to hear that. Give me those papers." He signed my orders and said, "You got your sea bag?"

"Yes, sir."

"You guys take him ashore." I'd already arranged it, but McCann was showing off his rank.

It was about three o'clock in the morning when they took me ashore and dropped me off. I was at the train station by four o'clock, before anyone on the ship was even up. The officer of the deck wouldn't even know I was gone until eight o'clock, and by then I'd be on a train toward Chicago.

Now, if I'd stayed in the Navy instead of getting out when I did, I'd probably have made first class immediately, and then two or three years after that, I'd have become a chief petty officer. From there I could have become a warrant officer, and then chief warrant. A chief warrant officer is about the best grade you can get in the Navy because you make as much money as lieutenants make but without paying for your uniforms like commissioned officers do. A chief warrant officer doesn't really have any duties. All he does is tell the warrant officer what needs to be done; the warrant officer tells the chief petty officer, who tell the first class, who tells the second class, who tells the third, who sees that it gets done. As you can see, your rank indicates how much work you will have to do. And as chief warrant officer in disbursement, I probably wouldn't have worked two hours a day until retirement. But I didn't want to stay in the Navy. I enlisted when I was seventeen and I was just coming up on twenty-one. I wanted to get out and be in the civilian world.

I got home, took my thirty days of leave, and reported into Toledo when it was over. This meant I changed from Com 12, which was San Francisco, to Com 9, which was the Great Lakes district, because Toledo was in Com 9's district. When I reported, the guy said, "God, Dick, I don't know what to do with you. We've got a full complement. I got guys like you sticking out my ears. Let me wire Great Lakes and see what they want to do with you. In the meantime, go back home for another week."

Well, that was fine with me, another week of leave.

I don't remember if it was then or another time when I was home on leave, but Mom and Wayne and I were uptown in Dundee at a little bar called Old John's Saloon. Uncle Brad and Aunt Elsie were there, and they said, "Come over to the house." They lived just a short walk from the bar.

When we got to Aunt Elsie's, she said, "What would you like to eat?"

"I don't know. What have you got?" I said.

"I've got some good fresh eggs."

"That sounds wonderful." In the Navy, I'd been fed nothing but powdered eggs.

"How many do you want?"

"Well, six," I said.

That tickled her. She laughed and made me six eggs and a couple slices of toast.

We sat there talking, and I finished off those six eggs like they were nothing. God, they tasted good.

"Are you still hungry?" she said.

"A little."

"Well, would you like some more?"

"Yeah."

"How many?"

"Six."

She fried six more, and I ate them. In the years to come, she'd tell that story often: "Little Dickie ate twelve eggs."

But they tasted so good. Man they were good.

After my extra week of leave was up, I reported back to Toledo and the guy said, "Dick, report to the University of Michigan. We're closing down the officer program and you can be of help there."

I reported in at Ann Arbor. They put me in West Quad, which was a nice dormitory, and gave me three rooms. One had a table and a desk, another had a private bathroom and a little kitchenette, and the third had two bunks. I didn't have a roommate so I had the bedroom to myself.

My duties consisted of inventorying books they weren't going to use anymore. I'd have everything finished in the first hour and then I'd stand around. Finally they said, "You can be officer of the deck." That meant all those college guys at U of M, studying to be commissioned officers, had to sign in and out with me to report where they were going and what time they were coming back. They had certain hours they had to be back by. All I had to do was watch them sign out and say, "Don't forget to be back, boys." Then I was off duty for the rest of the day and the next day as well. That turned out to be plush duty. On my weekends off, I'd hitchhike to Dundee.

In the Navy, officers and seamen alike had a knack for cursing, lacing nearly every spoken sentence with profanity. Now, home among my family and other civilians, it was a habit I needed to eliminate.

I stayed at U of M three months. But I was foolish. I should have enrolled in college. They were accepting anyone who wanted to enroll at that point. Some of my books would have been the same ones I was inventorying, so I wouldn't have had to buy those. But I had interviewed with the Ralston Purina Company and had a job secured for when I was discharged from the Navy. So my only thoughts were, *I'm going to get this job, make money, and buy a car.* I'd never had a car. I was twenty years old and I wanted a car. To hell with college. I had a job and was going to make money, what more would I want?

I needed someone to kick me right in the ass.

It turned out Wayne's heart attack had been a bad one, after which he couldn't work for a year. He and Mom lost their gas station business. She couldn't run it, and I was still in the Navy. They couldn't hire any help because all the men were still in military service or working defense jobs related to the war effort.

Once I was back in Michigan, I learned Wayne had been having other problems with his health and gallbladder before the heart attack. They were deep in debt, and one of the doctors was pressuring them to pay.

Then I found out they'd been charging groceries and owed the grocer $130. It doesn't sound like much now, but it was a lot back then. That was another factor in my decision to take the job at Ralston Purina instead of enrolling in college. After all Mom had done for me, it was only right for me to help them. Servicemen received a $500 discharge bonus from the state, and I used it to pay off their debts.

When the doctors said it was okay for Wayne to work again, he got a job driving truck for the College Inn canning company in Dundee. The craziest thing was that Wayne could read and write, but he couldn't understand a map. He drove truck navigating by landmarks. He'd look for an intersection with a familiar building on the corner to know where he should turn. This was before expressways, so highways were just two-lane roads. He'd make his way from Dundee to Chicago and back by finding key points along his route. He got sick again, but he recovered and continued to drive for them.

Chapter 17
Racism

I'd be remiss in describing the changes I witnessed in the twentieth century if I didn't mention race. The racial description "Afro-American," which is popular today, did not come into use until the 1990s, and before the late 1960s, "black" was usually a slur. In the period before and after World War II, "colored" was considered the polite way to indicate someone of African descent, preferred in those days over "Negro" or more derogatory names.

Today my wife and I live in a multiracial community. Our next-door neighbor, one of the nicest people we know, is Jamaican. Our neighborhood also has Asians and African Americans. But that was not the way America was in my youth, or even for decades after I was grown.

The first thing the Navy showed me, besides discipline, was how limited my schoolboy experiences had been. Michigan villages where I grew up—Ida, Dundee, Deerfield, and Petersburg—were rural farming communities. In Michigan, people of color stayed in larger cities where they found good jobs in automobile factories and other industries. There weren't any colored kids living out in the country in the Midwest, so there weren't any in my grade schools.

Monroe factories employed men of all colors, and their families lived there, but the colored had their own community. The first time I met colored kids my age was when I attended Monroe High School. There were two in my study hall and another class. I'd see them around school with their friends, but they didn't socialize outside their own group so

I never got to know them. Also, I was only at Monroe High for one semester before my parents divorced and I transferred to Dundee, which was all white.

From what I've told you, you can imagine how naive I was at seventeen. The North, where I grew up, was not overtly segregated like the South was. In Michigan, there weren't separate schools or restrooms or water fountains for different races. In fact, I didn't encounter segregation in that sense until I entered the Navy. But during World War II, the US Armed Forces *were* segregated.

When I arrived at Great Lakes Training Center for basic training, not only were colored people given separate quarters but white Northerners were assigned to a different floor of the barracks than white Southerners. Once we finished basic, the separation of Northern and Southern servicemen was dropped, but the segregation of black and white persisted. This was twenty years before the Civil Rights Act passed.

Even aboard ship, the Navy assigned "coloreds" a separate mess hall and quarters. For many, their jobs on the ship involved waiting on the white officers, so we never had an opportunity to mingle. You might see them up on deck or during general quarters, but you didn't know their names.

After I finished basic training, the Navy sent me to Alabama, and later to Louisiana. There I saw gas station restrooms labeled "White" and "Colored." Train stations had separate water fountains. Movie theaters had signs that read "White Only" and "Colored Only." Signs I'd never seen in Michigan.

With the preceding in mind, you will understand how my worldview completely flipped the first time I went ashore in Panama. We tied up in Cristóbal, Colón. The officer divided us into two groups, giving my group liberty to go ashore while the others stayed onboard to stand watch. The next night, my group would stand watch while the other group got liberty. The officer told us to be back by twenty-three hundred hours (11:00 p.m.).

We left the ship, and the first place we headed was the USO (United Service Organizations). USO clubs were places servicemen could go when they were on liberty. They had free coffee, music, dances, social events, and sometimes movies. Cristóbal had a big USO, but it was early, four o'clock in the afternoon, so there wasn't anything happening. They had a pool table, so we played a couple of games, but we were seventeen and eighteen years old—we wanted to see the town. Somebody said, "We ought to get a beer."

Everyone thought that would be the thing to do, so we strolled around until we found a pub. We walked in and everyplace I looked, there was a white guy with a black gal and they'd be kissing and hugging. I'd never seen it before, but no one I was with said a word about it. We bellied up to the bar and ordered our beers. We stayed there a little while and then moseyed down the street to another bar. The next place was the same scene.

We finally returned to the USO, and by then a little band was playing. Here there were only white girls, seven or eight, and they were snatched up in a hurry. Maybe you got a dance and maybe you didn't. So we stayed there a little while, ate a little food, and then wandered back to the ship.

It was decades after the war before we Americans would change our attitudes about race. Too many still haven't. Sometimes people fear another person for no reason other than a difference in skin color. I'm going to tell a little story on myself in this regard.

A few years after I left the Navy, I had gotten married and my wife and I were driving from Monroe to Dundee at about two o'clock in the morning. We were on South Custer Road, which had no streetlights. At the intersection with Ida-Maybee Road, a colored man stood in the middle of the road trying to flag us down. I had an old Plymouth coupe with a manual transmission. I downshifted into first gear and slowed the car to a crawl. I told Eileen to lock her door. He wanted to ask a question and started to grab my door.

"You get your hand off that door or I will drag you right down the road," I said.

"Wait a minute, boy, wait a minute, boy," he said, jogging alongside.

"What do you want?"

"I just want to know how to get to Ypsilanti."

"You get in your car and follow me, and I'll show you where to get the road to Ypsilanti."

So he followed me into Dundee. I stopped just short of going over the bridge, right underneath a streetlight that lit the whole area.

When he opened his car door, the dome light came on. I was never so embarrassed in my life. All I could see were tiny little eyes. He must have had seven or eight kids. I felt like a darn fool and never acted like that again.

After the twentieth century ended and the twenty-first century began, America elected Barack Obama president, something no one would have imagined possible fifty years earlier. I voted for him—twice. He was an intelligent man, perhaps great, whose presidency met resistance at every turn. While his opponents might claim they were only playing party politics, I suspect many of them were racially biased but dared not admit it.

When I was in my late seventies, I began volunteering as a chaplain at Alachua General Hospital in Gainesville, Florida. My patients were of all different races, cultures, and religions. Praying with ill patients of every race and religion, I gained an understanding my upbringing and work life had not afforded.

I'll tell more about my chaplaincy later, but let me share one story now.

While I was chaplain, I met Gainesville musician Cathy Dewitt, who was in a program at the hospital called Arts in Medicine. She and other musicians visited patients' rooms, played music, and sang. These programs engaged patients and stimulated the environment of healing care.

One day when I arrived in the chaplain office, I learned I was needed on the cardiac floor. A Haitian patient wanted a chaplain to come up and pray for her, but she couldn't speak English. I had no idea what language they spoke in Haiti, but I surely didn't speak it.

As I headed to the patient's room, I saw Cathy and another woman from the Arts in Medicine program in the hallway. I stopped them and said, "I've got a problem. Do either of you speak a foreign language?"

The woman with Cathy said she spoke Canadian French.

"Well, I have a Haitian patient who wants me to come up and pray for her, which I would be glad to do, but she doesn't speak English and I don't know how we'll communicate."

Cathy's coworker said, "If I'm not mistaken, Haitians speak a form of French similar to Canadian French. Perhaps we can do something."

The three of us entered the patient's room. We introduced ourselves, but it didn't mean much because she couldn't understand. I told her I was there to pray for her, and the woman from Arts in Medicine translated. Somehow, it got tangled up in translation and the patient thought she was supposed to pray for me. So she told me to sit down.

I didn't know what she wanted, but she pointed to the chair, so I sat. Then she commenced to pray over me.

When she finished, I realized where it had gotten confused. I got up and said, "Now I want to pray for you." I motioned for her to sit down. Then I prayed for her.

When I look back on that day, I wonder what race relations would be like if people prayed for each other even when they have obvious differences such as language.

Chapter 18
Courting Eileen

While stationed in Ann Arbor, I was off duty on weekends, so I'd come home to Dundee after work on Friday. I had two ways to get there: take a bus from Ann Arbor to Dundee—but that cost money—or hitchhike, which was free. If I had my uniform on, it was easy to get a ride. I wouldn't have my thumb out five minutes before some patriotic soul would pick me up.

My best friend from school, John King, was already out of the Navy. We'd get together on the weekends when I came home. John had gone on a few dates with Eileen Eblen, a girl from Monroe, and was really impressed with her, but now he was dating his future wife, Coleen. He thought Eileen and I would hit it off.

John and Coleen were into roller skating. I knew how to roller skate, but I couldn't skate waltzes and do all the fancy things other people did. John told me he would invite Eileen to go roller skating with us so I could meet her. But he said, "By God, you behave, and don't try anything funny. She's a *good* girl, and I'd be really mad if you did anything to embarrass her."

"John, I wouldn't do anything like that."

"Well, I'm just telling you, by God." So he and Coleen and Eileen and I went roller skating one evening.

After that night, I dated Eileen two or three more times, but it was challenging. I didn't have a car, so I had to hitchhike to Monroe. Fortunately, her house was only a few blocks from downtown, and we could walk to the movies.

Eileen Eblen, 1947.

It wasn't until after I was discharged from the Navy in May of 1946 that I started dating her regularly. By then, John's brother, Tom Woodruff, had a car and was dating his future wife, Jean, so we'd double date with them to go dancing.

Eileen and I both had strong mothers who had worked hard to raise us without our fathers. Her dad died at age thirty-eight, leaving her mother with three kids and no income. Her mom, Ruth, got a job working in a

Greek restaurant. (Eventually, Ruth would open her own restaurant.)

Eileen was only fourteen-and-a-half when her dad died, but she got a job as a counter clerk at a White Castle–type restaurant called the Triangle. Her sister, Jerri, was three years younger, and her brother, Ronnie, was six years younger. So it was just Eileen and her mom making any money.

Her situation seemed similar to my own. My dad wasn't dead, but as far as I was concerned, he might as well have been. I hadn't heard from him since before I enlisted. My whole time in the Navy, he never wrote me one letter.

Eileen had quit school when she turned sixteen and took a full-time job as an operator at the telephone company. This was considered a good opportunity. Telephone operators were exclusively women, and many women continued their careers at the phone company for years after they married.

Let me explain Eileen's job. Before cell phones or even dial phones, if you wanted to make a phone call, you lifted the telephone handset and an operator came on the line. The operator was sitting at the phone company in front of a large switchboard composed of rows of jacks like the type you see on electric-guitar amplifiers today. You told the operator the number or person you wanted to reach, she plugged a cord into her switchboard to connect your line to the line of the receiving party, and then she toggled a switch that caused the person's phone to ring.

If you wanted to call someone outside your local area, the operator connected you to the long-distance operator. The long-distance operator contacted the switchboard in the other city, and the operator there connected the call on her end. Long-distance calls were charged by the minute, and the rate varied by the distance to the city you called.

Eileen and I weren't going steady or anything serious, but I liked her. Then I almost blew it.

While I'd been stationed in New Orleans, ten or twelve of us would go out dancing once a week. A pitcher of beer cost fifty cents, so we'd each pitch in a quarter and buy enough beer and chips for everybody. We'd spend the evenings dancing, and I became friends with Ruth Winkler and two of her pals, Connelly and Schuman. They were in the WAVES, the World War II women's branch of the United States Naval Reserve. Ruth was from Wisconsin, Schuman from North Dakota, and Connelly from Detroit. We became close friends—not boyfriend-girlfriend close, but good friends.

After I was discharged from the Navy, Ruth came to Detroit to visit Connelly. They got to reminiscing about the fun they'd had dancing in New Orleans. Ruth had my phone number in Dundee and called to ask me if I'd be available Saturday night.

I said sure. Although I had a date with Eileen Saturday, I figured I could break it. I'd just tell her I couldn't get there.

Now, I knew Eileen worked at the telephone company. What I didn't know at the time was that the long-distance operator who handled Ruth Winkler's call worked right beside her. She said, "Eileen, aren't you and Dick dating?"

"Yes, we have a date for Saturday night."

"You might want to listen in," she said. "This is kind of interesting."

Eileen plugged in and overheard the whole conversation. Later, I called her and told her I couldn't make it. I had something else come up. Very icily, she said, "That's okay." But I wasn't paying attention to her tone.

I hitched to Detroit, danced all evening, and came home. The next day was Sunday. I caught a ride to Monroe, and when I got there, Eileen was cool—very, very cool.

"What did you do last night?" she said.

"Oh, nothing much, just hung out."

"Who with, Winkler and Connelly?"

Uh-oh. I knew what must have happened.

"Well . . . yes. We were all in the Navy together and Ruth was in Detroit for the weekend. We just wanted to touch base and renew our friendship."

"How close a friendship?" Eileen said.

"Just good friends, that's all." I wanted to get away from that conversation. "You want to go to a movie?"

"I don't think so."

"Did you want us to stay here?"

"No. Why don't you go home?"

So, I hitchhiked home, thinking, *I really blew this.*

I had been calling Eileen about every two days, but I waited four or five days before I called her again. I tried to play it upbeat. "Would you like to go out? Tom and Jean are going dancing and asked if we want to double up with them."

The phone was silent a long minute. Finally, she said, "That will be okay." She never brought the matter up again, and I sure didn't.

Right out of the Navy, I started working for Ralston Purina. Then Tom and Jack Woodruff told me the government would pay for us to take flying lessons. Back then there were little airports all over. Monroe had three. So Tom, Jack, I, and another guy signed up. We all progressed at about the same rate, but Tom and Jack got their licenses before I did. Because they lived in Monroe, it was easier for them to run out to the airport and complete their required hours.

Once Tom Woodruff got his license, he was never content with smaller planes like the Piper Cub or Taylorcraft. He wanted to fly Cessnas—that's where the speed was. One day while I was at work, Tom flew over Ralston Purina and buzzed me real low. Then he circled and came around again. He banked his plane on edge and poured the fuel to it, but he didn't have enough air speed. Tom wasn't paying enough attention and it dropped right out from under him. His plane ripped off the top of a barn, which knocked the wheels off his plane. He crashed in a field. The engine flew fifty feet away, and the plane tore all to hell.

I was the only one in the office, so I jumped up and raced toward the plane, thinking it was about to explode and I needed to pull him out of it. Before I reached the crash, Tom was out of the plane, running and jumping tall farm fences like a startled deer. He didn't even realize he'd run by me. I turned and shouted, "Tom!" But he kept going. When I caught up to him, he was white as a sheet.

We had to call the state police, the airport, and the Civil Aeronautics Board. They sent people out who took pictures of the plane and the site. I thought, *Well, Tom's done it now. He's not going to be able to fly.* But by God, he drove out to the airport the next day and said, "I'd like to have a plane," and they gave him one. He flew for an hour, came back, and landed.

It may surprise you to know that when you're flying in a small plane, you can hear what is said on the ground quite well. When I was soloing, I'd fly over Mother and Wayne's house real low, 150 to 200 feet. They'd come outside, and I'd yell, "Hi Mom!"

I'd hear her say to Wayne, "He's too low. He better pull up."

Eileen and I continued to date, and it was going good. I was excited about flying and wanted to share it with her. I could fly solo, but I didn't have my license, so I couldn't take passengers along. But I had a friend who had a plane and could take passengers, so I offered to pay for his gas if he'd give Eileen a ride. He said sure.

I drove her to meet him at this little farm airport near Petersburg. They took off, but they didn't come back. And they didn't come back. They were gone a long while.

After they finally landed, he explained that they had flown over Monroe, then toward Detroit. On the way back, he was low on fuel and had stopped at the airfield on North Custer Road to refuel.

I teased her for a long time after. "By God, I pay a guy to take you up and the first thing you do is disappear."

* * *

Eileen's mother, Ruth (Thornsberry) Eblen, was a force to be reckoned with, a strong-willed, self-sufficient woman like my mom. She liked me from our first meeting. Everything went well until one particular night.

I'd finally bought my own car—on credit. Eileen and I went on a date. When I brought her home, we got out of the car, walked up on the porch, and reached for the doorknob. Ruth yanked it open and said to Eileen, "Get in here. You're not married yet." Ruth grabbed her by the arm, pulled her in, and slammed the door.

I left confused. What the hell was going on?

Once Eileen was in the house, her mother lectured her about girls who sit in cars. Eileen said, "We weren't sitting in the car. We just now pulled in the driveway."

There were two parallel driveways alongside Ruth's house, hers and her neighbor's. Eileen and I didn't know the neighbor girl had come home earlier with her boyfriend. Ruth hadn't seen who it was, she only knew that a car pulled in about nine o'clock but Eileen wasn't in the house yet by eleven.

Eventually, Eileen convinced her mother it wasn't us, but Ruth never apologized for protecting her daughter's reputation.

Eileen and I dated for a year and a month before we got married.

Dick and Eileen wed on November 6, 1947, in Dundee, Michigan.

Chapter 19
Early Married Life

I thought Eileen was the most remarkable person I had ever met. I knew she was the one for me, so I asked her to marry me.

I was making $190 a month at Ralston Purina and she was still working at the telephone company. We decided if we lived in Monroe so she could continue to walk to work, we'd do all right.

She and I each bought a new suit to get married in. We had a small wedding, officiated by Reverend Griswald at the Congregational Church in Dundee. Sheldon Morrin, who had tried to enlist when I did, was my best man, and his wife, Alice, was Eileen's maid of honor. Mother and Wayne, Eileen's family, and my boyhood friends, John King, Tom Woodruff, Cal Zorn, and their wives attended. I didn't invite Dad.

For our honeymoon we drove to Grand Rapids, about four hours away, and stayed at the Pantlind Hotel. It was a nice hotel, ten stories high, which to us was a skyscraper. We checked in and were just getting settled in our room when the fire alarm sounded. I heard sirens outside, looked out our window, and saw ladder trucks and pumper engines pulling up. During 1946 and 1947, newspapers had been filled with stories about big hotel fires in Chicago, Dallas, Atlanta, Iowa, and Mexico City. Our room was on an upper floor, and we worried about how we'd escape. The hotel staff told us guests to stay in our rooms. We felt sure we were about to become another disaster headline. It turned out the popcorn machine had caught fire. The firemen put it out and left.

Dick and Eileen honeymooned at the Pantlind Hotel in Grand Rapids, Michigan. (Source: Grand Rapids Public Library History & Special Collections Archives.)

We stayed there on Saturday and Sunday. On our way home on Monday, Eileen's period started and she got ferocious cramps. I said, "What can we do for them, Hon?"

"If I had a hot water bottle, it would help."

We stopped at a drugstore. I let Eileen rest in the car while I went into the store. I didn't know about any of the things in the feminine aisle, but I found a rubber bottle with all sorts of tubes. It sure looked like it had everything. My face completely red, I paid the druggist and said, "Can you fill this with warm water?"

He gave me a funny smile and said, "Yes, I could."

I took it out to the car, and she put it on her stomach. It relieved her cramps, but I'd spent the last of our money buying it.

I kept an empty cigar box in the car, into which I'd toss loose change. I opened it and counted the coins, $2.34. I bought two dollars' worth of gas to get us home. Eileen had a paycheck coming, so when we reached Monroe, we stopped at the telephone company to pick up her pay. Luckily for us, employers paid in cash in those days.

Just before the wedding, we'd rented a little three-room upstairs apartment so we'd have a place ready to start our life together. Equipped with a wash basin and a toilet, but no bath, it cost us fifteen dollars a week and wasn't worth half that. For heat, it had a tiny coal stove in the living room that held less than a peck of coal.

We hadn't bought groceries before we left on our honeymoon, so I suggested we just pick up some hot dogs. Eileen agreed.

When we arrived at our new apartment, she headed to the kitchen and got out a saucepan. A few minutes later, she said, "Dick, come here."

I walked into the kitchen. My bride looked dismayed. "I don't know how to do this."

"How to do what?"

"Cook these hot dogs."

I thought she was pulling my leg. Her mother owned a restaurant for goodness' sake. "What do you mean, 'How do you cook hot dogs?'"

"I've never cooked them."

I laughed. "You fill the pan with water, put the hot dogs in it, turn on the burner, and you are good to go."

"How do I tell when they're done?"

"When they're boiling, that's good enough. You can shut it off. Then we'll make sandwiches with them."

I couldn't believe it. It had never dawned on me that Eileen wouldn't know how to cook. But because Ruth ran a restaurant and did all the cooking, Eileen had never learned. Also, she found her mother's recipes incomprehensible. Ruth would tell her, "Take a scoop of this, a dollop of that, and a dash of this." Eileen could never duplicate it.

Once we were settled, Eileen bought a recipe book and asked my mother to teach her. Mom taught her how to measure shortening, pack brown sugar, sift flour, all those things. Eileen became a darn good cook, but of all the deserts in her cookbook, she had favorites. Anytime we had bananas, she'd make banana cake. If she had lemons, we'd get lemon pie.

That winter, we had a heck of a time keeping warm. Although we were both warm enough at work, that puny stove at home didn't hold enough coal to heat our apartment. But we didn't care. We were happy. We were in love and cuddled for warmth.

Eileen was very easygoing, content with every step of our life, and never complained. She was a delight to live with and never demanding. The least little thing made her happy. For example, we went to Fink's radio shop together and picked out a little tabletop AM radio. It had good sound and every station it brought in was clear, which satisfied her. But it cost twenty-four dollars and I didn't have the cash. So, we put five dollars down and paid five dollars a month. That was our first credit purchase as a couple.

Shortly after we married, our car was confiscated. One Friday after work, I dropped the car off to be serviced at the dealership where I'd bought it. I said, "Now, can I pick it up tomorrow before noon?" They said yes. But when I came back Saturday morning, I found signs posted everywhere: "Do Not Enter by order of the Federal Bureau of Investigation."

It took me a couple of days to find out what was going on. The owners of the car dealership had been selling stolen cars. The car they'd sold me belonged to somebody in Ohio. Plus, it turned out they'd financed it twice. I was stuck—no way to get my car back, and no way to get out of paying the bank. The banker said, "Sorry, but you have to pay us. It's not our fault you bought a stolen car. This is already in the government's hands and they're not going to pay for it." Consequently, I ended up without a car. It was a good thing I hadn't bought a more expensive car from them or I'd have been deeper in debt.

The automobile manufacturer Kaiser-Frazer took over the former Willow Run bomber plant. They were offering higher pay than Ralston Purina so I quit my job because I could make two-and-a-half dollars an hour working on the assembly line at Kaiser-Frazer. That was big money then. I bought an old Chrysler to go back and forth to work. But thirty days after I started at Kaiser-Frazer, they cut three thousand jobs. Since I didn't have any seniority, I was laid off. To make things worse, I'd worked there just long enough for the union to deduct a fifteen-dollar initiation fee and fifteen dollars more for union dues from my last paycheck. I was pissed.

After the car fiasco and my lost job, we didn't have two nickels to rub together. We'd only lived in the apartment three months, but we decided we couldn't afford it anymore. We found a two-story house in Dundee on Toledo Street. The landlord wanted thirty dollars a month, which was better than the fifteen a week we were paying for the apartment in Monroe, but it was a crappy old house that needed paint. I made a deal with him: "If you'll buy the paint, I'll paint the inside of the house." He agreed, and I painted the whole interior.

The kitchen had a small, apartment-sized four-burner stove and a table with four chairs. There was also an old icebox instead of a refrigerator. You put block ice in a door at the top and it would keep food in the lower section cool. At the bottom, a drip pan collected water from the ice as it melted. That had to be emptied or it would overflow.

The bedroom windows had finger-width gaps between the windows and sashes. Only the strips of wood at the top and bottom kept them from falling in. So, I bought putty for ten cents a pound, rolled it into strips, and puttied the widows shut. Sealing the gaps and keeping out the cold air helped keep the house warm—there was no heater.

Uncle Herman knew where I could buy a second-hand Heatrola, a big cast-iron stove that would hold an entire bushel of coal. It was a heavy beast no one wanted to move, so it was being sold cheap. Uncle Herm and Uncle Ed brought it over on a trailer. It weighed over seven hundred pounds. I wanted to help carry it, but Uncle Ed said, "No, Herm can take that end and I'll carry this end." He picked up the heaviest part, where the legs were, and Uncle Herm grabbed the top, where the chimney pipe attached.

Uncle Ed said, "You get tired Hermie, just let me know and I'll set her down so you can rest."

The whole time they carried it, Uncle Ed never said, "Set her down." But Uncle Herm saw his brother was tired. "Don't you want to set it down, Ed?"

"No, I don't need to, but if you're tired, just say so and we'll set her down."

Neither Uncle was going to give in first. They got it inside and set it up in the living room.

Our used Heatrola held a lot more coal than I had money to buy, so I came up with a plan. I took my utility trailer to a sawmill near Azalia, Michigan, about ten miles from Dundee, and bought their scrap. When sawmills cut the bark off logs, the slab of wood with the bark is useless. For two dollars they'd sell me as much scrap as would fit on my trailer. I stood three- and four-foot-long slabs upright along the front and sides of the trailer to act like a trailer rack. I stacked shorter pieces against them to keep them from falling. This allowed me to pile wood on the trailer higher than normal.

After I unloaded the wood in my garage, I went to see Uncle Herman, who drove truck for Waterstreet Coal and Oil Company. "Uncle Herm, are there any empty coal bins they're cleaning out where I could buy the coal dust real cheap?"

"As a matter of fact, we have two. There's not much coal in them, mostly coal dust, so they'll probably let you have it for fifty cents."

I backed my trailer up to the bin. Uncle Herm powered up the front-loader and filled my trailer.

Now I was all set. I'd stack slab wood in the Heatrola, get it burning nicely, then cover the embers with coal dust. I learned to be careful, though. One time I used too much coal dust. It smothered the fire and generated a gas that exploded. Suddenly, *boom*! The stove door flew open and smoke poured out, and the room was covered in soot. I was more careful after that. Still, the coal dust set the chimney pipes on fire a couple of times and I had to disassemble and clean them after I put the fire out.

Eileen was still working when Kaiser-Frazer laid me off, but by this time she was pregnant with our first child. I looked and looked for work, but with all the GIs home from service, there weren't any jobs to be had. Finally, I got hired by Chromite, an outfit that stamped imitation tile out of zinc plates. They embossed the zinc plates in a press and gave them a couple coats of lacquer, and they looked just like tile.

My job was running the stamping press. I'd insert a sheet of metal and push a button, then the press would slam down. When it rose up, I'd pull the embossed sheet out and put in a blank one. Those presses would often double trip. If they tripped while the operator's hand was in there, he lost his hand—a lot of people had. So I needed to move quickly.

The problem was that I couldn't pick the sheets out of the press wearing the little rubber finger covers they gave me. They made the sheets slip and I didn't want my hand to get caught, so I worked without them. But about two hours of handling the plates without protection would wear holes in my fingers and they would bleed. My hands would heal on weekends, but as soon as I returned to work on Monday, the wounds would reopen.

I was the highest-producing press operator Chromite ever had. I'd produce 2,000 to 2,500 sheets a shift, but they didn't give me any more pay for my efforts. I was killing my hands for the whole sum of a dollar an hour. Forty hours, forty bucks. I worked at Chromite for four weeks. Then I got a chance to catch a job with Kelsey-Hayes Wheel Company, and I took it.

Kelsey-Hayes manufactured wheels and brakes for the major carmakers. They had just opened a factory in Monroe but didn't intend to keep it long-term. They had bought it as a favor for their largest customer, Ford.

You see, during World War II the US government built lots of factories to ramp up industrial production of war materials. After the war, the government sold these to private companies but required the buyer to run the plant for at least two years before being permitted to resell it. To ensure equitable distribution, the government limited the number of surplus properties any one company could purchase in a given area.

Ford wanted this Monroe plant since it was located on Lake Erie and had both harbor and rail facilities, but Ford had already bought its maximum quota. So Ford told Kelsey-Hayes to buy the plant and run it two years, and then Ford would buy it for more than they'd paid.

My job as a time clerk at Kelsey-Hayes was a real improvement over that terrible job at Chromite. Time clerks kept track of how long a machine was down and calculated how many pieces it could have produced during the time it was down. I was earning fifty cents more an hour and not losing skin off my fingers. But I was broke until my first paycheck. Fortunately, Eileen had learned to make baking powder biscuits that melted in your mouth. She sliced two biscuits in half and made me sandwiches with this pickle and mayonnaise spread that was the cheapest thing we could buy. That was my lunch at work.

One of the men I worked with thought they were fried pies and tried to trade his meat sandwich for mine. I was too embarrassed to tell him what they were. I said, "No, I've just got these two and I'm going to eat them both."

For the rest of that pay period I made it a point to eat lunch by myself. I didn't want anyone to know I was living on biscuits and pickle spread.

Chapter 20
A Baby

In August of 1948, Eileen had false labor. It looked and acted like the real thing. I rushed her to the doctor, and he said, "Take her to Toledo Hospital—I'll meet you there."

We got to the hospital and waited from seven in the morning until ten o'clock at night with no sign of the baby. Eileen's water never broke, but she suffered strong labor pains. The doctor said, "We don't know when this baby's coming. Take her back home."

For the next two weeks, she stayed at Mother and Wayne's while I was at work so Mom could watch her. Finally, Richard came out. We nicknamed him Ricky.

With a new baby, I needed a better car. I got rid of the Chrysler and bought a Plymouth coupe. Beneath the rear window, it had a recessed shelf where we'd make up a bed for the baby. He couldn't roll out, and that spot got all the heat from the heater. We'd go down the road and he'd sleep, toasty warm and happy. Today that seems unsafe, but children's car seats weren't invented yet. For their whole childhoods, our children stretched out in the backseat and took naps while we drove.

After Ricky was born, Dad called one day to ask if he and his wife, Reba, could come over.

He'd married Reba Zion in August 1940. Their wedding had been on Les Cheneaux Islands in Michigan's Upper Peninsula. I hadn't been invited. I met Reba once, briefly, after they wed, but I hadn't seen them for seven years.

Wedding photo of Reba Zion and Dick's father.

I held back my ire, said yes, and hung up.

Dad and Reba arrived, and it was awkward at first. Not on Eileen's part. She was friendly and outgoing. She and Reba chatted, and then Eileen got Ricky out of his crib and asked Dad if he wanted to hold his grandson. We made up from there, but it took a little while. They came to see us two or three times before we visited their house.

Dad was good with woodworking. After we reconciled, he came over and helped me build a two-shelf cabinet in the kitchen. Next, we built a frame under the sink with shelves to hold our dishes. We hung a curtain around that. The landlord was a real piece of work, though. He came over one day, saw the improvements, and said, "Very nice, I should raise the rent." And he did.

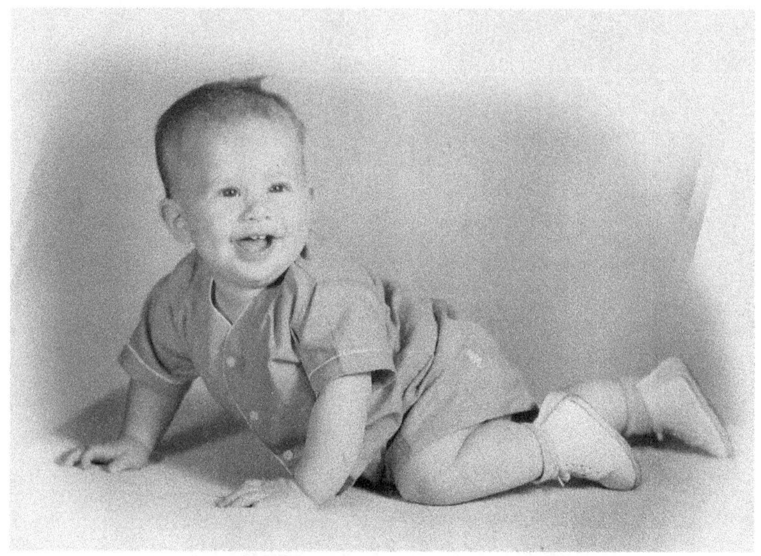

Richard (Ricky) Gartee.

Once he started to crawl, Ricky kept Eileen on the run. Rooms on the first floor of our house were all connected. He could go from the kitchen to the dining room to the living room, then through our bedroom and the bathroom before returning to the kitchen. Eileen would be doing something in the kitchen and Ricky would crawl off. She'd have to stop and search for him. She might not find him at first because he'd hide behind a chair or duck behind a cupboard.

One day she came in the kitchen and he was sitting with the door to the icebox open. He'd gotten out the butter and smeared it all over his head. He'd also opened the syrup and poured that in his hair. He picked up an egg and smashed it on his head, too. There he was, a gooey, icky, sticky mess, smiling big as cuffy, having a good time.

After he learned to walk, Ricky only got harder to catch. For some months he'd been taking a shortcut across the kitchen by running under the table. Then he grew.

One day, while his mother was after him, he dashed under the table and smacked his head on the underside rail of the tabletop. It knocked him right on his butt. He didn't cry. He just rubbed his forehead, stood up, and ran at it again. Same result.

Eileen was still laughing about it when I came home from work.

From his first Christmas, Ricky was fascinated with the Christmas tree. By the next year, when he started to talk, he'd say, "Pret—tee." The glass balls and the lights reflecting on them just thrilled him. He'd sit there for an hour, never bothering a soul, just going, "Pret—tee."

The following year, when it neared time for Santa Claus to come, he said, "All I want for Christmas is a snow shovel."

We'd already bought his presents, but I found him a child-size snow shovel at the local hardware store.

A day or two before Christmas, Michigan had a nice snowfall, an inch or two, and not too wet, so it wasn't heavy. Eileen and I debated whether he should get his present early. I said, "Let's give it to him today, while the snow is still soft and he can enjoy it. All he's been talking about is Santa Claus remembering to bring him a snow shovel."

We had his presents hidden in the garage, so when Ricky left the room to do something, I slipped out the back door, brought his snow shovel around the house, and set it on the front porch. On our front door we'd hung a set of old-fashioned sleigh bells as a Christmas decoration. I gave those bells a hard shake and yelled, "Ho, ho, ho!" I dashed around the house and came in the back door.

Meanwhile, Ricky had run to the front door as fast as his little legs would carry him and tried to get the front door open. Eileen fooled with the lock, delaying until I arrived, then she opened the door for him and there was that snow shovel.

Oh, he was excited. "How did Santa know I wanted a snow shovel?" We put on his snowsuit, boots, and mittens, and out we went to shovel snow.

* * *

I worked at Kelsey-Hayes a little over two years, until 1949 when they sold the plant to Ford, as agreed. They moved the factory to McKeesport, Pennsylvania, so I got laid off. I started to sign up for unemployment, but the man at the unemployment office told me to sign up for a veterans program instead. World War II veterans could get twenty dollars a week for up to fifty-two weeks without a waiting period. If I signed up for Michigan's unemployment, I'd have to wait two weeks before payments began.

Eileen was pregnant with our second child, so yeah, sign me up for that one. I needed the money right away.

The man filled out the veteran benefit forms and said, "You'll get a check next week."

Weeks passed, and I never received a check. We were running out of food. I borrowed ten bucks from Mom and Wayne to buy flour and basics. We lived on biscuits and pancakes. It was Christmastime, and Eileen's mother gave us a big ham. We ate that ham every way possible—baked ham, ham and potatoes, ham and cabbage, and then Eileen made soup out of the leftover bone. Still, no money came. I couldn't afford gas to drive there, so I called the man at the unemployment office every week saying, "I didn't get a check."

After four weeks, the guy said, "Come in and see me tomorrow morning."

When I got there, he said, "I don't know what's happened, Dick. We've checked your record, and you should have been getting money right along. Here's what we'll do. We're going to give you the four weeks we're behind right now so you can pay your rent and buy groceries."

I left for home happy as hell with eighty bucks in my pocket. I got home and in the mail were four twenty-dollar checks. I phoned the guy and said, "I've got to bring your money back."

"Why?" he said.

"I got home and all four checks were in the mailbox. They belong to you because you gave me eighty bucks."

"No," he said. "The money I gave you came out of a different fund. Don't worry about it. Keep the checks and the eighty bucks. Use it, and it will be money well spent."

Eileen and I were on a high. We drove to the grocery store and bought everything we needed. We stocked up, but we didn't waste a penny. We paid the landlord and kept back enough for the following month's rent. I still didn't have work, but we had all our bills paid and a full pantry.

After a couple months without finding work, I took a day job wheeling concrete for a contractor who was pouring a doctor's driveway. I mixed the concrete out by the street and then pushed it uphill in a wheelbarrow. He and another guy spread and smoothed the concrete. If I got behind, one of them would come down and help mix, but I did all the wheeling. They got as much of the driveway done as they could for that day and stopped work. They'd finish it the next day.

I awoke the following morning and could not straighten up. My hands, sore from gripping the wheelbarrow handles, would not close. My arms wouldn't move, either. Eileen called the man and told him I couldn't work because I couldn't walk. He said that was okay, and he'd pay me for the one day.

Ricky and baby sister, Sharyl.

Chapter 21
Baby Two and a Job in Tecumseh

A Michigan adage says that either March comes in like a lion and goes out like a lamb or vice versa. In 1950, March began like a lion. On the day Eileen gave birth to our daughter, the forty-eight-degree temperature would have seemed downright balmy four weeks before Easter were it not for the twenty-five-mile-per-hour winds. Despite the blustery weather, we were surprised and delighted by our pretty little girl—surprised because in those days, doctors had no test to predict a baby's sex ahead of time. Every delivery was a mystery revealed.

Eileen wanted to name the baby Nicola Lynne, but try as she might, my mother could not get her tongue around the syllables. We thought about it some more and came up with Sharyl, which Mom had no problem saying.

I was still out of work. As soon as Eileen got Sharyl home from the hospital and could take care of the baby on her own, I drove to Tecumseh, Michigan, about fifteen miles from Dundee. I'd heard Tecumseh Products Company was hiring.

Tecumseh Products manufactured compressors for refrigeration and air conditioning equipment and had become the largest supplier in the world. The Tecumseh city limits sign read, "Refrigeration Capital of the World." I turned off the main drag and drove south until I found the factory.

A line of guys waiting to apply for jobs stretched the entire length of the street. It was a Friday, and I thought, *I'm not going to get in line there. I'll never get to see anybody.* So I walked into the front office. The receptionist said, "May I help you?"

"Yes, you can. I'd like to see your office manager."

"What is it about?"

"Well, I'm looking for a job, and I think I've got experience he can use."

"If you'll have a seat, I'll call somebody."

She called Raynor Kerr because he had posted two job openings for payroll clerks. When he came up, I showed him my discharge from the Navy and a citation I had received from the naval station in Toledo. We talked for a half hour about my experience in disbursement and payroll for the Navy. He said, "You going to be home tomorrow?"

"Yes."

"You have a telephone?"

"Yes." I gave him my number.

"Can you come to work Monday morning if we hire you?"

"Yes."

"Okay, I'll run this past the personnel department and we'll see what we can do about it. I'll call you at three o'clock tomorrow."

When I got home, Eileen said, "How did you make out?"

"I'll tell you, Honey, it was the biggest bunch of bullshit. This guy talked to me for a half hour, then said, 'Go home, and I'll call you at three o'clock tomorrow.' Nobody calls anybody at three o'clock on a Saturday. That was just to get me out of there."

The next afternoon, Eileen and I were waiting at the house. When our old clock reached three, she got excited. "It's three o'clock. He ought to be calling."

"He's not going to call. I told you that was all BS."

Then the phone rang. It was Raynor Kerr. "Dick, can you be at work at seven o'clock Monday morning?"

"Yes, sir."

"Anything wrong with you physically?"

"Not to my knowledge. When I got out of the Navy a couple of years ago, I was sound as a dollar, and I presume I still am."

"Well, be here at seven a.m. We'll send you to the company doctor. If you pass your physical, you not only have a job but I'll pay you for the time you spent at the doctor's."

"Okay, it's a deal," I said.

The rest of the story is that I worked there for thirty years.

I liked working for Raynor and we became friends. He and his wife, Arlene, would visit us in Dundee, or we'd go to their house in Tecumseh and play cards. Our children started calling them Grandma and Grandpa Kerr. Raynor liked to smoke fat stogies while we played cards, and their smell would drive Eileen mad.

My job was good, but our money was still tight. One Friday night, I had a single beer left in the icebox. The entire drive home, I was thinking, *Boy, I got this cold beer waiting for me.*

When I got home, my beer was gone. Eileen told me Ricky had taken it out, somehow got the cap off, and started drinking it before she found him. She dumped what was left down the sink. So, there was no beer.

Eileen had just finished telling me her tale when there was a rap at the door. It was Raynor and my coworker in payroll, Fred Westfall. "We thought we'd come down and have a cold beer with you."

"I haven't got any beer," I said.

"You haven't got a beer?"

"I had one, but Ricky got into it."

"Oh, don't blame that poor little boy for you not having any beer," Raynor said. "Fred, I guess we have to bring our own beer."

Fred opened the brown paper sack he was carrying and took out a six-pack. "Yeah, here, have a beer. You got to bring your own damn beer when you come to Dick's." They had a big time teasing me about that.

Stealing my last beer wasn't Ricky's only interference with my bad habits. Grapes grew in the backyard of the house on Toledo Street. I'd never made wine before, but I had grapes, so I thought, *Well, why not make them into wine*?

I got a crock, mashed the grapes in it, added sugar, filled it with water, and let them ferment. I scraped the foam off and left the mixture to ferment some more. When I decided it was ready, I put it in bottles. It had the most beautiful red color you ever saw. It looked like it just had to be perfect, but it was sour as hell, almost vinegar. I could hardly stand the taste, but I kept one bottle just to show people the color.

I woke up one morning to the sound of Ricky giggling. He'd gotten out of bed and was in the dining room sitting next to a cupboard where I kept the bottle of wine. Somehow, he'd managed to get the cork out and was sitting there drinking that terrible, sour old wine. Laughing, having a big time. He'd only drunk a little, but enough to give him the giggles.

There was another vice of mine that Ricky impeded. I smoked in those days and had a collection of pipes, a clay meerschaum and several other nice pipes. Eileen heard splashing and found Ricky in the bathroom washing every one of my pipes in the toilet. They had to be thrown away, and that ended my pipe smoking.

Raynor Kerr had a sense of humor and, throughout the workday, the guys in our department would rib one another.

Fred Westfall and I weren't making much money. We'd started at a buck an hour and were probably up to a dollar fifteen an hour, but the company would allow merit raises. I'd say to Fred, "It's been about six months since we had a raise. I think we ought to put the pressure on Raynor again."

Raynor would come in with a joke. "Boys, I heard a good one."

He'd tell it and we'd keep a straight face. I'd look at Fred and say, "I don't see anything funny about that, do you, Fred?"

"No."

"For another nickel an hour, I could probably laugh at it."

"Yeah, for a nickel or dime an hour I would laugh at it, too," Fred would say.

We'd keep this up for four or five days, every time Raynor told a joke. Next thing you know, we'd get a nickel merit raise.

One year, as the deadline for income tax approached, there was lots of joking about it among the guys in our office. "You better get your income taxes filed or the Treasury Department will be looking for you."

A man in a dark suit came into the office and said, "I'm looking for Raynor Kerr."

The fellow at the desk nearest the door pointed across the room. "That's him, right there."

The suit walked over to Raynor, pulled out a badge, and said, "Mr. Kerr? FBI."

Raynor looked like he was going to crap his britches.

Raynor wasn't in any trouble. They were looking for someone or checking to see if a person had been working at a certain time. Raynor, as the head of payroll, had the time cards for every employee there. But the incident gave us something to tease him about for a long time afterwards.

Of course, Raynor had things to tease me about, too. One Sunday afternoon, Eileen and I were playing cards at the Kerrs' home when Raynor's wife, Arlene, said, "What's Ricky got?"

Eileen and I looked across the room, but our son and his sister were playing harmlessly.

"No," Arlene insisted, "he's eating something."

About that time, Ricky pulled a cold, greasy pork chop out of his pocket, took a bite, and put it back in his pocket. We'd had pork chops for dinner and he'd saved one.

Monday, Raynor told everyone at work, "Poor little boy isn't sure when his next meal is coming—has to keep a spare pork chop in his pocket."

Chapter 22
In-Laws

Comedians on TV used to tell lots of jokes about dreadful mothers-in-law, but that wasn't true for us. Eileen loved my mother and depended on her for advice and help with the children. Eileen's mother, Ruth, loved me as much as she ever loved anyone except her own children. And I loved her.

Ruth was a remarkable self-made woman who ran her own restaurant. She wouldn't take guff off anybody.

Like my mom, Ruth had persevered through difficult times and didn't shy from hard work. Ruth was born in Kentucky into a family of ten kids. When she was four years old, her father, Andrew Thornsberry, lost his sight and became unable to work. It was probably cataracts or glaucoma, but in 1912 ophthalmology wasn't very advanced. Her mother supported the family as a midwife, and it fell to Ruth to keep house and take care of her blind father while her older siblings worked the garden and fields.

When she was eighteen, Ruth married Marvin Eblen. Two years later, Marvin left Kentucky to find work in Monroe, Michigan. Once he secured a job, Ruth and baby Eileen joined him. The Eblens settled in Monroe and had two more children, Geraldine (Jerri), and Ronnie. When Ruth was thirty-four, Marvin died.

A widow with three kids to feed, she found work as a dishwasher and assistant cook in a Greek restaurant. Later, she became head cook at another restaurant. Then a man named Del King opened a new restaurant and asked Ruth to work for him. While there, she learned restaurant management. After a time, they made an agreement for her to run his place on commission.

Ruth decided she'd open her own restaurant and partnered with her best friend, Clara Edmondson. The restaurant was a success, in part due to the Southern recipes on her menu. Henry Ford had sent busses into the South to recruit workers for his factories and bring them to the North. By the time Ruth and Clara went into business, a sizable portion of the Monroe workforce was from Kentucky. Ruth's chicken and dumplings and homemade pies were comfort food to the transplanted Kentuckians. Ruth soon owned two restaurants, and she also bought two houses as rental properties.

One of her restaurants was on the east side of Monroe near several bars. She'd get a lot of drunken customers when the bars closed. One Friday night, a drunk was giving the waitresses a hard time. Ruth came over and told him to leave or she'd throw him out.

He stood up and laughed in Ruth's face because he was a good-sized man and she weighed 105 pounds. Ruth grabbed him, one hand on his collar and the other on the seat of his pants, and took him right out the door.

A few moments later, the police officer who worked her beat came in for coffee. His waitress said, "You should have been here a minute earlier."

"Why?"

"Ruth threw out this drunk."

"Where is he?"

"I don't know. She sent him out by the seat of his pants."

When Ruth came out of the kitchen, the cop said, "Ruth, why didn't you call me? I'd have taken care of him for you."

She said, "Shit, if I needed your help to throw him out, I'd have probably been dead by now."

Ruth's other restaurant was next to the bus station, and she did good business there. Besides her regulars, there were customers every time a bus arrived. But one night she was walking home from there alone when a man grabbed her by the arm and demanded her money. She was only a couple of houses from her home so she hit him and fought him off, and then she ran into her house and called the police. The man was long gone by the time the police arrived, and she didn't know who he was. After that, I gave her a blackjack for protection. It was a leather-covered bludgeon made of lead, with a flexible handle. Wayne had given it to me. I don't know where he got it from, but if you hit someone with it, they were going down. Ruth carried it in her pocketbook for years.

Ruth worked long hours at her restaurant and took her meals there, so she didn't keep much food in her house. When we came to visit, she'd often have us meet her at the restaurant and eat there before going to the house.

One week, Ruth called us before we left for Monroe. She said she was at home, but we should stop at the restaurant for lunch before we came over as she had nothing to feed us. So we did. Our waitress was new and didn't know who we were. After the meal she brought the check, and I paid it. I wasn't about to tell someone I'd never met that I didn't have to pay because I was the owner's son-in-law.

When Ruth found out what I'd done, she showed up at our house for breakfast the next weekend with a sack of groceries. "If you're going to pay for your food when you come to see me, I'm going to do the same." It was a real sticking point for her, and no one in her restaurant ever dared give us the check again.

When you visited Ruth, she expected you to eat. If you said, "We'll be there at two in the afternoon," there was something to eat when you arrived. Even if you dropped in for a surprise visit, she'd call over to the restaurant and send you to pick up an order.

In 1950, Eileen's younger sister, Jerri, married Stan Billock. This left Ruth's sixteen-year-old son Ronnie on his own while she worked at the restaurant. Since our two-story house on Toledo Street had an extra bedroom upstairs, Ruth decided Ronnie should live with us while he finished high school. We agreed. Ronnie graduated from Dundee High School in 1952 and entered the Milwaukee School of Engineering. He completed one year there and then enlisted in the Navy because he hoped the Navy would further his training in electronics. He was right. As soon as he was discharged, he was snapped up by IBM and had a lifelong career with them.

Eileen's brother Ronnie joins the Navy.

Ronnie bought a sporty Chevrolet convertible while he was in college. When he enlisted in the Navy, he left it with his mom. He kept telling her the car couldn't sit, it needed to be driven. But Ruth didn't know how to drive. Stan tried to teach her a couple of times, but she wouldn't do what he said and they got angry with each other. After I heard that, I wasn't about to try. She and I got along well, and there was no reason to invite discord.

One day, while she was bad-mouthing Stan over his driving lessons, he said, "Go, take your driving test."

Stan took her to the driver's license office, which, in those days, was the police station. He got in the backseat and the cop who was testing her got in the front. Ruth knew all the cops in Monroe. They ate in her restaurant.

The cop said, "Go up here and turn left." Ruth did. He said, "Up here, turn right." She turned right. All the while, she drove slowly, and a car was tailgating her.

The cop said, "Stop." Ron's car had power brakes. She hit them hard.

Convertibles have a steel frame across the top of the windshield where the retractable roof latches, and in those days, cars didn't have seatbelts. The cop hit his head on the frame. Stan bounced against the back of the cop's seat, which flew forward. The tailgater slammed into the rear bumper, and the cop got another jolt.

Although the cop didn't want to give the driver behind them a ticket, he *had* been tailgating. So the cop got out, madder than hell, chewed the driver out, and then let him go with a warning.

He got back in the car and said, "Ruth, take me back to the station."

She said, "Well, it's about time you made up your mind. Why didn't you say you wanted to go there in the first place? That's where I'd have taken you."

She drove back to station and the cop told her to park. He got out and said, "Stan, take her out someplace and let her drive around until she gets used to this thing, but don't bring her back to me. Ruth, you've got a license."

When Ronnie came home for a visit, everyone gathered at Ruth's house for a family dinner. During the meal, the conversation turned to her infamous incidents of dealing with unruly customers. Ruth said, "Oh, I'm not like that anymore."

"You're not?" Ronnie said.

"No. Just the other day I let a woman call me a bitch and get away with it."

"How did that happen?"

"She was halfway down the street before I could get to the door."

* * *

In the 1950s, silver dollar coins were still in circulation. Although most people carried paper money, some of Ruth's customers occasionally paid their bill with silver dollars. She would save these and give them to her grandkids, Ricky, Sharyl, and Lynda (Stan and Jerri's daughter).

Later, when we visited Mother and Wayne, Mom gave the kids nickels to buy candy. Ricky handed his back to her and said, "Grandma, I want one of the big nickels." Ruth's silver dollars.

As our kids got older, they loved going to Grandma Eblen's restaurant because she permitted them to order anything they wanted for free. Ricky ordered fried shrimp because Eileen never made shrimp at home. Sharyl, though, would order a dill pickle sandwich. The waitresses could never get over it. She could have anything in her grandmother's restaurant, and what she wanted was two slices of bread with butter and those dill slices restaurants put on hamburgers.

One Saturday when we visited Ruth, she told the kids they couldn't watch TV because her set wasn't working. Wayne had given Ricky a little pocket tool set. It had a screwdriver with interchangeable straight and Phillips-head blades, a small crescent wrench, and a tiny pair of pliers. Ricky got out his tool set, determined to fix her TV, and Ruth was going to let him.

"Don't let him do that," I said.

"Oh, he won't do any harm," she said.

I said, "He's going to take that thing apart."

I knew from experience. When Ricky was just a toddler, we had a Formica kitchen table with chrome legs and matching chairs. These were very popular in the 1950s; everyone had a kitchen set like that. The back of the chair was fastened to the chrome frame with two screws that had heads the size of a dime. Ricky would take his thumbnail and work on those until he got them unscrewed. I'd get a screwdriver and tighten those screws as tightly as I could turn them. The next night, I'd come home from work and find the back of the chair hanging cockeyed and the screw on the floor. How his little fingernail stood up against that screw, I never understood.

Chapter 23
Perpetual Crises

I had a good job at Tecumseh Products, but all was not perfect. Eileen had a heart problem—the result of contracting rheumatic fever as a child—that wasn't discovered until she was carrying our first child. She gave birth to Ricky and, eighteen months later, Sharyl. Then, five months after Sharyl, she became pregnant again. The doctors told her she couldn't have that one. Choose—her life or the baby's. We knew our two kids needed her as a mother more than we needed a third child. She took great pride in her children, loved them dearly.

* * *

On Memorial Day in 1951, Ricky was two-and-a-half and Sharyl had recently turned one. Eileen put Sharyl in a high chair while she boiled eggs to make potato salad for a picnic later in the day. She had already prepared fried chicken for us to eat cold, so once she finished the potato salad, she wouldn't need to cook the rest of the day. We could just laze around and take it easy. But that didn't happen. In an instant, the day turned into a disaster.

Ricky climbed up on Sharyl's high chair and they fussed. She gave him a shove and he lost his balance. As he fell, he grabbed the pot handle and boiling water drenched him. He screamed, Eileen screamed, and Sharyl started crying. I realized his flannel pajamas were holding the scalding water to him. I had to get them off. Eileen panicked. Then I did, too, because when I pulled his PJs open, the flesh came off his chest. There was blood everywhere. I had never been so scared in my life. Eileen got a soft baby blanket, and I wrapped him in it. "Grab Sharyl! We're going to the doctor's!"

The next thing I knew, we were racing to Dr. Williamson's. I don't even remember getting in the car. Dundee had no hospital. Dr. Williamson's medical office, which was in his home, was the town's only medical facility. I ran in with the baby in my arms: "Ricky got burned!"

I started to open the blanket, and more skin peeled off with it.

Dr. Williamson took one look and said, "Go to Toledo. I'll meet you there."

Toledo, Ohio, thirty miles away, was the nearest city with a major hospital. I drove like a bat out of hell, but the doctor beat me there. I don't know how he did it. Dr. Williamson had told his wife to call a burn specialist while we were en route, and the specialist met us at the hospital.

I didn't think Ricky had a prayer. The next time I saw him, he was bandaged up like a mummy. Scary.

They kept him hospitalized for a month. Fortunately, Eileen's brother, Ronnie, was living with us and would watch Sharyl while Eileen and I visited Ricky. The longer he stayed in the hospital, the harder it got for us to go when visiting hours were over. He'd stand in his hospital bed, crying, "Please don't leave me. Please don't go home." Hardest thing I ever did was to walk away with Ricky begging us to stay.

A nurse named Mary was his favorite. She'd put him on the gurney while she delivered sheets and towels to the rooms, and he'd ride up there like he was big stuff.

Ricky had to have more than his share of injections and grew to fear them. Four teenage boys were in a ward down the hall, and when it was time for his shot, Ricky would duck away from the nurses, run into the boys' room, and hide beneath one of their beds. The boy in the bed would drape his blanket over the side so Ricky couldn't be seen. A nurse would come in and say, "Have you seen Ricky?"

"Not in here."

Away she'd go looking for him, and Ricky would laugh.

His burns healed enough that he could be discharged, but his scars formed keloid tissue that caused them to grow excessively. In those days, the treatment to shrink keloid scars was radiation. So our three-year-old son was given massive doses of radiation, probably more than anyone should have in a lifetime.

* * *

We didn't have it easy with Sharyl, either. She started having small seizures when she was young. We took her to the hospital and a specialist drilled two holes in her skull to look at her brain. When he was done, the specialist explained to us that in every developing fetus, there is a pouch at the top of the pharynx (throat) called Rathke's pouch. It eventually loses connection with the pharynx and forms the pituitary. In some cases, the developing wall doesn't fully fill the pouch, leaving behind a small cleft. The cleft can develop a benign, fluid-filled growth on the pituitary gland called a Rathke's cleft cyst.

The doctors discovered that Sharyl's seizures only happened when she got excessively tired, so they put her on a child's dosage of phenobarbital, a couple drops in orange juice. At first we had to give it to her every day, but eventually we only gave it to her if we saw her becoming too tired. But her doctors warned me, "She'll never live past thirty-seven." Fortunately, they were wrong. Sharyl is now a sixty-eight-year-old grandmother.

* * *

When Ricky recovered from his burns we bought him a tricycle. He had a terrible time learning to pedal it. We'd try to get him to put his feet on the pedals and push, but when it didn't move, he grew impatient and put his feet on the ground to walk it. Sharyl watched with envy, but he was very possessive of his trike.

We'd say to Sharyl, "Would you like to sit on Ricky's tricycle?"

He'd say, "No," and run over and sit on it. That was *his* tricycle.

So we bought one for her. She'd been carefully observing Ricky's attempts to ride. As soon as she got hers, she climbed right on and took off pedaling.

Sharyl Gartee

There was never a child easier to potty train than Sharyl, either. One of her grandmothers gave her a pair of silk panties for a present. Eileen discovered that Sharyl would sooner bust a gut than go in those panties. All we had to do was keep her in silk panties and she was potty trained.

Sharyl was tight with money, though. As far as Ricky was concerned, money was just something to get candy with; it was a waste of time for him to hold on to a nickel. I'd give the kids ten cents and take them to the little neighborhood store to buy penny candy. Ricky would eat all of his as soon as he got it. Sharyl would eat a little bite at a time. Three days later, when Ricky was all out of candy, she'd go into her stash, get a piece of candy, and eat it in little nibbles, holding it up in front of him, just tormenting him. Finally, I told her, "It's all right that you save your candy, and it's all right for you to go into the bedroom and eat a piece when you want, but you can't tease Ricky with it." She quit after that.

When the kids were a little older, I developed a trick to teach them fairness, and to control how much candy they ate. I'd buy a single candy bar to be shared between them. I'd unwrap it and hand them a butter knife. The rule was that one child got to cut the candy bar in half, but the other child got first choice. Oh, how grueling their decision making, how precisely they measured the cut.

* * *

In addition to Eileen's heart condition, Ricky's burns, and Sharyl's seizures, my stepfather, Wayne, was frequently hospitalized for heart attacks and gallbladder attacks. I blamed his gallbladder attacks on the stupid things he ate. He'd open a can of oily sardines and eat them with a handful of peanuts for breakfast.

When Wayne wasn't having a heart attack, Eileen was. At one point I questioned, *What's wrong here? Other families aren't having one person after another in the hospital.* Eileen would get out and Wayne would go in. Wayne would just get out, and Eileen would go back in.

CHAPTER 24
TIME STUDY

I worked at Tecumseh Products under Raynor Kerr for two or three years. One day, he said, "Dick, I'm sorry, but they're making me lay off people. I have to lay off you, Fred Westfall, and two other guys. It won't be a long layoff, just the summer months when business is slow. As soon as we start back, you've got a job."

I was off work about a week when I got a call from Virgil Tucker, the company's assistant treasurer. He told me who he was and asked me to come in and see him. When I arrived, he took me to Paul Breitenwischer's office. Paul was Secretary of the company. Paul said, "Dick, I understand you're darn good with math."

"Yes, sir, I do all right."

"Have you ever thought of doing something besides payroll? You know, in industrial engineering there is a field called time study. It involves a lot of math. We think you'd do well at it if you'd like to try it. It doesn't pay the biggest pay in the world; it starts at three hundred dollars a month."

Well, three hundred a month sounded pretty good to me.

Paul continued, "But we'll expect you to take some college courses. We're revising the time-study department and sending the men to Wayne State University in Detroit and the University of Toledo."

Time and motion study, as I was about to learn, is direct and continuous observation of the time it takes to accomplish a task, which is measured with a timekeeping device. In those days, we used a stopwatch.

The goal is to find more efficient ways of performing a task. Time and motion study is based on the ideas of Frederick Taylor and Frank and Lillian Gilbreth. The book *Cheaper by the Dozen*, and the film based on it, contain many humorous examples of Frank's application of efficiency techniques to his home life.

Tecumseh Products created a "piece-rate" incentive program that paid workers a bonus beyond their hourly pay for producing an above-average number of good pieces. Time-study measurements were used to establish the baseline and calculate the piece rate for each machine operation. This also allowed the company to know the actual manufacturing cost per compressor.

Members of the Tecumseh Products Time Study Department 1954 to 1957. Pictured left to right: Perry Wirick, Harold Hornsby, Dick Gartee, Louise Matheny, Clarence Bumpus, Doc Morden, Bill Kuhlman.

Five days after I started in the time-study department, the head of the department got fired. He was replaced by Clarence Bumpus, the president of the union, whose knowledge of time study came mainly from contract discussions and union disputes. Clarence added two more union guys, Doc Morden and Harold Hornby. They had been on the union board with him, but they likewise knew nothing about time study.

The company divided us into two groups. Clarence, Joe Springer, and I went to Wayne State University twice a week for evening classes. The others attended University of Toledo. At the end of the semester, we passed our final exams. The Toledo and Wayne State groups graduated at the same time.

I took to time study like a duck to water. It wasn't long before I had responsibility for everything from the white room assembly area to the back of the plant. The rest of our department was flocked up in the machine shop and service departments.

Tecumseh Products had been founded by Ray Herrick, a master toolmaker who worked in Michigan's booming auto industry during the 1920s. Herrick's reputation led to his rapid advancement into supervisory positions, and he became friends with Henry Ford.

Next, Ray became manager of a small-engine company in Hillsdale, Michigan; later, he and another toolmaker, Bill Sage, formed Hillsdale Tool & Machine Company to manufacture refrigerator parts. Initially, Bill, his wife, and Ray owned equal shares, but eventually Ray bought controlling interest. However, they'd started the company during the Great Depression, and it was near bankruptcy by 1934.

The city of Tecumseh had a 30,000-square-foot abandoned foundry with a dirt floor and a strong need to bring jobs to the community. The citizens of Tecumseh helped renovate the building, clean up the inside of the plant, and pour a concrete floor without charging for labor. Ray moved his factory there and renamed it Tecumseh Products Company. My boss in time study, Clarence Bumpus, had been with Ray in Hillsdale and had helped set up the plant in Tecumseh.

When the first machines were delivered, the company didn't have forklifts or any equipment to move them. These were huge machines, ten feet in diameter and eight feet tall. The men used pry bars to lift the front edge of a machine and then slid scoop shovels under it. The rest of the guys pushed the machine from the back while the men in front kept the scoop shovels in place and steered it into position. Then they'd anchor it. A lot of that work was done gratis by the people of Tecumseh. They had nothing to lose—without a factory, they had no jobs.

Ray got the plant open, and Henry Ford helped Ray secure a line of credit from a Detroit bank. Ray focused the company on manufacturing hermetically sealed refrigeration compressors. By the end of the Depression, plant production exceeded one hundred thousand compressors a year. During World War II, they limited compressor production to those used in military equipment and switched to manufacturing ammunition shell casings and parts for aircraft engines.

After the war was over and servicemen returned to civilian jobs, the demand for refrigerators to replace iceboxes zoomed. Window air conditioners were invented, and they used Tecumseh compressors. By the time I started with the company, its annual production was over two million compressors and sales had reached $72 million a year.

I feel fortunate to have worked for two great industrialists. The first was Henry Ford, whom I saw on several occasions when I was a teenager, and the second was Ray Herrick. Without Ray, America would still have gotten refrigeration, but it might have taken another ten years to evolve.

Ray kept on top of everything at Tecumseh Products. When a certain compressor model wasn't selling as he thought it should, he gathered everybody in the factory and said, "Boys, I'm going to have to ask you to work harder. I'm not going to pay you any less, I'm not going to pay you any extra, but we're going to put out more compressors. Tomorrow morning, I'm going to cut the price two dollars a unit, and I can't do it unless we make more compressors per shift."

He'd cut the price, and we'd sell compressors.

The city of Tecumseh got a good deal and a generous friend when it convinced Ray to move his company there. In business, he was tough-minded and stubborn, like Ford and other self-made industrialists of his time, but to his community, he was generous beyond imagination. He built a hospital, a new library, and new school buildings, and he also donated money to rebuild and expand dozens of local churches.

I'd worked at the company for a couple of years when Ray offered his employees a free lot in a new subdivision, Herrick Park, plus $500 toward building a house. Or you could apply $500 toward the cost of a lot in any other Tecumseh subdivision. I didn't care for Herrick Park, but we found a quarter-acre lot in Tecumseh Acres for $500. We'd have to wait though, until we saved enough money for a down payment on the house.

When Eileen's mother learned we were looking at a house in Tecumseh, she gave us a check for $500, which enabled us to buy right away. I wanted to repay her, but Ruth wouldn't have it. She said she'd helped Jerri and Stan get their house, and the check was our Christmas gift. We bought the house and lived there until our kids were grown.

We liked Tecumseh, but it was small, not exactly a shopper's mecca. Its business strip consisted of two hardware stores, two dime stores, two jewelry stores, two drug stores, several restaurants, and a men's clothing shop. One year, Eileen needed to buy a nice dress to wear to a wedding. I don't remember what year, but the kids were still young. A Federal Department Store had just opened in Monroe, so we drove there.

Federal's was a chain based out of Detroit that offered a larger selection of merchandise than local stores. The ladies' department had a seating area on a dais with chairs where the husbands waited while their wives tried on dresses. It took Eileen a while to find the one she wanted and the kids grew restless, hopping on and off the dais. I tried to keep them seated, but they were bored. Finally, one of them said, "Tell us a story."

"Yeah," said the other, "a story."

At the moment, I couldn't remember any children's stories, but they were pressuring me. I had to make up something quick. "Okay, once there was a boy and girl who had a dog named Meow and a cat named Bowwow. When they wanted to play, they'd call out, 'Meow, Meow,' and the dog would come running into the room going 'bowwow, bowwow!'"

The kids started giggling, so I continued. "And if the children wanted the cat, all they had to do was call, 'Bowwow!' But when Bowwow came and Meow saw him, Meow would bark, 'bowwow, bowwow.' Then Bowwow's fur would stand up, and he'd go 'meow, meow, meow.' This would, of course, make Meow bark even more. With Meow going 'bowwow, bowwow' and Bowwow going 'meow, meow,' they chased each other around the house: 'meow, meow, meow' and 'bowwow, bowwow, bowwow!'"

Oh, the kids thought this was the funniest thing they'd ever heard. They were rolling around the dais from laughter when their mother came out of the dressing room carrying her new dress in a garment bag emblazoned with the store logo.

"Mommy, Mommy, you have to hear this story. Tell it, Daddy! Tell it again."

I gave her a shortened version. She smiled and rolled her eyes.

Chapter 25
Old Wounds and New Traditions

We had our new house in Tecumseh. Ricky started kindergarten and decided he was to be called Rick—he was a big boy now. Two years later, Sharyl started school, too. I was thirty years old but still dealing with fallout from my parents' divorce. Christmas day had become an ordeal. We'd open presents with the kids and then, before they could play with their toys, we'd pack the kids into the car. We'd go to Mother and Wayne's, have breakfast with them, and open presents there. She was trying to outdo Dad, so the kids would get a trunk load of presents. But I'd have to take their toys from them before they hardly started playing so we could jump in the car and rush to Monroe.

Ruth would have a big dinner for us, and more presents for the kids. When she cooked at home, she couldn't break the habit of her restaurant years. Ruth would prepare three different meats: ham, turkey, and roast beef. She expected you to eat all three.

Then we'd leave there and go to Dad's. Reba didn't want to be outdone, so she'd serve a big meal, and they'd also have a load of presents for the kids. By then, the kids were tired and we were all full of food up to our eyebrows. One year, after a whole day of this, Rick got cranky and threw one of his presents.

I grabbed him by the arm and yelled, "You stop that right now."

I no more than did that and the thought hit me, *What are you doing? This is Christmas. The kid hasn't had a chance to play with a single toy. He's worn out.*

So I said, "Well, we're going to head home."

I told Eileen that night, "This is the last Christmas we are ever doing this. From now on, Christmas is going to be at our house."

The conversation was forgotten until the following December. Mother was sitting in our kitchen when she raised the subject of Christmas plans. "What time are you coming on Christmas?"

"We're having Christmas here," I said.

"You're having it here? Who's coming?"

"Everybody is invited."

"Who is everybody?"

"You and Wayne, Ruth, Stan, Jerri, Lynda . . . Dad and Reba."

Mom, suddenly serious, looked at me and said, "I'm not coming."

"Mom, you and dad got divorced and I had nothing to say about it. You raised me the way you wanted me raised. These are my two kids, and we're not going to drag them from house to house all day. We're going to have Christmas at my house, and you and Wayne are invited. You know I love you deeply, and we'd love to have you come, but if you don't, that's strictly your choice."

Out of the house she ran, crying. Got in her car, slammed the door, and drove away. We didn't hear anything from her the rest of the week and into the next week—unusual, because Mom and Wayne only lived about twenty miles from Tecumseh and visited frequently. One Friday she came into town to buy groceries. She walked in our house, sat for a few minutes, then said, "We'll be here for Christmas."

I said, "Great! Wonderful! It wouldn't be Christmas without you, Mom."

Stan's family celebrated Christmas on Christmas Eve. When they came home from midnight Mass, they'd open their presents and eat with his family, so this plan was fine with Stan and Jerri. They could sleep in and then get up and drive Ruth to our house for Christmas dinner.

Every Christmas, the company gave each employee the choice of a free turkey or a canned ham. Wayne was now also working at Tecumseh Products, driving a fork-lift. So he chose the ham and saved it for a later holiday, and I took the turkey for our Christmas dinner. These were large birds that easily fed twelve, plus leftovers. Eileen prepared the turkey the night before and then got up at five o'clock on Christmas morning to put it in the oven.

Mom and Wayne arrived first. They brought in a big armload of presents, and the kids opened them up. We served coffee and rolls. Eileen and I got busy preparing dinner. Then Dad and Reba arrived. They sat on one side of the room, Mom and Wayne on the other, a wall of awkwardness between them. Reba tried to make a little conversation, but Mother just stared out the window and limited her communication to yes-or-no answers. Dad and Wayne weren't so bad. Wayne could talk to anybody, and he soon had Dad chatting up a storm, but Mother was having a wretched time. I had to do something.

As I've said before, both the Rathkes and the Gartees were card-playing families, and they especially liked euchre, a four-person game. I went into the kitchen, where Eileen was cooking, and said to her, "This is awful. I'm going to get a euchre game started. After we've played a few hands, you call for me to help you with something and I'll get Mom to take over my hand."

I returned to the living room, set up the card table, and said, "Reba, I believe you and I can beat any two people in this house in euchre. Be my partner and let's whip these old men."

Wayne said, "Ted, are we going to let them get away with that?" And so we started playing.

Each team had scored a couple of points apiece when, right on cue, Eileen called from the kitchen. "Dick, I need your help. Can you come here?"

"Yep." I looked around and said, "Here, Mom, play my hand out. I've got to help Eileen for a minute."

I handed her my cards, told her what trump was, and left for the kitchen. She couldn't refuse.

Eileen and I puttered around for a while getting dinner ready. When we looked in the living room, the four of them were playing euchre as if no one had ever been angry at anybody. From that day on, there would never be a problem with my parents sharing Christmas at our house.

They continued playing cards until Stan, Jerri, Ruth, and Lynda arrived. The kids opened more presents, and then we set dinner places at the card table for the kids. With leaves in, our kitchen table was just big enough to seat the nine adults, but it was a tight squeeze.

After we got through that Christmas, I wouldn't say Mom and Dad ever became friends, but they were cordial and we could have family events without anyone's nose getting out of shape. One time, they even teamed up to help me kill and clean seventy-five chickens.

Max Goode, from Dundee, worked at Tecumseh Products. He'd been raising leghorn chickens and decided he was losing money and would get rid of them. I bought the whole lot.

On Saturday, I picked up the chickens in cages and brought them home on a utility trailer. Mom and Wayne, Dad and Reba, and Eileen and I processed them in the backyard. I set up an old washtub over a fire, filled it with water, and heated it to boiling. We killed the chickens, dressed them out, and put them in our freezer. I gave each of my parents some to take home.

Wayne and I did most of the killing and plucked most of the feathers. Dad would then draw them (take the guts out). Finally, Reba, Mom, and Eileen washed the chickens and prepared them for the freezer. Rick and Sharyl were around, but they didn't help. They were feeling sorry for all the chickens that were getting killed.

We were working along, and it was going much faster than we anticipated. The cages were almost empty. We were amazed that we were nearly done.

I went to get a rake so we could clean up all the feathers. Our quarter-acre lot had a large garden, a small orchard, and a shed I had built to house the garden tractor, lawn mower, and yard tools. When I reached the shed and opened the door, a dozen chickens came at me.

The kids had been "rescuing" them from their cages and hiding them in my shed. Saving those chickens' lives.

* * *

Independence Day became another holiday when my parents would join us and get along with each other. My boyhood friend John King and his wife, Coleen, had two children near the same age as our kids. John had discovered Lower Huron Metropolitan Park near Belleville, Michigan, and suggested it would be a good place for a large group picnic. The park covered 1,258 acres spanning both sides of the Huron River. It had wooded hills, ravines, streams, springs, a cable suspension footbridge, and an Olympic-size swimming pool with lifeguards and diving boards of different heights.

With the Fourth of July coming up, we decided everyone should meet there in the early morning. John and Coleen brought their kids and John's parents. I invited Mother and Wayne and Dad and Reba. Stan and Jerri brought their daughter and Eileen's mother. Cal Zorn, another friend from grade school, came with his wife and children. The park had ample parking and extra-long picnic tables. We dragged several tables together, set up grills and camp stoves, and started making breakfast. Mom peeled, sliced, and fried potatoes. Dad knew a butcher who sold slabs of bacon, and he brought enough to feed everybody. He hand-cut the bacon in thick slices and Reba fried it. John and I got several pans of eggs going while other people set the table and made toast.

How do you make toast without electricity? We had a pyramid-shaped metal apparatus with holes in it, like a cheese grater. You placed it on the camp stove burner and put a slice of bread on each side. When one face of the bread was toasted, you flipped the bread over and toasted the opposite side. You could toast four slices of bread at a time.

After breakfast, we cleaned up the dishes and set up horseshoe and lawn dart games. The kids ran off exploring the woods and creeks, finding tadpoles and other creatures. When the swimming pool opened, they went swimming. Meanwhile, the adults played cards.

In the afternoon, we fired up the grills again and cooked hamburgers and hot dogs. Each family had brought dishes to share—potato salad, coleslaw, Jell-O salad, baked beans, cupcakes, and pies. We made the kids wait one hour after eating before they were allowed to swim again, so they played tag and ran around the park. As soon as the hour was up, they raced off to the pool and stayed there as long as we let them.

At the end of the day, we got leftovers out of our coolers, ate a little more, then packed our picnic supplies and returned to our respective towns to watch fireworks.

From that day on, Fourth of July picnics at Lower Huron Park became a tradition, and we celebrated this way for many years. Mom and Dad got along just fine, especially in a big group where there were other people to talk to.

* * *

Michigan is an exceptionally beautiful state with lakes and forests that make ideal vacation spots. Michigan's Upper Peninsula, with pristine forests and dozens of waterfalls, is the land Longfellow writes of in *The Song of Hiawatha*. Eileen and I vacationed there with our kids several summers.

I wasn't making big money, so we traveled inexpensively. We'd rent a cabin and use it as a base of operations. In the mornings, Eileen packed a cooler with food for the day. We'd have breakfast at the cabin and then take day trips to waterfalls and other sights. At noon, we'd stop at a roadside table. I'd light the grill and cook hamburgers or whatever she'd planned for us. After lunch, we'd jump in the car and head for another destination, then return to the cabin by evening. Except for gasoline and the cabin rental, we could travel all week for the same cost as eating at home.

Mom's brothers and sisters liked Hubbard Lake in the northeastern part of Michigan's Lower Peninsula. We would rent several cottages and vacation together there. The men fished and the women and kids swam. In the evenings, we'd cook the day's catch for dinner and then play euchre.

Wayne Schroeder and Brad Munson show off their catch during a vacation at Hubbard Lake.

Eileen would fish, too. But she didn't like to put the worm on her hook. One year we vacationed at Houghton Lake with John and Coleen King and their kids. We were all fishing one morning, and when we came back to the dock, Eileen left a worm on her hook. It was a dried, shriveled husk by the afternoon, but she wasn't about to remove it. She just cast her line out and got a hit right away. She took the fish off and the bait was still there, so she left it on and cast again. The rest of the afternoon she caught fish after fish with that desiccated old worm.

My Dad's brothers also liked that part of the Lower Peninsula. Uncle George, who I had threshed with as a kid, sold his farm in Deerfield and bought a place fifty miles east of Houghton Lake near Rose City,

Michigan. It was a nice two hundred–acre farm with a small private lake.

Uncle Ira, the brother Dad lived with in Wyoming when he was a teenager, found a four hundred–acre parcel a mile or two from Uncle George's. Uncle Ira bought it in a tax sale. Then the state started to build highway M-33 through Rose City. They needed gravel for the blacktop to pave it, and Uncle Ira's land had a lot of gravel. He sold the state enough gravel to pave eight miles of road, and he raked in the money.

Uncle Ira loved to tell how he walked into the Buick dealer with the money he'd made on gravel in his pocket. He looked a car all over and said to the young guy waiting on him, "Sonny, I'd like to buy that car right there. How much you want for it?"

The salesman told him, but Uncle Ira didn't like the price. "No, I'll give you this much for it."

Eventually, they settled on a figure and Uncle Ira said, "Let's go."

"No, you can't take it today. We got to do this and that to prep it."

"Sonny, who do you think you're talking to, some guy who just fell off the turnip wagon? I want that car today." He pulled a big roll of cash from his pocket and started counting out bills. "I don't get the car, you don't get this money."

"Well, you know, they got my car ready," Uncle Ira would say, and then he'd laugh.

Whenever we visited Uncle Ira, he always had fresh venison—year around. We'd get to his house and he'd say to my aunt, "Anna, why don't you put on some potatoes and make us a venison pie or a roast?"

When the game warden found a deer hanging in his barn, Uncle Ira told him, "They're on my land. I feed them and I eat them."

The game warden fined him, but Ira always had deer meat.

The summer Sharyl was four and Rick was five-and-a-half, we vacationed at Uncle George's. I mentioned earlier, his land had a small lake. It was overstocked with fish. Rick had brought a little rod and reel on the trip. One morning I took him to fish. He had no more than thrown in his line when he caught a nice-sized bluegill. I unhooked it and said, "We'll put that back in and see if we can catch a bigger one."

He cast his line in again and immediately hooked another fish. When he pulled it out, it was even bigger. I took it off the line and threw it back.

Rick got perturbed. "What are you doing?"

I explained, "Uncle George doesn't allow anybody to take the fish out of his pond. We have to put them back in after you catch them."

He threw his pole down and stormed off toward the house. He was done with fishing.

Chapter 26
Insert Scalpel, Open Heart

Eileen's heart continued to weaken, and in late 1956, we were told open heart surgery was her only option. At the time, heart surgery was fairly new. The surgeon who performed Eileen's came out of Toronto, Canada. Few doctors in America could do the procedure, and Canadian hospitals were ahead of US hospitals.

Unlike today, when many heart procedures can be done by running a catheter up the femoral artery, back then they had to split the ribcage and actually cut open the heart. Open heart surgery was in its infancy, and they didn't have heart-lung machines that could keep the patient alive for hours while they worked. From the time the surgeon started, he had only twenty minutes to repair the valve and close her up.

Her surgery was scheduled for early 1957 at Toledo Hospital. Before admitting her, the kids and I took her out for one last dinner at the classiest restaurant in Toledo. While we were waiting for our food, Rick said he had to go pee. Eileen pointed to the restroom, and said, "You're eight years old. You can go by yourself. The men's room is right there."

Rick entered the restroom, and minutes later the door flew open. In a boisterous voice filled with wonder, he said, "Mom! You ought to see. They've got colored marbles in the urinals—red and blue and yellow." The whole restaurant laughed.

When we finished eating, we drove to the hospital and checked Eileen in. The surgeon operated the next day. It didn't end well. I learned later that a piece of plaque came loose during the surgery. While she was in recovery, it moved through an artery and into her head, stopping the flow of blood to her brain. They paged a neurologist. He took one look and recognized what was going on. He injected something to stop the obstruction from moving any further until they could dissolve it, saving her life.

The heart surgeon frustrated me, though. The smartest person in the world is useless if he can't speak anything but jargon. I got so angry because this brilliant surgeon seemed incapable of explaining what happened to Eileen without resorting to Latin medical terms I'd never heard —and I took Latin in high school. I tried to get him to use simpler language, but he dismissed me, saying, "Talk to your family doctor."

When I cornered Dr. Williamson, he used terms I did understand. "There was plaque in her heart. A piece of plaque got loose and traveled into her head to the junction where the artery divides into branches that feed the left and right sides of the brain. The plaque lodged there, cutting off blood to one side of her brain."

It was touch and go for a while. Eileen was in a coma for eight days. They say patients don't know what's going on while in a coma, but she must have. They had to tie her hands down because even though she was unconscious, she would pull loose all the tubes and cords that were connected to her. She hated being tied and struggled against the bindings. I'd talk to her, trying to get her to relax, telling her everything was going to be all right, not knowing if she heard me, not knowing if what I was saying was true. She'd calm down, but it wouldn't be long before she'd be struggling again.

I had to hire private nursing care for her around the clock. The nurses worked shifts, and when the one who worked the midnight shift changed the dressings, Eileen somehow sensed that the nurse had put the shears in her uniform pocket. Evidently, Eileen deftly slipped them from the nurse's pocket and hid them in the folds of her sheet, intending to cut herself loose—in her sleep. The only thing that prevented it was that the nurses took inventory of supplies at the end of every shift. The nurse realized her scissors were missing. She checked both pockets, returned to

Eileen's room, and looked to see if she'd laid them anywhere. No shears. She pulled back Eileen's covers and there lay the shears, right at the end of Eileen's fingertips.

The bills for Eileen's heart operation and nursing care piled up. I was at the hospital in Toledo when I got a call from work that Ray Herrick wanted to see me. "Can you be here by eleven o'clock? He wants to see you this morning."

"Yes, I can." When the head of the company calls you in, you go. So I drove back to Tecumseh and walked into his office. It was just Ray and me. He said, "Dick, how is it going?"

"Well, it's pretty tough right now." I proceeded to tell him how Eileen was doing.

He asked the company treasurer to come in and said, "Dick, don't you worry about those bills. We're going to write you a check for the entire amount you need to pay off everything."

"I thank you, but I'm sorry—I couldn't accept that check."

"Why?" he said.

"Because I work for you. I don't want charity. I'm grateful, and if you'll help me out but allow me to pay it back, then I'll take the money."

Ray turned to the treasurer. "You let him pay it back any way he wants to. If it's a dollar a week, that's good enough."

So I did. I paid back every penny. I didn't want to feel I was obligated to him. But I thought it was awfully nice of him. Ray had over three thousand employees in the Tecumseh plant alone. For him to concern himself with the troubles of a single individual showed what kind of man he was.

* * *

The most trying year of our life together was definitely 1957. When Eileen came out of the coma, her left side was paralyzed. She needed to go to rehab, but in those days the only hospital that did therapy was the Crippled Children's Hospital in Toledo. She was transferred there and stayed for three months. It was very hard on me. I would work all day, stop at home to see the kids for a few minutes after work, then drive like hell fifty miles to Toledo to get there by visiting hours. I'd stay until they kicked me out and then drive an hour back to Tecumseh. I'd fall into bed and then get up to be back at work by eight in the morning.

As hectic as my schedule was, it wasn't nearly as hard emotionally as visitation. The therapist would have Eileen sew leather lace around a billfold, but her hand didn't work. She'd get mad and throw it. When I'd visit, she'd be angry about what had happened to her and take it out on me. "Why don't you just go home? You don't love me. If you did, you wouldn't leave me here."

There I was, doing all this driving, trying to give her all the time I had to spare, and she just resented it. I'd go in the next day and she'd be all lovey-dovey, as if she hadn't said a word. She'd want to hold me, cling to me, and show me what she'd made that day.

Our house at that time only had two bedrooms—Eileen and I had one, and our children shared the other. Sharyl was in first grade and Rick in third. Mother and Wayne lived on Wamplers Lake, twenty miles away, too far to take the kids back and forth to school. So they borrowed a small travel trailer from one of their neighbors and parked it behind our back porch. This gave Mother and Wayne a place to stay while she watched the kids for me during Eileen's recovery.

What a big help it was to have Mom and Wayne there. Our children missed their mother, and their dad was hardly ever present. The kids' teachers had their classes make get well cards for Eileen. But it wasn't until she came home that we realized how upsetting it had been for them. All of us had been barely holding on.

Yet, could any of us understand what it was like for her? A beautiful young woman, not yet thirty, waking up to find her mouth drawn down on one side, a hand that wouldn't hold anything, a left foot that dragged when she walked. She was frustrated with the challenges she had to overcome.

Eileen progressed to where she was walking, and they let her come home. She limped a little if she got tired. I could look across the room and tell her condition. We'd go to her mother's or my mother's and visit for a while, but when the left corner of her mouth started to droop, or if her left hand lost its grip on something, I knew she was tired. Her hand wouldn't hold things automatically the way our hands do. She had to consciously direct her left side. When she got tired and stopped telling it what to do, it would just stop working. I'd notice and say, "Eileen, don't you think we've visited long enough? We ought to start for home and get a night's rest." She wouldn't argue. She knew.

Her condition improved to where we could go to a dance. She couldn't dance long, maybe three dances. We'd sit out the rest, then have a last dance and go home. She got along marvelously if she didn't overdo it.

She was truly a remarkable woman. I never met another individual like her. Quick to smile, quick to laugh, and I don't think she ever held a grudge against anybody. I knew I'd been right when I asked her to be my wife.

Chapter 27
Two Fast Rides

By the following summer, Eileen had started driving again. She wasn't supposed to drive long distances, but one day during school vacation, she put the kids in the car and took off for Monroe. The kids were fighting with each other over something in the backseat. She got distracted and had a head-on collision. I got a call that my wife was in Monroe Hospital. Since she had just totaled our only car, Mom and Wayne drove me there. Just as we arrived, I saw two orderlies loading Eileen into an ambulance to rush her to Toledo Hospital. I shouted for Mother and Wayne to take the kids and I jumped in the ambulance to go with Eileen. I never had such a ride in my life. The driver was going eighty miles an hour down two-lane roads, siren wailing, cutting in and out of traffic all the way to the hospital.

Eileen had a broken jaw and ribs. She was hospitalized for five or six days, and I needed a car to get back and forth, so I bought the first good deal I found. It was a Ford, not brand new, but it was like new with low mileage. It had a Ford Interceptor V-8 engine, a special high-performance model that Ford made for police cars.

In those days, a new car was a topic of conversation even if the car wasn't brand new. When anyone in the neighborhood came home with a different car, the neighbors would stop by to admire it. The first time you visited relatives with your new car, everyone would come out to the driveway to look it over. Men would often pop the hood and stare at the engine. Sometimes relatives would pile in and you'd take them for a drive around the block.

Dick's brother-in-law Stan Billock loved cars.

My brother-in-law Stan was a real car enthusiast. He did his own mechanical work on his cars and was always tuning or tweaking his engine. Our first trip to Monroe after Eileen's accident, we visited her mother and then stopped out to Stan and Jerri's. Naturally, the new car got attention. Stan looked it all over, and I said, "You want to take it for a spin?"

"Sure do."

Stan slid into the driver's seat and I got in on the passenger side. Jerri and Eileen didn't care to go, and the kids were playing in the basement with their cousin, Lynda. Stan and Jerri lived on the outskirts of Monroe at a place called Stony Point.

Stan headed out the county road and said, "Have you opened this baby up?"

"No."

"Let's see what an Interceptor V-8 can do."

I didn't know if I wanted to.

Stan jammed the accelerator to the floor. The force of acceleration slammed us into our seat backs. In seconds, the speedometer needle was as far right as it could go. Trees along the roadside looked like a picket fence. I glanced at Stan, and he was grinning ear to ear.

The downside of the Ford was that as the speedometer needle went up, you could watch the needle of the gas gauge move down. That model of the Interceptor engine also had poorly designed cams that wore out quickly. When I replaced the cams for the third time in two years, I thought, *That's enough.* The next day, I traded the Ford for a 1960 Chevrolet—my first new car.

Chapter 28
Vacation Travels

Shortly after I bought the new Chevy, we offered to take Mother and Wayne with us on vacation in Michigan's Upper Peninsula. They had never been.

Michigan's two peninsulas are separated by Lake Huron and Lake Michigan. The closest point to cross is the Straits of Mackinac, a five-mile stretch of turbulent water where the two Great Lakes meet. In the past, the crossing was made by car ferry when the weather was warm. When the lakes froze in winter, there was no service. The ferries carried a limited number of cars at a time, so there was always a wait. On our previous trips, we had arrived at the ferry docks early, parked our car in the queue, and eaten breakfast while we waited our turn.

This trip was different. The Mackinac Bridge had opened. Stretching five miles, between Mackinaw City and St. Ignace, it was the world's longest suspension bridge. It had taken four-and-a-half years to build and cost $99.8 million, plus the lives of five workers.

We paid our toll and were treated to stunning views: the sun rising over Lake Huron on our right, magnificent Lake Michigan on our left, the Straits of Mackinac two hundred feet below us. In less time than the ferry would have required, we exited the bridge and drove into St. Ignace.

Michigan's Upper Peninsula is peppered with waterfalls. We showed Mom and Wayne all our favorites. The magnificent Upper Tahquamenon Falls, two hundred feet across and fifty feet high, is colored with stripes of gold from tannins in the water. We showed Mom Lower Tahquamenon, Miners Falls, Munising, and many others, but what caught her eye were the rocks. Big rocks.

Michigan was formed by ice-age glaciers that moved and crushed vast amounts of rock. Plow any farm, rake any lawn in Michigan, and you will turn up numerous stones the size of your fist or larger. Mother had outlined her flowerbeds and the edges of her driveway with four- to six-inch stones she painted white. She'd scold anyone whose tires made a mark on one. "Stop driving over my stones."

Throughout our trip, whenever Mom saw an eight- to ten-inch "boulder" on the roadside, she'd make me stop and put it in the trunk for her. By the time we started back across the bridge, the hundreds of pounds of rocks in the trunk canted my new car like a missile ready to launch. I made fun of Mom for a long time about hauling home all those rocks.

Even as adults, Mom and I never outgrew our habit of teasing each other. I'd still sneak behind her while she cooked and tie her apron strings in knots. Rick started imitating me, and soon there were two of us doing it. She could seldom prepare a meal for us without struggling to get the knots out of her apron when she finished cooking.

Mom and Wayne owned a nice two-bedroom house on Wamplers Lake, about twenty minutes west of Tecumseh. We'd go there nearly every weekend. Wayne bought a boat, and the kids and I learned to water ski. Eileen tried once or twice but wasn't able to stand up and found herself skiing in a squatted position. She decided she'd rather ride in the boat and watch the skier.

One Saturday, we came to visit and found Mom tending her garden in the backyard. After watering her tomato plants, she threw down the hose. I picked it up, sprayed her, twisted the brass nozzle to shut off the water, and dropped the hose. I took off running. She grabbed the hose and chased me, intending to get even. Her next-door neighbor, watching the scene unfold, slipped into the yard, turned off the faucet, and disconnected the hose. As Mother chased me around the house, the hose kept coming. It never occurred to her the hose wasn't that long.

Finally, I let her catch up. I held up my hands in surrender. "Are you going to spray me with water?"

"You better believe it."

She twisted the nozzle on. Nothing came out. She tried twisting it the other direction. That didn't help. Her frustration reminded me of the time she threw cooked potatoes at me for teasing her.

* * *

After Eileen recovered from the heart operation and subsequent left-side paralysis, she had a few years of good health. But not long after we returned from the Upper Peninsula, her heart started acting up again, and there was nothing more that doctors back then could do for her. Still, she loved our travel vacations, so we bought a sixteen-foot travel trailer. It was "self-contained" with gas and electric lights, a propane refrigerator, a freshwater tank, and a flushable toilet. There was a full-size bed for Eileen and me and a bunk bed for Rick, and the dinette converted into a bed for Sharyl.

One feature we especially liked was that the full bed was always set up instead of being a pullout bed or a couch that unfolded, which many other trailers had. This meant that whenever Eileen felt she needed to rest, we could pull off at a roadside table and she could lie down while I made lunch or snacks.

Dad and Reba also bought a travel trailer. So, our first long trip with our trailer was to camp with them in Great Smoky Mountains National Park. Nowadays National Park campgrounds have "bear-proof" dumpsters, but in the 1960s they just set barrels with heavy lids between concrete posts. The black bears had learned that if they whacked the side of the barrel with their island-size paws, the lid would pop off. Throughout the night, we would hear *whomp—clang, whomp—clang* as the bears foraged through the campground garbage.

Our trailer had a screen door plus the exterior door. One warm night, we propped the outer door open and used only the screen door. We hadn't been in bed long when Sharyl, whose bed was across from the door, said in a loud whisper, "Dad! I think something's out there."

I slid out of bed, grabbed the flashlight, and shined it through the screen door. On the other side was a raccoon peering in like a burglar casing the joint. The light made him scamper off, but Sharyl wanted the door closed thereafter.

The following summer, the 1964 New York World's Fair opened. This was a big deal. We decided to go. We found a campground in Bayonne, New Jersey, and commuted to the Fair every day.

That fair was a marvel. If you have been to EPCOT at Walt Disney World, you have a good idea of what it looked like because Disney patterned a great deal of EPCOT on the 1964 Fair. In fact, four of the main attractions at the Fair were created by Disney and are still in operation in Disney parks. These include an Abraham Lincoln exhibit (now the Hall of Presidents), It's A Small World, the Carousel of Progress, and the Ford Magic Skyway ride in which guests rode in Ford convertibles past scenes featuring dinosaurs, cavemen, and a futuristic cityscape. Parts of the Ford ride were later incorporated into other Disney attractions.

The similarity doesn't stop there. The Fair had water fountains that danced, and nightly fireworks, some of which came out of the fountains. There was also a monorail and ground vehicles similar to those that Disney parks now use to convey guests from the parking lot to the park entrance.

Exhibits at the World's Fair came from eighty nations, twenty-four US states, and forty-five corporations. The longest line was for the Vatican Pavilion, where Michelangelo's *Pieta* was on display. It was the first and only time it had ever been allowed to leave St. Peter's Basilica. It is a magnificent sculpture, well worth our wait in line.

That summer, Rick was a month shy of sixteen and Sharyl and her friend Judy, who joined us on the trip, were fourteen. We allowed them to roam the Fair on their own on one condition: they had to stay together. They couldn't split up. Rick's main complaint was that girls had to pee too often.

* * *

Mother and Wayne weren't big travelers. Vacations at Hubbard Lake with her sisters and going to the Upper Peninsula with us were the biggest trips they'd ever taken. They were in their sixties when I convinced them they should take my trailer to Indian River to celebrate their upcoming wedding anniversary.

I loaned them my travel trailer, and we swapped cars since mine was already wired for trailer lights and brakes. I showed Wayne how to hitch the trailer to the car and how to level the trailer when they parked at the campgrounds. Once they were in the car and couldn't see what I was doing, I slapped a big "Just Married" sign on the back of the trailer. As they pulled out of the driveway, Eileen and I waved goodbye, smiling and laughing.

They were driving north on US 127 through Lansing and into St. John, Michigan when two guys pulled up beside them, saw their age, and started laughing. The men had beer in their car, and one of them held a bottle out the window and shouted, "You want a beer?"

Wayne said, "No, thanks." He turned to Mom and said, "My, people up here are friendly. Those guys just offered me a beer."

As they continued up the road, people smiled, waved, and tooted their horns. When they stopped for gas, folks congratulated them, but they never caught on. They assumed everyone was congratulating them on their wedding anniversary, never questioning how anyone would know.

They arrived at the state park and the ranger made a reference to it, but they still didn't get it. In the morning, Mom walked over to the campground showers wearing her long nightgown and bathrobe. The women there smiled real big and asked, "Did you have a good night?"

She came back from the showers thinking, *Wayne was right, People in northern Michigan are certainly friendly.*

Wayne, who had happened behind the trailer while she was gone, said, "Come here a minute" and showed her the sign.

They stayed one night and drove back home. They'd had their big trip, and one night was enough.

Chapter 29
Promotion to Mechanical Engineering

I stayed in the time-study department for five years. In the course of my regular work, I'd see where combining one operation with another would save steps and labor. I would draw up proposed layouts to make the factory run more efficiently and then take them to Joe Herr in process engineering. He'd look at my drawings, okay them, and have the machines moved the way I'd suggested.

The engineering department had a man retiring. Joe said, "Dick, if you would be interested in coming up here and working for Carl Fossbender in mechanical engineering, I think the time is right. We could get you in there."

"I'd like to try it. I think I could do well. I'm doing some layout work now."

"I know what you're doing," Joe said. "I'll set up a meeting with Carl."

I should explain. Manufacturers need two types of engineers, those who design a product, like a compressor or an engine, and others who design the mechanical processes by which the parts are machined and assembled into a finished product. Mechanical engineers and process engineers are the latter type.

Initially, Carl really didn't want to hire me, but he talked to Morgan Ford, Joe's boss. Morgan said he trusted Joe's opinion. Joe was a plant engineer who oversaw all of the assembly processes, and he convinced Carl that I ought to have the job. I started working for Carl in 1960 and stayed in mechanical engineering until 1970, when I was promoted and sent to set up a new plant in Somerset, Kentucky.

As Joe had pointed out to Carl, I'd been doing this type of work right along, so moving to the engineering department was no problem. I liked the work, and during the time I worked there, I came up with new inventions that the company patented.

My first major task was to improve the way rotors were put on the compressor crankshaft. Until then, we had pressed them on, which was slow and sometimes damaged the rotor's fine electrical wires. I realized that by induction heating the rotor, it would expand and slip onto the crankshaft in exactly the correct position. When the company saw what I'd come up with, they instructed me to write up the process for a patent.

Next, we needed a power-free conveyor system that would allow an item to move along the assembly line until the worker tripped a lever to stop it. The person could work on the piece and then release a solenoid so the item would continue down the line to the next station. Once I had it designed, I asked the vendor who made our assembly-line equipment how much they'd charge to build it. They wanted over a hundred thousand dollars, but I didn't have that kind of budget. So we built it in-house and also obtained a patent on the process.

I never earned money from the patents. When you invent things for your employer, the inventions belong to the company.

One year, large air-handler units needed to be installed on the factory roof. The units were so large and heavy that if we tried to wheel them across the rooftop, they'd crash through the roof. Joe Herr's plan was to weld in place the frames the air-handlers would rest on, then lift the units up and set them on the frame. The problem was that the air-handlers had to be positioned over the center of the plant, and a crane boom that would reach that distance didn't exist. Also, there were high-voltage power lines in the way.

The mechanical engineering department came up with a solution. Once the frames were ready, we'd lift each unit by helicopter, fly it over the roof, and set it down on the frame. Ray Herrick opposed the plan, thinking helicopters would be too expensive. So Joe and Carl waited until Ray was scheduled to be out of town. But Ray hadn't left. He'd only stopped get his hair cut before coming into the office.

Tecumseh had a little two-chair barbershop in a triangle-shaped building on South Evans Street, three blocks north of the plant. It was owned by Garner and Roe, two fast, efficient barbers who kept up banter between themselves and their customers all day. A lot of us got our hair cut there.

That morning, Ray sat in the barber chair and Garner, while clipping Ray's hair, said, "I hear you got a little excitement going on at your factory today."

"What do you mean?" Ray said.

"Well your guys are putting big units on the roof with helicopters."

Ray shot out of the barber chair, grabbed his hat, and headed for the plant.

When Ray showed up, Joe thought, *We're all going to get fired for this.* But Ray never said a word to Joe. He watched the helicopter set one or two units, then went into his office.

For each trip, the helicopter carried only enough fuel to place one unit. Between lifts, it was refueled with the minimum quantity necessary for the next. This way, in the event the helicopter crashed, there wouldn't be excess fuel to explode.

Once all the air-handlers were fastened in place and the helicopter left, Ray called Carl to his office. I'm sure Carl expected that he and Joe were being fired.

"Damn fine job," was all Ray said.

Another time, Joe was told the company needed a new warehouse. He worked on the plans, had them drawn up, and got the construction bids. Joe took everything into a management meeting, but Ray didn't even let Joe begin. He looked around the table, and said, "You guys all want a warehouse?"

"Yeah."

"Well, take your own damn money and buy it." Ray got up and walked out.

All of Joe's work was for nothing. But the company did need another warehouse. So the next year, management had Joe present the project to Ray again. The same result.

Finally, one year Ray and Joe were both out of town. Jack Clark (who worked for Joe) grabbed the appropriation, took it to the guy Ray left in charge, and got it signed. Jack sent a man to get a camera and two of the chrome-handled shovels the company used for ground-breaking ceremonies. Then Jack had pictures taken of him and me breaking ground. We pasted the photo on a card and captioned it: "Engineer out of town, young engineers fill in and break ground for a new warehouse." We left the card on Joe's desk.

Ray could seem tight with the company money, but what started from an abandoned foundry with a bare dirt floor grew through his industriousness and intelligent business decisions. While I worked there, the company had refrigeration compressor plants in Tecumseh, Michigan; Somerset, Kentucky; Tupelo, Mississippi; and Marion, Ohio. We built gasoline engines at plants in New Holstein and Grafton, Wisconsin. We had stamping plants in Toledo and Acklin, Ohio, plus another in Indiana. We had a plastics plant in Detroit. We owned Little Giant Pumps and Peerless Gear. Plus, we had thirty-four licensee plants throughout the world. At the time I worked there, the company was completely debt-free and had sixty million dollars in a slush fund that Ray established to be used only if the economy hit hard times and the company was failing, or as protection to prevent a leveraged buyout by another company. After Ray's death, his son Ken took over, and he did a good job.

Long after I retired, Ray's grandson, Todd, took over. He decided the company needed to get into business in Europe. He was wined and dined by European business leaders who convinced him to disregard the engines and refrigeration compressors that were the core of Tecumseh's business. Instead, he concentrated on the electric motors that go inside the compressors. He bought four European companies and, once he acquired them, he discovered that they didn't have all he needed. So he kept putting money into them until he bankrupted Tecumseh Products Company. To me, it was unbelievable. His grandfather must have turned over in his grave two or three times. The plant in Tecumseh was sold and demolished to build condos and a strip mall.

Even though I didn't own the company, or even have stock in it, it hurt when, by the end of the twentieth century, the plant was gone. It was disheartening to give a major chunk of my work life to building up a place that employed so many people and then watch it be pissed away by poor decision making.

Chapter 30
Impermanent Cure

The benefits of Eileen's heart surgery didn't last long. Throughout the 1960s, she was admitted to the hospital at least once a month, sometimes every few weeks. And Eileen was a pistol. The nurses told her she couldn't have salt or ice. She'd save the little cups they delivered medicine in, fill them with water, and set them outside the window in winter to make her own ice. She also started carrying a small salt shaker in her purse so she'd have her own salt when she was hospitalized.

When she wasn't in the hospital, she rested at home and could do very little. I got up every morning, packed the kids' lunches, fed them breakfast, sent them to school, and left for work. After school, Sharyl would iron clothes and start supper. Both kids did dishes. On Saturday I cleaned house.

I'd taken over housecleaning several years before, when the kids were younger. I told them to pick up their toys one Saturday, but neither of them paid attention. They were too busy doing something else. After about the third time that I told them and they didn't do it, I took a large trash bag into their room and started bagging every toy on the floor. Sharyl came in just as I threw one of her dolls in the bag. She said, "What are you doing?"

"I told you to pick up your toys. I guess these aren't any good. We'll just throw them in the trash and let the garbage man take them."

I continued gathering toys. She started crying and ran to get her brother.

Rick grabbed his little trucks. "You can't do that with our toys."

"Sorry, I told you to pick them up."

I packed up every toy on the floor, folded up the bag, carried it outside, and set it next to the garbage cans. I came back in the house and resumed cleaning.

Pretty soon they came to find me. "We're sorry. We'll keep them picked up."

"Okay, bring them in and put them away. But the next time I have to pick them up, they stay out there."

I had no problem with toys after that. I'd say, "Hey, kids, time for Dad to clean house." They'd pick up their toys right then.

I don't know why, but Eileen's heart attacks always came at night. She'd wake me up at one or two o'clock in the morning and say, "I've got chest pains. I've got to go to the hospital."

I took her to the hospital so frequently that they let me admit her myself. I'd fill out the paperwork while the nurse took her to her room. I'd leave the admission papers on the desk and the doctor would sign them when he came in the morning. Through it all, Eileen never complained, never said, "Why me? Why is this happening to me?" She just accepted it.

One night she woke me up at one o'clock with chest pains. I took her in and they put her in a room with another lady. When I finished the paperwork, I walked down to her room, and as soon as I entered, I knew something was wrong. I heard the other patient gasping and thought, *I've got to get Eileen out of this room.*

I ran and found the nurse. I said, "We've got to get Eileen out of there."

"Why?"

"The other patient is dying—right now."

The nurse ran into the room, took one look at the patient, and called for another nurse. I started pushing Eileen's bed out the door. The nurse helped me move it into the hall and closed the door. She and the second nurse attended to the other lady in the room, and sure enough, she died.

I didn't want Eileen in the room seeing that. She'd been too close to death too many times herself. I didn't tell Eileen what happened until she got home.

Our kids had a rough struggle because Eileen's hospitalizations didn't always allow us to do the things we'd planned, and they missed their mom. On days when Eileen was in the hospital, I'd visit her during my lunch break. After school, the kids walked to the hospital and visited with her until I picked them up after work. We'd have supper and then go back for evening visiting hours. If the kids hadn't finished their homework, they'd stay home and only I would go back.

Sharyl's teen years were hard. Rick got a job flipping burgers in a restaurant to earn pocket money while Sharyl tried to make up for her mother's absence by helping around the house. I remember when Sharyl cooked her first turkey by herself. She thought it had been in long enough to be done, but when she took it out, it was bloody. She cried.

"It's all right," I said. "Just put it back in the oven a while longer."

Sharyl got her driver's license but hadn't driven alone much. One night she asked for a ride to choir practice. I said, "Take the car, drive yourself." Our church was only two miles from where we lived.

"You mean it?"

"Yeah, sure, take the car. Come back when it's over."

So she drove herself to church. When she put the car in park and lifted her foot off the brake, the car rolled forward a little. The church had a heavy chain strung along the parking area, and the front of the car hit it. Sharyl came home crying. I said, "What are you crying about?"

"I wrecked your car, your brand-new car."

"Are you hurt?"

"No, I'm not hurt." Blubber, blubber, blubber. "I wrecked the car."

"Well, what did you do to it?"

"It rolled into that chain in the parking lot."

"Let's go out and look at it."

We did, and there wasn't a scratch anywhere. "You didn't damage the car. See? Not even a mark."

She kept crying. "Aren't you going to yell at me?"

"No reason to; you're all right and the car isn't hurt." I finally got her consoled.

* * *

As the years passed, Eileen's heart condition worsened. She still loved to travel, but in the later years, her heart wasn't strong enough to let her walk very far. In 1967, we heard there would be a World's Fair in Montreal, Canada. We had so enjoyed the 1964 New York World's Fair that we decided to go to Montreal. So we hooked up the trailer, took Sharyl, and left. Richard didn't go with us—he was in college by then and no longer called Rick.

While we were at the fair, Eileen had an episode and I had to take her to the French-Canadian hospital. I didn't speak French, and the doctor there spoke very little English. To communicate I showed him Eileen's pills and pantomimed what I was saying: "Her doctor said take two pills and wait one hour. If she's not okay, you can admit her." He didn't want to wait, but he finally agreed to it.

I knew from experience that the sooner we got the pills in her and got her lying down, the sooner everything would go back to normal. And it did. He had someone who spoke better English come out and tell me I could take her back to the campground, but she had to go to bed, and the next day she was not to go back to the Fair unless she used a wheelchair. She was not to walk.

She didn't want to get a wheelchair, but we did it anyway. The part she disliked was that people in wheelchairs were taken to the front of the line. It bothered her that she got to jump the queue while everyone else waited like cattle. In her mind, we belonged in line with them.

The other time she got upset over her weak condition was at Munising Falls State Park in Michigan's Upper Peninsula. It was a pretty, fifty-foot-tall waterfall, but unless you climbed stairs up to a viewing platform, you couldn't see the whole falls. At the bottom, where we were, you only saw a small outflow from the falls. I looked at the steps—Eileen would never be able to climb them. So I told her to get on my back and put her arms around my neck as though riding a horse so I could carry her up.

She resisted, but I said, "If we don't go up, we can't see the falls. But if you don't want to go that's okay."

"No, we're here, so we'll see it." That was her attitude.

Up we climbed, with her on piggyback. But it was the last time she let me carry her. She had her pride, and it embarrassed her.

If I've made it sound as if we never did anything, let me correct that. In addition to our travel vacations, Eileen and I both bowled. I was on two teams and bowled twice a week. Eileen bowled for several years when her health permitted. Later, I won a set of golf clubs and tried golf for a few years.

We bought a Lowrey organ in 1968. It came with six lessons. Sharyl played clarinet in the high school band, and she taught me how to read music. I'd sit down with a sheet of music and read it to her like a book: "A, C, B, F . . ." If I made a mistake, she would correct me and show me where the key was on the keyboard.

I wasn't one of those people who play by ear, but if I knew the tune and had the sheet music, I could practice it a couple of times and be able to play the melody with my right hand. For the bass clef, I just played chords with my left hand.

I got so I played pretty decent. I even wrote six or seven songs. Not that they were masterpieces.

Chapter 31
Learning What I Didn't Know

By 1970, Carl Fossbender, who hired me in engineering a decade before, was vice president of the company. Carl held a meeting with me and Lloyd Roebeck, who was to be the plant manager of a new factory Tecumseh Products was building in Somerset, Kentucky. Throughout the meeting, I thought we were discussing my transferring there as a plant engineer. I assumed I'd be responsible for laying out conveyers and production lines and would report to a boss like Joe Herr.

When we got around to wages, I'd have insisted on more money if I'd understood what they expected of me. But I didn't. When the interview finished, Lloyd said, "Now, you realize what you are going to be?"

"Plant engineer?"

Lloyd shook his head. "No, you're going to be the master mechanic."

The master mechanic is in charge of the entire plant, mechanically —machines, electric, construction, production, gas, environmental protection, everything. If I'd known that's what they were talking about, I wouldn't have settled for $16,000 a year.

I'd be my own boss in Somerset, reporting directly to Carl, not Lloyd. Because the way Tecumseh Products structured management, heads of departments in other cities reported to the main office in Tecumseh.

Eileen and I sold our home in Tecumseh and bought a brand-new three-bedroom house in Somerset. She was thrilled to death. For the first time, she owned a dishwasher, and all her kitchen appliances matched. The house had a full basement and wall-to-wall carpets in every room except the kitchen. She got to choose the colors of the walls, carpets, and drapes and buy all new furniture. She really thought she was in high cotton.

Not me. I knew I was in deep. I wasn't prepared, didn't have the knowledge required to build and set up a brand-new factory. When I arrived in the summer of 1970, the plant was still under construction. There were a multitude of things about which I knew nothing.

As a process engineer, I understood workflow and assembly lines. Suddenly, I needed knowledge about electrics, solid waste disposal, and air and water quality. I had to learn on the fly about transformers and how to get the electricity from outside to where I needed it in the plant. Plus I needed to build a staff and lay out the machine and assembly lines.

I hired an engineer, a chief electrician, and a maintenance superintendent. I milked those three for every bit of knowledge I could. I constantly read textbooks and articles. If people came in with information, I'd sit with them, pick their brains, and then compare it to what I read.

I had a lot of hard choices to make between what needed to be done and what the company had allotted money to do. For example, they put in half the number of transformers needed and provided no money to run long-distance 440-volt electrical lines to the machines.

We could use long cables, but I didn't want cables strung all over my plant. Electric cables have a resistance per foot, and the longer the cable, the larger the resistance. When current flows through the cable, the resistance results in a voltage drop according to Ohm's law. The better choice for distributing electrical power in a factory is bus duct, a sheet metal duct containing copper bars capable of conducting substantial current of electricity.

I also didn't want my electricians working around high voltage without being protected, and cable has to be bare wherever it connects. If a man touched a bare wire carrying 440 volts, he would be seriously injured or die. Bus duct cost more than cable, but it would be safer.

My first big battle was over the electrical transformers. The contractor had quoted transformers for the front and back of the plant, and even poured concrete pads for them, but never installed them. Instead the contractor put three transformers in the middle. Suddenly, I needed to learn how to calculate electrical loads and losses.

Even with bus duct, the farther electric current has to go and the more equipment you hook on to it, the bigger the load on the transformer. I talked to our chief engineer and the head of the electric company. Although the actual loss wasn't as severe as I calculated, it was as close as I could estimate with my limited knowledge.

Carl came to Somerset with Gene Eldritch, who had developed the original cost estimates to build the Somerset plant. Gene was unhappy with me because, as master mechanic, I'd been overriding his estimates on a lot of items. Gene was only worried about money. He'd told management the plant would cost a certain amount. Now, I was saying, "No, I need to spend more, especially for the transformers."

We held a meeting, and I brought in the contractor who had installed the transformers. In the middle of the meeting, Gene said to me, "Here you are, don't know your ass from a hole in the ground, arguing with a guy who studied electricity in college, been in business for twenty years, and you're telling him how to put in transformers."

"No, I'm not telling him how to put in transformers. I'm saying under the current set up I will have to run bus duct or cable a long distance to where the machines will be located, and the present plan will only supply enough electricity to run one production line. We are scheduled to put in a second and third line. All I'm asking is, where is all that electricity going to come from? We need to plan for it now."

Gene got mad as hell.

"Dick, why don't you let us discuss this for a few minutes," Carl said.

So I left the meeting. When Carl came out of the meeting, he said they'd decided I was right. The economical thing to do was to put additional transformers on the front and back pads.

I'd won, but now I had to learn another whole thing. To accomplish what I wanted, I needed to bring the power company into it and have the city supervise the installation to make sure it conformed to safety codes.

While trying to locate the ground for the three transformers that were already operational, the electricians discovered something wrong with the way they were grounded. They killed the power immediately, gave the electricity time to discharge, wired an alternate ground line, made sure it was working safely, and then started digging. They discovered the ground had never been connected. If one of my workers had rammed in a rod, he'd have been become the ground conduit and been electrocuted.

As long as we were improving our electrical setup, I arranged for us to have two sources of electricity, the Somerset generating station and another from Russell Springs. That way, if Somerset had a power failure we could switch to Russell Springs and keep our plant running.

Once the outer walls of the factory were up, we used temporary walls to separate one area into a crude office. We heated it with kerosene heaters, but the heaters weren't sufficient and we had to work with our coats on.

I was constantly overwhelmed by the tasks at hand. I monitored the plant construction to make sure everything was put where it belonged. I had to buy all the conveyors, equip the entire machine shop, and find boilers that burned not only natural gas but also fuel oil. The refrigeration units for air conditioning and dehumidifying the white room assembly area had been calculated incorrectly in the plant design and were undersized.

To add to the pressure on me, I was engaged in battles with the state on solid waste and the city on water disposal. The machine shop would generate gallons and gallons of water that had to be cleaned. We had only half the water treatment equipment we would require and nothing in the budget to buy more.

Chapter 32
Somerset

Somerset was a small town, similar in size to Tecumseh. A handful of millionaires there had made fortunes owning coal mines, but before Tecumseh Products opened, working people in the area only made four dollars a day. Hard to believe that in 1970, four dollars was a day's wages in Somerset. Hadn't the Great Depression ended thirty years ago?

Eileen liked it there. We found her a doctor and had her medical records transferred to him. She bought a poodle and named him Pierre. She loved that dog and really enjoyed having a new house, but Eileen's heart condition was worse than ever.

I worked seven days a week trying to get the plant operational, which left no time for me to clean house, and Sharyl was hundreds of miles away in nursing school. So we hired a housekeeper to come in weekly.

Eileen continued to be hospitalized frequently. When she wasn't home, Pierre would follow the housekeeper from room to room watching her work. The woman quit. She said, "That dog keeps eying me as if I'm a thief."

We only had one car, but with Eileen's poor health, she needed to have a car. I couldn't afford to buy anything new. I found an old used Dodge that burned a little oil but was good otherwise. I drove it to work and left her our newer car.

Finally, we got the factory open, but I continued working ridiculous hours because the plant was so much more complicated than I had anticipated. There were so many areas that I'd never been educated in and lacked even the foggiest understanding about. I can't count the times I sat in my office reading textbooks and regulations as I tried to figure something out with nobody to ask. No one at the plant knew any more than I did, so all I could do was read about each new challenge as it came up. From solid waste disposal to Occupational Safety and Health Administration (OSHA) regulations to waste water treatment, I learned on the fly.

I had responsibility over everything mechanical in the plant and was accountable for noise level, water, solid waste, liquid waste, gas, air quality, and more. Additionally, I had no experience in machining. For instance, how a diamond bore or a drill should be sharpened to do a job. My difficulties were compounded by all the new hires.

When a plant opens in Michigan, 90 percent of the employees hired have previous factory experience. The workers available to us in Somerset, however, were primarily coal miners or farmers who had never seen the inside of a machine shop. They too, were learning on the job, which only made my job so much harder.

We might have had a machine running very well and then, an hour later, it wouldn't produce a good piece because an operator had loaded a piece in wrong, knocking everything out of alignment. So we'd have to realign the whole machine—start over as if it were a brand-new machine. We'd get it running correctly and some other operator down the line would mess up his machine.

When Tecumseh Products selected Somerset for its new factory, the city wanted to build a new wastewater treatment plant, so the company donated one million dollars toward the cost of a new facility. But by the time we started production, the city still wasn't ready to treat the water.

We cleaned our water and discharged it into a creek behind us. Next to us was a stamping plant. They also discharged water into the creek. The Somerset refinery dumped into the same creek, too. I hired a chemist, Dick Johnson, and had him go to the creek every morning and draw a quart sample of the water we discharged. He'd test it, cap it, label it with the time and date, and save it.

One day, Lloyd called me to his office. Officials from the city were there ranting and raving. "We've got foam on the creek knee high," they said. "It's coming from this plant." They intended to shut us down, right now.

"How do you know it's from this plant?" I said.

"Well, we just do."

I called Dick Johnson up to Lloyd's office and said, "Please walk that creek until you find where this is coming from. I want you to take someone from the city along—he'll help determine whose discharge line is whose."

Well, Dick did that, and he traced it all the way to the next town, Ferguson, where a battery plant was dumping raw acid into the creek. The contamination flowed downstream to a refinery where the oil they put in reacted with it, producing deep foam.

When they returned and told me they'd found the cause, I asked the city official to wait while I phoned his boss at the wastewater department, who had been at our plant earlier. I asked him to come back out. When he arrived, I took him to where we had our water samples stored. I said, "You see these quart jars are all dated? This is what we dump after we treat our discharge water. You need to go to Ferguson and stop the battery plant from dumping their acid, and when you're done, go talk to the refinery about the oil they're discharging."

He left like a whipped pup. They resolved it and we were able to keep running. But there always seemed to be some issue coming up.

Wastewater wasn't the only problem I had with the city. The company had signed an absurd contract with the city of Somerset to pay them a flat rate of $1,750 a month for water usage, but we were only using 20,000 gallons of water a month—less than two average families. So, we were paying considerably more than we should have. Lloyd wanted to break the contract, but the city wouldn't give. They thought we were using ten times that much. The difference came from how they interpreted the water meter readings. My maintenance superintendent and I got down in the pit where the meters were located. I said, "Don, what does that meter look like to you?"

"It's a three-decimal gallonage reader," he said.

This meant the meter had eight dials, a decimal point and then three more dials for three decimal places.

The city said, "We don't have a meter like that in Somerset. All our meters measure only two decimal places. You're reading the meter wrong."

We had vicious arguments about this at city council meetings. Then one guy insulted me. "That's the trouble with you Yankees. You come down here thinking you know everything in the world, and you don't even know how to read a water meter."

Boy, that got me up out of the chair. I looked him right in the eye, and said, "I'll tell you what, you bring your water meter man to my office tomorrow at eight o'clock. I'll take both of you out to our meter, and if he tells me I'm wrong, I'll buy it. But if that meter has three decimal place dials, then Lloyd gets to renegotiate the amount we're paying for water and you will abide by our readings."

He snapped back, "We'll go right now if you want."

"No, it's too dark at night," I said. "Tomorrow morning, eight o'clock."

Next morning, they were there. We walked out to the pit. I said, "I'm not even going to get down there, you just go down there and see for yourself."

He sent his man down to look. The guy was down there about two seconds. He came back up and said, "That's a three-decimal water meter."

I didn't say a word to embarrass them. I just said, "You agree it's a three-decimal meter system?"

"If he says it is, it is."

"Okay, thank you. Let's go back to the office and see Lloyd for a minute." We returned to Lloyd's office. I said, "You want to tell him or you want me to tell him?"

"No, we'll tell him. It's a three-decimal meter. I can't imagine where you got it from, but that's what it is."

"Lloyd, I will leave you to negotiate the new water contract," I said, and then I left the room.

I had my minor victories over various officials but suffered defeat in the struggle Eileen and I fought for so long—her health. She never complained when they'd call me from the plant at three o'clock in the morning and I'd have to leave her home alone while I went in to solve some problem. But for me, whenever Eileen was in the hospital, our house was lonely. I would come home after visiting hours and play the organ for an hour or two to relax.

* * *

Eileen holding her first grandchild Jeff Beal.

Sharyl wed Norman Beal during her senior year of nursing school. From early on, she had wanted to be a nurse. She studied hard and maintained a high grade point average. When she graduated and pinned on the stiff white cap nurses wore in those days, we were proud parents. Soon she and Norman gave us our first grandson, Jeff.

Eileen was so pleased that she'd lived long enough to hold her grandchild.

Together, we took one last big trip. We toured California, visiting

Yosemite and Death Valley.

When we got back from our California trip, Eileen held on as long as she could, but I could see she didn't have long. I called her family in Michigan and Ruth and Jerri came down. Richard was traveling, and I didn't reach him until after Eileen passed away.

The morning she died, I was in the hospital room with her and her chest was filling up with congestion. The nurse said, "We need to suction you out."

"No," Eileen said.

"Yes, we need to," the nurse said.

I told her, "You're going to feel better."

Eileen said, "You just don't know."

The nurses held her down and suctioned her out. Afterwards, I saw her pillow wasn't positioned very comfortably. I said, "Would you like me to fluff this pillow for you?"

"Yes."

I raised her head, fluffed the pillow, and laid her head back down. "Are you comfortable?"

She said, "Yes," took one breath, and died.

Eileen had known suctioning out would not do her any good. She was dying—no point doing it. She knew what neither the nurses nor I did: she lacked oxygen. After she took her last breath, her skin turned black. Her face, neck, and all the exposed skin I could see was dark. The nurses asked me to leave the room so they could clean her up before letting Ruth and Jerri see her. By the time we came back into the room, her normal color had returned.

Eileen and I had twenty-six great years together. Not always easy, but definitely not easily forgotten. She was a very special woman. Perhaps the thing that allowed her to endure chest pains and poor health was an experience she had in 1957 during her coma. Years later, she revealed to Sharyl that while in the coma, she feared that she was dying and her children would grow up without their mother. Eileen said God spoke to her and told her she was not dying yet, she would live to see her children grown. Indeed she did.

Chapter 33
So Alone

After Eileen passed, I felt so alone. I had no family in Somerset. Sharyl and Norman, Mother and Wayne, and my aunts and uncles all lived in Michigan. Dad had retired, and he and Reba were traveling America in their travel trailer. Richard lived in Florida.

We hadn't made any close friends in Somerset. I'd spent most of our two years there at the hospital with Eileen or at work. And I couldn't really make friends with my coworkers. I was privy to too much confidential information about future plans for the Somerset plant. I was kept apprised of what changes we would implement and when. Also, there were guys in the Somerset office who would repeat everything they heard, trying to make themselves look important. Lowell Doyle was probably my closest friend in Somerset, but we worked together so I couldn't blow off steam about work with him.

Work was like being in a pressure cooker all the time. Ninety-seven percent of the appropriations for the Somerset plant went through me. I didn't report to Lloyd Roebeck, the Somerset plant manager, but directly to Carl Fossbender, the VP in Michigan. While that gave me a lot of leeway to do what I needed, it also created tension because the plant manager couldn't order me to do something. But I always worked with Lloyd to address plant issues.

Usually this involved me going out onto the factory floor and clearing him and a half-dozen others out of the way so my men could get in and fix the problem. Lloyd would be over on the side ranting, raving, and cussing about a machine not running, and my men would already have it fixed. I'd tell the operator what I wanted him to do, and as soon as the piece came out, I'd hand it to the inspector and have him check it. We'd run several more and he'd check them. I'd ask, "Are you satisfied it's running good pieces?"

"It looks like it," the inspector would say.

I'd tell the operator to go ahead, and he'd be running it while Lloyd was still demanding they get it fixed or he was going to know why. I'd walk over to him, and say, "Lloyd, you can go back to your office. It's running, and it is passing inspection."

When I left the plant at night, there was nothing for me to do at home. There weren't hundreds of TV channels back then, no such thing as a VCR or DVD movies, and not a program on TV that I cared to watch.

I was glad we'd brought the Lowrey organ with us when moved from Tecumseh. With Eileen gone, it kept me sane after work. I'd come home, scrape together something to eat, and then play the organ for hours upon hours, until bedtime.

One Friday I looked ahead at the weekend and I sure didn't want to stay home and eat whatever I scrubbed up for my dinner. I also didn't want to sit in a restaurant by myself. I noticed Doris Green, Lloyd's secretary, clearing off her desk and getting ready to go home.

Normally, I didn't have much interaction with Doris because Lloyd's office and mine were separate. When he and I had meetings, my secretary took the minutes, not his, so I only knew Doris well enough to say hi.

I said, "I don't suppose you'd like to go out to dinner tomorrow night, would you?"

She thought a minute, and said, "Sure, I'll go out."

Saturday night I picked her up for dinner, and that was the first time I'd seen her house. Doris and her kids were living, let's say, "thrifty."

After that night, as we continued to date, she told me about her life. She'd grown up in a family of migrant workers who picked cotton in the south, apples and cherries in Michigan. They moved wherever the crops were ready. And it wasn't just the parents working. The whole family picked, including her.

She'd married and divorced George Green. They had two children, Greg and Pam. By the time we started dating, Pam was eleven and Greg was thirteen.

Doris said George was a pretty smart engineer, but he couldn't control his drinking. When he was sober, he was a great guy. When he was drunk, he did whatever it took to get another drink. Once, she'd visited her mother in Missouri and returned home to find he'd sold their furniture to get money for a booze party. After their divorce, Doris had put herself through community college and got the job as Lloyd's secretary.

Greg idolized his dad because he was a hunter and a fisherman. George didn't care if school was in session; if he wanted to take Greg fishing, he'd take him out of school. And that was fine by Greg.

Pam wanted to be loved by her dad, but he never seemed to give her much attention. When he'd come to visit, it was all *Greg this* and *Greg that*.

Doris and I continued to date. We took square-dance lessons, attended square dances, and bowled. I asked her to marry me.

At first she said no. Then she thought about it and said, well, yeah, she would.

I wrote Sharyl and Richard letters explaining while some people might judge me for remarrying only six months after Eileen's death, I could not bear to be alone any longer.

Doris and I married on March 2, 1973, and she, Greg, and Pam moved into the house I'd bought with Eileen. It was a nice suburban ranch-style home, less than three years old. The kids liked it, but Doris didn't. She felt she was being looked at all the time because houses were closer together in a subdivision than she was accustomed to, and people from work who lived in our neighborhood drove by the house daily.

Dick and Doris wed on March 2, 1973, in Somerset, Kentucky.

We'd been married about a year and a half when, in 1974, the United States had a shortage of natural gas production. This meant I had to reconfigure the plant so it could run on natural gas part of the month and propane the rest of the time. I had to learn about propane and build a propane field. We poured foundations, installed two propane tanks, thirty thousand gallons each, and bought vaporizers to turn propane into a form of gas compatible with our equipment. I also had to get fuel oil so we could change over and run the boilers on fuel oil when necessary. The amount of responsibility was horrendous.

After natural gas production declined almost 6 percent in 1974, the Federal Energy Administration stepped in and the Federal Power Commission set priorities on gas use. Lloyd and I flew to Washington, DC, with Tommy Thompson, the company's vice president, to fight for our natural gas allotment.

At the hotel, Lloyd put down his credit card and got his room. Tommy did the same. When it was my turn, I took out cash, counted out the amount of the room bill, and gave it to the clerk. He pushed it back, and said, "No, I can't take that."

"Why?"

"We can only give you a room if you have a credit card."

"I don't have a credit card."

I'd never needed one. When I traveled for Tecumseh, I always drew cash from the company to cover my expenses before I left. I slid the money toward the clerk again. And he shoved it back at me.

Tommy handed the clerk his card, and said, "Here, put his room on my card."

I picked up my cash and handed it to Tommy. When I got home, I got a credit card.

* * *

Not long after that, Doris wanted us to sell the house and move elsewhere. She'd never warmed to living in a subdivision.

"Well, how do you feel about living out in the country?" I said. I'd wanted a little farm my whole life.

"That would be all right," she said.

I searched the surrounding area until I found a piece of land where I thought we'd be happy. So, I took her out and showed it to her. She agreed it looked like a nice place to live. It was up on a mountain and there was a lot of privacy, a small pond, and a barn, but no house. We'd build our own design. One side of the land was 1,200 feet from the edge of a national forest, and there was a creek on the lower corner of the property. I made an offer for the land. The seller told me it was twenty acres, but I knew that wasn't right. I stepped it off and made a counteroffer based on my estimate of thirteen acres. Finally, we settled on a price.

At work, I drew up house plans based on our house in Somerset but changed anything I disliked. For example, I didn't like that our kitchen and dining room were combined, so I added a half wall to separate them. I designed more shelving and cabinet space for the guest bath and enlarged the size of the bedrooms.

I completed the drawings and got a quote. The builder came in at a very good price. I said, "Okay, when can you start?"

"I'll start next week. I'll go out this week and stake it out."

Later in the week, he called me. "You better come out here."

We met at the land, and he said, "We can't build this house where you want it."

I had picked a lovely spot on the edge of a hill overlooking our bottom land. "Why?"

"Well, the house would chop off and come straight down in back. There'd be no place to put a porch and no way to get out of the back of the house, so everything would have to go in and out the front. It doesn't lay right. The house is too long to put the basement where you want it. If you put the garage in the basement, it would cost an arm and a leg to bring the driveway around to it, and require an ungodly amount of concrete."

"Okay," I said, "give me about three weeks and I'll see what I can do."

Instead of going home that night, I returned to the plant. I called Doris and told her I wouldn't be home for supper. I started to work up another scheme for a house built into the hillside. The biggest trees on the property were where the land sloped downward. If I didn't put my house there, I wouldn't have any shade as the rest of the property had been cleared for farming. I envisioned a house with a stone face on the front and back, and lots of glass, big windows across the back with fireplaces upstairs and down.

I worked on the drawing that night, and then next morning. Every day I got to the plant early to put a little time in on the house plans before work started. When I had the design just as I wanted it, I took the plans home and showed Doris. She thought it looked pretty darn good.

When I took my revised plan to the contractor, he got excited. "That will be fun to build. Yes, we can put it right where you want because the sliding doors on the rear wall of the basement will give you an entrance on the back of the house, and the deck off the back of the top story will create a shaded patio below."

Construction started, and I had the well put in. The well driller drilled down two hundred feet. He said, "I got you a good well—you're not going to be able to run a car wash or anything, but it will be adequate."

The house was completed and we moved in, but the first time we flushed the toilets, we discovered we had no water. Now I had a real problem, four people living in a house without water. The only thing to do was build a cistern with a filter wall. As soon as it was ready, I had water trucked from town. That turned out to be expensive. We were using six truckloads a month at fifty bucks apiece—three hundred dollars a month for water unless it rained. So, I had a different well driller come out.

He said, "The problem with that other guy was he missed the seam of water. He passed right through it."

"Okay, where do you say the water will be?"

"I've hit good water in this area at a hundred feet."

I told him to go ahead. He put in a hundred-foot well and hit a dry hole. I said, "What do you think you have to do now?"

"Well, I must be close. I'd like to go another twenty-five feet."

Another twenty-five feet—no water. Again, I said, "What do you want to do now?"

"I don't know," he said, "I don't know where the water is. I'd swear it was right here."

"We haven't got a well, have we?"

"No," he said.

Meanwhile, the first well started putting out water, not much, about 20 percent of what I needed, and muddy. So, I went to town and bought a good filter system to clean the water, and that cut how often I had to fill the cistern.

* * *

Back when Wayne retired, he and Mom had sold their house on Wamplers Lake and moved into Tecumseh, about two blocks from where I lived.

Then, when I moved to Somerset, they'd sold the house in Tecumseh, bought a mobile home, and lived in a trailer park on Devils Lake in Michigan for five years, but they were older now. They moved their trailer to Somerset to be near me.

Wayne loved that I now owned a farm. He'd come out and putter around. He liked to drive my old Farmall tractor, and he painted the barn for us. Doris didn't have a problem with Wayne. He got along with everybody. But she and Mom didn't get along. Pam liked them both, and they liked her and Greg, too.

I raised chickens and had five cows. I put in white pine evergreens, but the cows loved to lie on the pines, which crushed them. I got 1,200 walnut trees from the forestry service and planted them, but the cows pulled up every one. A cow would pull a seedling out, taste it and spit it out. Go to the next one, forget that they didn't like walnut seedlings, uproot it, chew and spit it out. They kept at it until they ruined my whole forestry project.

Dick's grandsons driving his tractor on the farm near Somerset, Kentucky. Pictured left to right: Jeff Beal, David Beal, Ryan Beal, Richard Beal, Dick Gartee.

Chapter 34
A Bellyful

Lloyd Roebeck, the plant manager, retired and his replacement was a guy who had absolutely no knowledge about industrial machining or running a plant. He had been working for Chrysler supervising a system of warehouse conveyers. His experience was limited to getting parts on and off a conveyer and stacked in the right location for easy retrieval when needed.

This guy, I'll call him "Mr. Nasty," had the morals of an alley cat. I personally heard him tell a secretary, "I got a guy coming in tomorrow and I want you to take him out and show him a good time, and you understand what I mean."

She left his office crying.

We didn't get along from the word go. Every day it was a fight. It got so I hated to go to the daily production meeting because he'd have all his foremen there and he'd play a little game of "get Dick."

He'd claim everything was wrong in the plant, but there was really nothing wrong. He'd make a big issue out of little things that were already fixed before I came to the meeting.

I'd had it right up to my neck. Meantime, we had real, ongoing issues to take care of, like water quality.

In a meeting one morning, he took off on me, swearing and calling me curse names. I sat through it, thinking, *I'm not taking any more of this.*

As soon as the meeting was over, I went to my office and told my secretary, "Anybody asks for me, I'm out for the rest of the day."

When I got home, I told Doris, "I'm resigning from this job tomorrow. I can get a job somewhere else and make a good living. I can't take it.

This plant manager is not my kind of guy, and I don't have to put up with his swearing, cussing, personal attacks."

She didn't say anything. She knew because she had worked there. Fortunately, she now had a job at the Social Security Office so she didn't have to deal with him like I did.

That night, I wrote out my letter of resignation. The next morning I typed it myself before anyone else was in the office. I kept a copy for the plant manager and put the original in the daily company mail run to Michigan headquarters, addressed to "Tommy Thompson, Company Vice President."

When "Mr. Nasty" arrived, I said, "I need to see you for a minute before we start the day."

"Okay," he said.

"In your office, please."

I followed him into his office and handed him an envelope. "Here."

He opened it and read the letter. "What the hell does this mean?"

"It means I will not be working here two weeks from today. I'll give you two weeks to hire whoever you want, and they can just take over from then."

He blustered. "Hell, I don't know if we need two weeks."

"Well, that's up to you," I said. "But what I'm offering is two weeks' notice."

"All right, we'll take the two weeks."

I left his office and called all my department heads together, told them I was leaving and would no longer be the master mechanic at the plant. They asked me where I was going and I said, "I have no idea at the present time."

I was in my office an hour later when my secretary came in and said, "Mr. Gartee, Mr. Thompson is on the phone and wants to talk to you *right now*."

I closed the door to my office and picked up the receiver. "Morning, Tommy."

"What the hell is going on down there?" he said.

"I've had a bellyful of the personnel running this plant. So, I have resigned from Tecumseh-Somerset."

"Are you mad at Tecumseh Products or something?"

"No, I'm not mad at Tecumseh," I said. "I just don't want anything further to do with this Somerset plant."

"Well, what are you going to do?"

"I don't really know, Tommy. I was looking for a job when I came to Tecumseh thirty years ago, and I guess I'm looking for a job now."

"Don't get excited," he said. "Go over this with me."

I told him what I'd written in the letter. "You'll have a copy today because I sent it up in the company mail run."

"Well, just stand pat. Don't say anything to anybody and don't do anything. I'll call you tomorrow."

The next morning, Tommy called. "Dick, I'd like you to come work up here."

"Well, what will I do up there?"

"We are about to start a new line for automotive-air-conditioning compressors. I'd like you to take over building the assembly line for that. Oversee it, buy the equipment, really get into it, especially if you see anything that needs to be changed in what we've designed so far. You'll still get your present salary."

That meant I'd be making a lot more money than when I left there to come to Somerset. I'd still be on the bonus system and have all my benefits. So I returned to work at the Michigan plant, but Doris didn't want to move to Michigan. Over the next months I took her there twice, and she wasn't even interested in looking. She didn't want to leave Kentucky. That left me commuting between Tecumseh and our farm outside Somerset, coming home on weekends.

During the week, I stayed with Cy and Harriet Desmet. Cy was the chemical engineer at the Tecumseh plant. They had a large house with extra bedrooms now that their children were grown. When I mentioned to Cy that I needed to find a place for the nights I was in Tecumseh, he generously offered to let me stay with them. I paid him a ridiculously low rent.

We fell into a funny routine. On the way home from work, we'd stop at the liquor store and Cy would poke through the wines until he came up with a bargain-priced selection. At dinner, he'd pour the wine and go through a whole tasting ritual, studying the color, sniffing the aroma, taking a sip, and swishing it in his mouth. Then he'd pronounce, "Not too shabby."

Cy and Harriet were wonderful, but after two months, I knew I couldn't keep working in Tecumseh with Doris living in Somerset. The other factor was that I quickly saw Tommy was using me. When I got there, he put me with Morgan Ford and Joe Herr, the two men I had worked for originally.

Tommy would call me into his office. "Well, Dick, how is it going today?" Gradually, he'd get around to asking me, "What do you think about this and this?" And what he asked about wasn't my area; it was Joe's or Morgan's area.

I had to answer carefully because I didn't want to get those guys pissed at me. They were my friends. Also, I didn't want anyone there to think I was a spy.

Every week I got a little more pressure. "Dick, did you see this appropriation Morgan and Joe had on this project? Did they go over it with you?"

"No, they did not go over it with me." Why would they?

"Please sit here for a minute, look at it, and tell me what you think."

I thought, *This is not right.*

Then Tommy told me I could have either of their jobs. He said, "Morgan's getting close to retirement age, I can arrange it. Or, if you want Joe's job, Joe's got bad health."

Well, I didn't want to get either of them kicked out to make an opening for me.

I held on until December. Then I wrote Tommy a letter notifying him that I was retiring as of the thirty-first.

I left Tecumseh Products and opened my own engineering business. I named the company Double D—Dick and Doris—hoping she'd feel included. It was the start of the Reagan recession, but I ignored that.

The first year, I sold General Electric a seventy-foot-long machine to make dishwashers at their Louisville plant. The equipment manufacturer wouldn't give me the full commission on it, claiming I hadn't been a representative of theirs long enough to make it my project. They had a point. When I started on the project, the engineering was complete and the purchase order had been drawn up. Still, I was connected and would have to do the follow-up. They paid me a $20,000 commission. The machine cost over a million dollars and my commission should have been five times higher, but I wanted to get my business going so I accepted it.

CHAPTER 35
BUENOS DÍAS

General Electric owned several factories in Mexico. One of them made refrigeration compressors under license from Tecumseh Products. Other GE plants made irons, toasters, and various appliances. GE contacted me and said, "We'd like you to go to Mexico City for two weeks as an engineering consultant for our refrigeration compressor factory. Look the plant over and tell us how we can get our present production up to two thousand units a day. Then, we'd like to put on a second shift and produce four thousand a day. When we reach that level, we'll buy some automated equipment to increase it further."

Since I sold automated equipment, they were dangling a little carrot. "But," they cautioned, "that will be further down the road."

"Okay," I said. It sounded like a good job. They agreed to pay me a daily rate plus all my expenses, and I could take Doris.

Our hotel was in a safe area of Mexico City, not far from the factory. The US Consulate was two blocks from our hotel, and every morning I'd see lines queued around the building of people who wanted to go to the United States. Engineers consulting at the other GE plants were in the same hotel and had brought their wives, too. Doris and I spent time with two of the couples. We shared a rental car and visited interesting sites, including the nearby National Cathedral and the National Museum. In the evenings, we ate dinners together in nice restaurants.

Fresh fruits and vegetables were plentiful, but we ate only food prepared by the hotel or a good restaurant, nothing sold on the street. We didn't want to get Montezuma's Revenge (dysentery).

In preparation for the trip, I studied Spanish at home and arrived in the plant the first day prepared to say, "Buenos días."

The plant manager shook my hand and said, too fast for me to catch a word, "Buenosdíasseñorcómoestáusted?"

Chagrined, I said, "No comprendo. Do you speak English?"

"Yes."

"Good. The company is supposed to provide an interpreter. I'd like to meet with her beforehand, and then I'll meet your engineers and spend the rest of the day getting acquainted with your equipment and the layout of the plant."

That was agreeable to him. He checked on my interpreter. "She won't be here until eleven. If you want to walk through the plant now, we can meet back at the office when she arrives."

"I'd like to get started," I said.

He introduced someone who would show me around. The man gave me a tour of the whole plant. I felt as if I'd entered a time capsule. In the nineteenth and early twentieth centuries, machines in US factories didn't have their own motors. Instead, machining equipment was powered by connecting pulleys and belts to a jackshaft, a long shaft that rotated overhead and ran the length of the line. American companies had quit running off jackshafts fifty years ago, but this plant still used one.

When we returned to the office, my translator had arrived. We got along right off the bat. I knew after ten minutes that she was not only fluent in English but she also had the vocabulary necessary to describe engineering concepts. I told her that I intended to discuss issues in meetings with plant personnel and also demonstrate things. "It will be up to you to explain what I'm acting out."

With her in tow, I proceeded to the machine shop.

Right away, I noticed that machinists had to leave their stations to sharpen their own tools. There was no one to do it for them, nor was there a spare tool that could be changed out to allow the operator to keep running. No wonder the plant wasn't making its production quotas.

About eight stations down the line, I watched an operator working feverishly to get the finish bore properly aligned to make a perpendicular hole in cast iron pieces. An inspector was measuring his output, but none of the operator's adjustments made the correct holes.

I picked up one of the pieces, studied it, and thought, *The problem is not here.* I began working my way back down the line. When I found it, I returned to the inspector and the frustrated machinist and said, "Follow me."

I took them to the beginning of the line and had the inspector check a piece coming from the rough-bore machine. It was off. "The problem is not with your machine," I told the operator. "Here is the problem. If this station bores the hole off-center, there is nothing you can do at the finish bore to correct it. The inspector needs to get this machine to produce good pieces and everything else will fall in place."

Every day, I ate lunch in the cafeteria with the workers. In Mexico, the green hot sauce was spicier than the red sauce—really hot. The young men who sat with me, eighteen or nineteen years old, would ladle green sauce into their bean soup until it turned green, then eat it and never make a face. I'd put a few dabs of the red sauce in mine, and when I'd taste it, I'd grab for a drink of water. That cracked them up.

The people there were so nice. One young man who spoke no English had someone teach him four words before I left so he could say, "You come back quick."

Every night when I returned to the hotel, I would write notes about what I'd seen that day.

The consultants that preceded me had been giving only bits and pieces of information and then leaving. Previous consultants scribbled a few notes on a yellow pad, handed it to the plant manager, and said, "Implement that and I'll be back in two months."

Two months later, they'd come back, stay for another two weeks, and do the whole bit over again.

I didn't know that's what had been going on, and I wouldn't have done it anyhow. I tackled this job as if my own company had sent me to one of our plants and said, "We want you to straighten it out as much as you can."

With that mindset, I spent the first four days in their machine shop because they had terrible problems on the crankcase line. The biggest issue was sand holes in the cast iron. These inclusions or tumors in the metal occurred when the foundry poured hot metal into the form. The defects weren't apparent in the early stages of machining, but further down the line, as the cylinders that had been bored into the crankcase were honed, faults in the casting were revealed and the piece would have to be scrapped. The plant was throwing away 35 percent of its crankcases. To make it worse, the pieces would already have a half-dozen operations done on them before being scrapped, wasting the labor costs, too.

Teotihuacan Pyramids outside of Mexico City (Photo by J.J. Nanni – Pixbay.)

I had weekends free while I was consulting in Mexico. One Saturday, Doris and I drove forty kilometers with two other couples to Teotihuacan, an ancient city and site of numerous pyramids, thought to have been established about 100 BC. A long, wide avenue through the ruins terminated at the Pyramid of the Sun. At 233.5 feet tall, it is the third-largest pyramid in the world. We climbed a set of steep stone stairs to the top.

At the opposite end of the avenue was the Pyramid of the Moon, the second-largest pyramid at the site. Along both sides of the avenue stood many smaller pyramids with platforms at the tops used for ceremonies by the Teotihuacan people almost one thousand years before the Aztecs arrived. Further down the avenue, a large plaza of ancient temples included the ruined Temple of the Feathered Serpent, where we visited an archeological excavation that was underway.

Other tourist trips we took on my days off included the Basilica of Our Lady of Guadalupe, the National Shrine of Mexico, where in 1531 the Virgin Mary appeared four times to a peasant, Juan Diego. Juan's first three attempts to convince the bishop to build a church on the site fell on deaf ears. In her fourth appearance, Mary sent Juan to a normally barren hill and had him gather Castilian roses for the bishop in his tilma (cloak). When Juan unfurled his cloak before the bishop, the flowers fell to the floor and left imbedded in the fabric an image of the Virgin Mary. Today, Juan Diego's original cloak is housed in the Basilica. The circular floor plan allows the image to be seen from any point within the building.

Another day, we rode gondola boats through the canals of Xochimilco while serenaded by mariachi musicians who played traditional Mexican music. The canals wound through lush gardens, and the boats were a spectacle in themselves, brightly painted with floral designs.

When my two weeks were up, I told the plant manager, "I'd like you to schedule a meeting today for me to talk to all the foremen and superintendents in charge of each manufacturing operation. I also want to include your purchasing department." I cautioned him that the meeting would take the entire afternoon.

He said, "Sí," and gathered everyone.

I started with the sand-hole problem. "Your purchasing department must tell your supplier you cannot accept any more iron castings with sand inclusions. Tell them you will find another vendor if this continues."

"We can't do that."

"Why not?"

"We only have two suppliers for cast iron, and one of them casts our parts in the empty areas of the mold they use for General Motors' engine blocks."

"Well, it may cost something to get your own molds made, but this is your number one problem. You're scrapping 35 percent of your production right out of the gate."

I moved on. "Next, you need to buy roller conveyers to flow parts from machine to machine, and make some wooden pallets to ride on them. I'll give you exact dimensions in my report."

At this point, I pantomimed how operators should use the conveyors, loading a piece from the conveyor into their machine with one hand while removing the finished piece with the other. My interpreter described in Spanish what I demonstrated.

The rest of the afternoon, I continued through my list of recommendations. When I finished, I saw some long faces. For years, local engineers at the plant had envied the highly automated equipment in American factories. They'd hoped I'd say the way to increase production was to replace the machines in their shop.

"If you'll implement the simple changes I've recommended," I said, "your production numbers will go up."

After the meeting ended and the manager and I were the only ones left, I asked him, "Did I say anything to your men you didn't want me to say?"

"No, señor, you did fine."

He informed me that I was the first consultant to talk to his entire staff. My predecessors had been handing out advice in drips and dabs, milking the company for as many consultations as they could.

When I got home, I wrote a detailed report, including a complete layout of the plant. This wasn't an easy task. Since I no longer had access to my translator, I was having problems labeling the equipment. I called the man who'd hired me and said, "I'm sorry, but my report will be two days late. My English-to-Spanish dictionary is not helping me. For instance, a bore and a drill are two different machine operations, but the Spanish word is the same for both."

"That's okay," he said. "You can label the machines in English."

I sent copies of my final report to GE, to the Mexican plant manager, and even to the export division of Tecumseh Products, the licenser. I received feedback that everyone was pleased with the job I'd done.

Several months later, I had lunch with engineers from the General Electric plant in Louisville, Kentucky, where I'd sold the machine that made dishwashers. As I left the restaurant, I ran into one of the consulting engineers who had toured the pyramids with Doris and me. The man acted cold—barely acknowledged me. I said, "Well, how are you doing?"

"You ought to know, you SOB."

Dumbfounded, I said, "I don't know what you're mad about."

"Sure you do. You screwed it up for everybody." He proceeded to explain that two weeks after receiving my report, GE called in all the other consulting engineers, threw my report on the table, and said, "From now on, this is what we expect from all of you. No more scribbling a few lines on a notepad and saying that's your report."

Two years later, an interesting coincidence reminded me of my trip to Mexico. The 1982 World's Fair was held in Knoxville, Tennessee, only two hours southeast of my farm in Somerset, Kentucky. Sharyl and Norman brought their boys down from Michigan, Richard and his girlfriend came up from Florida, and we all went to the Fair. Who did we meet in the Mexico pavilion? My interpreter from Mexico City—small world. I introduced her to my family and had a great reunion with her.

Chapter 36
On My Own

Here is what most people don't know about a recession. If you have a job, you don't even realize the recession is on. If you don't have a job, you can't find one for nothing. That year, I quoted proposals that should have netted me $300,000 to $400,000, but none of them matured. I added industrial robots to my offerings, but I couldn't get those deals to go through, either. I could design robots to do everything my customers wanted, but nobody bought anything.

Meanwhile, my reputation was growing. I got called to go through a new General Motors (GM) plant in Dayton, Ohio. They were having problems with an automated line to assemble engines. GM brought me and another guy in as consultants. We were to go through the plant independently and not confer with each other. Then we would quote against each other on what it would take to fix the issues.

The jobs of the two GM engineers who had brought us in were in peril. They had to either get the line working or be fired.

After we had both toured the plant and prepared our quotes, they called us in to a meeting together and said, "Okay, who wants to go first?"

The other consultant said he would. What he told them was basically the same thing I'd written in my report. The current assembly line was a 250-foot-long contiguous unit. When an engine got screwed up, there was no way to take it off line so they had to shut the entire line down until they got the problem engine fixed. Meanwhile, the rest of the work stopped. The solution was to tear out part of the line and put in a couple of stations where they could slide an engine out of the work flow and let the others continue.

When he finished his oral presentation, I gave them mine in writing. "There it is," I said.

We had both identified the same problem areas and the same solution, and we had quoted nearly the same dollar amount.

"We're not going to spend that kind of money," the GM engineers said.

The other consultant replied, "I can't fix it unless you want to do this."

The engineers turned to me, and I said, "If you won't spend money to fix your problem, I don't want to be part of it. But thank you for inviting me. I'd like to just leave."

We both left, and neither one of us got a contract. We surmised that they made our suggested changes on their own.

A year after I came back from Mexico, Todd Herrick from Tecumseh Products contacted me. He was Ray Herrick's grandson, and at that time, vice president of their export division. He wanted a quote from me for an engineering consultation similar to what I'd done for General Electric. Except this time I'd be going to their licensee plant in Turkey, and I'd be overseas for six months.

I really didn't want to go. Eileen's brother, Ronnie, had been stationed in Turkey while he was in the Navy and told us of seeing bodies hanging from lampposts on the street. At least when he was there, the government executed criminals and left the body on display as a warning to others. It didn't sound like a place I wanted to be stuck for six months. But I couldn't afford to gain a reputation as a consulting company that wouldn't respond to a request for proposal, so I drafted an agreement I thought I could live with and submitted it. I wanted $400 per day, plus they were to fly me home every six weeks at company expense and pay me for the days I was stateside.

Todd called and said, "God, we can't afford you."

They sent another man instead, but he died at the airport. They had a devil of a time getting his body returned. After that, no one wanted to go.

They contacted me again and, without telling me about the man who died, asked if I would reduce my price. I said no. Later, I met with Todd, who said, "They wanted me to go over. I told them I wouldn't."

"What makes you think I'd want to go if you turned it down?" I said.

The second year in business I quoted $6.5 million worth of proposals. I lost an order that would have paid me about $25,000 and would have helped my business survive.

At home, Doris and I had our differences, but I didn't think they were great issues. I thought we were doing pretty well. She didn't like that I was working for myself, but she recognized that I was fighting to keep the business going.

Then, on New Year's Eve, she shocked me. We'd decided not to go out and instead have a quiet celebration at home. She was reading, and just to make conversation, I said, "Do you have any resolutions for the New Year?"

Doris laid down her book, looked at me, and said, "I decided I'm not going to live with you."

"Oh?"

"Yeah, I want a divorce."

I sat there, stunned. After a while I said, "Is this your final decision?"

"Yes, it is."

"Then there isn't much use of me saying anything, is there?"

"No."

"Okay," I said and just dropped it. The next day, I said, "When do you want all this to happen?"

"Well, I want to find an apartment in town. When I get an apartment, I'm moving out. I'll look for one this week."

The next thing I knew, we were divorced.

Afterwards, I felt a bit used. When I met Doris, she was a single mom trying to raise two kids on a secretary's income and irregular child support from an unreliable ex-husband. I thought, *She marries me, a man with a good income, stays until her kids are raised and out of the house, and then leaves.* Perhaps that was only my uncharitable thoughts and never her intent. I'm sure I wasn't the ideal husband for Doris. There was an age difference between us. My children were grown and hers were not. Marriage is not easy under the best of situations, and looking back, maybe neither of us tried hard enough. But divorce left a bitter taste.

Her daughter and I remained close. Pam lives in Florida now and regularly visits me. I haven't seen Doris or her son, Greg, in years.

Christmas 2014 – Dick gives stepdaughter Pam a painting he made of the farm they lived on when she was growing up.

Chapter 37
Thrice Wed

I hadn't square-danced in a long while. Dancing is an activity for couples, and after Doris and I split up, I didn't want to go alone. Friends kept saying, "Aw, come. You can dance with somebody."

I didn't want to do that. "No, I'm not going."

Then one night, Dee and Virginia Shepard called. "We're going to have square-dance classes, and we need you to help us out because we've got more women than men."

I said I would. I got there and they did have three or four women without partners. I helped teach the class, and in doing so, I met Mary Hutzel, a widow. She seemed like a nice person.

When there were square dances in the neighboring villages, like Monticello, Mary's friends would say to her, "Aren't you going to go? It's only fifteen or twenty miles away."

"I'd like to go, but I don't have a partner."

"Maybe Dick is going," her friends said.

Meanwhile, one of the couples would say to me, "Dick, why don't you bring Mary along?"

Next thing I knew, she and I were square-dancing together regularly.

The house on my farm had a large basement. To help new square dancers practice, I'd invite Mary and three couples over to square-dance. Soon she and I started going together to larger regional square dances as far away as Gatlinburg, Tennessee.

After six or seven months of square dancing, I asked Mary to marry me.

Dick and Mary wed on September 25, 1982, in Somerset, Kentucky.

Mary had converted to Catholicism when she married her first husband, but she told me she would change to my religion if I wanted to remain Presbyterian. I didn't think that would be right. She had raised her seven kids as Catholic, sent them to Catholic school. How could we tell them, "Mom's not a Catholic anymore?"

That's just going to disrupt the family, I thought. *Much simpler if I join the Catholic Church.* I talked to her priest, Father Toby, and asked what I had to do to join his church. He said take some classes, be baptized, and go on a retreat. I said I'd already been baptized, but doing it again wouldn't kill me. So I became a Catholic.

In my new church, I avoided getting drawn into too many duties. I'd learned my lesson at the Presbyterian Church in Tecumseh, where I'd taken on increasing numbers of activities until church burned me out. At the Catholic Church, I ushered and served communion. One year they wanted help to raise money to fix up the old school, so I assisted with writing letters and so on. But I kept things simple.

Although Eileen had died ten years before, I had remained close with her mother, Ruth. I took both Doris and Mary to meet her after I wed them. Ruth didn't warm up to Doris. She was polite, that was it. But Mary was similar to Eileen in a lot of ways, and Ruth really liked her.

My mother died in June 1982, just three months before Mary and I wed in September. Shortly after our wedding, Wayne came to live with us. He had to—he couldn't take care of himself.

At first we had an awful time getting him to bathe. Mary had a very sensitive sense of smell and she'd tell me, "I don't know what to do with Wayne. He stinks, and I can't stand it."

Wayne adored Mary, so I said to him, "Wayne, Mary loves you, but you've got to take a bath."

"I'll do it tomorrow morning."

He'd get up the next morning and never go near the shower.

Finally, we tried something different. I knew after he'd lost his fingers as a child, his mother had kept him close and told him what to do. Then he married Mom, and she told him what to do. He just needed a woman to tell him to take his bath.

Mary handed him his towel, clean underwear, pants, and shirt and said, "Now, go take your shower and put those on."

He'd go along like a little kid, shower and dress in clean clothes every day. Unless Mary forgot to tell him—then he wouldn't. But Wayne only lived twenty months after Mom died. He missed her deeply.

Meanwhile, our finances were stretched thin. Newlyweds starting out all over again. My third year in business, I'd quoted $7 million and had two surefire sales lined up for $350,000 each. I'd earn $70,000 in commission if both sold. These were proven designs my supplier had built for other plants that were working every day. But I couldn't get the customer to spend money on it because the Reagan recession had shut off all the company's funding sources.

By the end of my third year in business, I'd eaten through my savings and was borrowing money to keep my business stimulated. I couldn't get in the car, drive to the bottom end of Georgia, over to Tennessee, up to Michigan, and back to Kentucky without spending money. I still had General Electric as a client, and I'd have to go up there twice a month to take them to lunch. I'd arrive planning on two guys and end up with four. They'd always choose an expensive restaurant. With drinks and food, I'd end up with a $200 lunch bill.

I thought, *This is going the wrong way. Money is going down a hole and taking me with it.* The straw that broke Double D was a pending sale I had on a welding machine for $440,000. The commission would have bought me some time.

My customer called my supplier in Michigan and said, "We want another $1,500 off this machine."

The company said no.

"We can get it elsewhere for less," the customer said.

"Well, then, buy it from somebody else," was my supplier's response.

So my customer took his order to another firm.

If, instead of being stubborn, the company had consulted me, I'd have told them to take the $1,500 out of my commission. Because for the chance to earn $44,000, what was $1,500 to me? Nothing. And that money would have kept me going for a whole year.

I didn't have any other sales pending. I notified the two companies I was representing. "I'll give you my customer contacts and the projects I've got in the works, and it will cost you nothing."

The ongoing recession was bad. I sent over a hundred resumes. I had interviews where a guy would say, "We'd hire you, but you're too highly qualified for us and you'll want too much money."

"No, let's talk about wages." I was ready to negotiate, but companies wouldn't make an offer.

Things got so drastic I went to the local drugstore where we bought our prescriptions. The store had an advertisement for a man to stock shelves. I said, "I'll do it."

The owner looked at my resume and said, "Dick, I won't hire you."

"Why?"

"I can't afford to pay you that kind of money."

"I'm not asking for that. I'll take whatever you're paying." I didn't care if it was $1.50 or $2.00 an hour. I just wanted some cash coming in.

"No, I won't hire you. You'll just leave."

I threw down my papers and said, "You write up a contract and I'll sign it. I'll agree to stock your shelves for one year. If another job comes along, I might have to stock them at night, but I'll guarantee you one year."

"Oh, I can't do that," he said.

I felt pretty desperate, couldn't even get a job stocking shelves in a drugstore. So I took up insurance sales. They taught me how to sell insurance. I passed the insurance board exam and got my license. The problem was my conscience.

My territory was Eastern Kentucky, the poorest region in the state. I'd go into a person's house. Stuffing was coming out of their furniture, a couple of chicken bones on the end table, kids running around in diapers, older kids in bib overalls with no shoes. I'd tell a guy how much insurance would pay his family if he died, or another plan that would pay if he got sick. But in my heart, I knew as soon as I walked in his door that I shouldn't sell this man insurance.

A client's premium was fifty-eight dollars for the first month. That was my commission. But I'd look at that family and think, *He doesn't need to give me fifty-eight bucks, he needs groceries and some clothes for these kids.* And his situation wasn't because he was boozing or wasn't a hard worker. No one in Eastern Kentucky made any decent money. In a lot of those towns, the workers made only two or three dollars a day. I couldn't sell insurance because I couldn't bring myself to take what little money they had. I decided I had to do something different.

Chapter 38
Lord, Where Do I Go?

One day as I left home, I told Mary, "Well, I'm off to see if I can sell some insurance today. I can't say exactly where I'm going. I'll head toward Corbin and then wander until I find a likely place."

The traffic light at a T-intersection in Corbin, Kentucky was red. To my right, the road led to Williamsburg. If I turned left, I'd go toward Hazard and other little towns that might be better for selling life insurance. While I waited for the light to change, I said a prayer: "Lord, I don't know what to do. I can't keep selling this insurance. I can't do that to these people. They need their money worse than I do. Please direct me to something. I need a job bad. I put it all in your hands. Amen."

The light turned green. Without realizing what I was doing, I turned toward Williamsburg. I drove without a destination in mind, busy thinking, *What am I going to do?*

Roper had a factory in Williamsburg where they manufactured home appliances. I had never been to that plant in my life, but I suddenly found myself in their parking lot. There weren't many cars there. I shut off the engine and wondered, *What am I doing here?*

I always kept copies of my resume in my briefcase, so I decided that since I was here, I'd see if they had a job. I walked inside and said to the receptionist, "Can I see the man in charge of engineering?"

She looked puzzled but told me to have a seat while she found someone to help me. She disappeared. After fifteen minutes, a man came through the door she had exited. He was wearing the slacks and vest from a three-piece suit, but not the coat. His white dress shirt was open at the collar without a tie. Still, it was obvious he wasn't one of the factory laborers. He introduced himself as the vice president of engineering from Roper headquarters. He said the company had ten plants around the country and Williamsburg was just one of them.

"We're on shut-down here," he said. "We're changing the plant over right now. The man I'd like to have you interview with is not here. Let me see your resume. What kind of job are you looking for?"

I handed him my resume. He read the first four lines and said, "We've got three openings in engineering right now, and if your resume is accurate, I don't see a job you can't handle. But I don't want to hire for that man, I want him to hire his own men. So if would it be all right with you, could you come back next week when he'll be here?"

"Yes, I could."

"Monday he'll be crushed, and he may need Tuesday to get on his feet because we've made some big changes here. How would Wednesday be for you?"

"That will be fine." He could have said any day and I'd have been happy.

We made an appointment and I walked out of there on air. I'd had over a hundred resumes out and hadn't even gotten a tumble. Now, I had an interview at a company with three openings.

Cell phones didn't exist yet. I went to the nearest pay phone, dropped my quarter in the slot, and dialed home. When Mary answered, I said, "I'm on my way home. You are never going to guess what."

"Did you sell some insurance?"

"No, I've got better news than that. I've got a chance for an engineering job next week. There are three jobs, and I ought to get one of them. I'll tell you all about it when I get there."

Driving home, I could hardly contain my excitement. As soon as I arrived, I started telling Mary the story when the phone rang.

The caller said he was with American Greetings, a card manufacturer second only to Hallmark in size. "We've been going over your resume, and we have two job openings, both in industrial engineering. Would you be interested?"

Industrial engineering meant I'd be doing time study again, but on the other hand, the interview with Roper might not turn out. "Yes, I'm interested."

"Could you come for an interview Tuesday?"

Perfect, that's the day before my Roper interview, I thought. Then I said, "Yes, I could." We set a time, and I hung up.

Mary and I were discussing our turn of fortune when the phone rang again. It was Bill Foley, a headhunter I used when I was hiring for the Somerset plant. "Dick, I've got two openings I am trying to fill for a plant in Lexington. They need a plant engineer and a design engineer. I told them about you and they are eager to meet you."

"How excited are they, and when do they want to do this?"

"They'd like to talk to you Monday, if you can be there."

"I can do that. What time?"

"They would like you to meet with the plant manager before the interview, say eight o'clock. Would that be too early?"

"No, eight will be fine."

He told me the company name, Standard Products, and gave me directions to their plant.

I hung up the phone, and said, "Mary, you will never believe this, but I've now got interviews Monday, Tuesday, and Wednesday. I'm going to get hired someplace."

We were elated. What a load off my shoulders. I'd go to each interview and tell them I would give them my decision on Wednesday, depending on which paid the best.

Monday morning I arrived at Standard Products and the manager, Hoot Gibson, was waiting for me. He wanted me to tour the plant with him. They made the rubber molding around windows, windshields, and bumpers for the auto industry. I didn't know anything about the rubber extrusion and roll-forming processes used to make window seals. I'd never been exposed to that type of manufacturing. As we toured the plant, he said, "I want to show you our electrical" as if he was real proud of it.

He led me to a room where the plant's electrical circuits connected. I took one look and didn't like what I saw. Bare high-voltage wires were sticking out where anyone who stumbled against them would be shocked.

He gave me a couple of minutes to look it all over and said, "What do you think of it?"

I looked him right in the eye. "Not much. This is an accident waiting to happen. Somebody is going to get killed or badly hurt in here."

"What?" he said.

"See these bare wires? I can tell by the gauge of the wire, these are high voltage, probably 440 volts. You touch that baby—you'll get a jolt you didn't expect. Might knock you across the room, might knock you into another live wire. This is a bad situation."

He said, "Okay." We continued touring the rest of the processes throughout the plant. We returned to his office, and he said, "What do you think about the plant in general?"

"What do you mean, in general?"

"Our personnel and production."

I thought, *Well, since I already told him I didn't like the electrical, I may as well go the whole yard.* "Truthfully, I didn't think much of it. It looks like a country club to me."

"What do you mean, country club?" Hoot said.

"Everybody is standing around laughing, talking, playing. Not working. I don't know how you make a profit."

He didn't have a response to that. He said, "I want you to talk to our employment manager for a few minutes, then I'll get back with you."

While I was gone, Hoot got on the telephone with the vice president at the main office in Cleveland, Ohio, and apparently told him he wanted to hire me. The Cleveland office gave him some salary ranges and Hoot sent word he was ready to see me again.

When I returned to his office, he said, "We have two job openings—one is the plant engineer and the other is the chief engineer. Which one do you want?"

I asked him to describe each position. The chief engineer primarily worked with the auto company engineers and had to travel to Detroit every other week to meet with the car companies on their upcoming designs for new models to make sure the company got it right before it started to extrude rubber. The plant engineer job involved adding a new production line to the two they already had and building additions on the warehouse and office sides of the plant. That's the one I chose.

Hoot wanted to know how quickly I could get figures together for it. I didn't know anything about extruding or extruding equipment, but I knew factory construction.

"I could probably rough out the building requirements enough to start gathering quotes in two weeks," I said. "But the new extruding line will take longer to get plans together."

The rest I was winging. "There'll be equipment to get bids on and all that, but I can create a rough outline of what it will cost in a month."

Hoot said okay, and we started to talk about salary. His first offer was too low for that point in my career. I said no. We negotiated, he came up considerably. I took the job and canceled my other interviews.

Within a month, I worked up both the construction and equipment appropriations because I knew I had to have the money approved before I could do anything. I told Hoot, "It will cost a million four thousand for the building and another million for the equipment. Do you want me to put those in an appropriation request?"

"Yes," he said. "We'll take them to Cleveland headquarters."

I wasn't dressed for that. I'd come to work that day without suit or sport coat, just a shirt and necktie. But Hoot said, "We leave in an hour. I've got us a plane waiting at the airport."

It was a small four-seat private plane. We flew to Cleveland and met with Tom Judd, the VP. I told him what we proposed and gave him my appropriations. He looked them over and said, "Sounds like a pretty good figure, Dick. You feel it's reliable?"

"I know the building figures are extremely accurate," I said. "The equipment, I'm not as sure about, but I think the numbers are pretty darn close. I've put a little fudge factor in there, not much, but just in case."

He said he would look them over and get back to me in a day or two. Hoot and I flew back to Lexington, and Tom Judd called the next day to tell me both appropriations were approved. Without knowing anymore about me than my resume, they had just given me two million dollars to spend how I wanted.

Six weeks later, I got a telephone call from the chief operating officer of a company in Ohio. He said, "Dick, I'm looking for a man, and people tell me you're the one I want. I own the company and you would report directly to me. You will have the power to hire or fire anyone you want. I want you to straighten this plant out. Everybody I have talked to has assured me if there was one name they were thinking of, you were the guy who could do it."

"I'm sorry," I said. "I've just started this job for Standard Products. I have a couple of significant projects to do here and I have committed to it."

"If you're talking about money, Dick, name your wage. You'll get that plus a bonus every year."

"That part sounds fantastic," I said, "but I can't accept it. I made a commitment to this company, and they have trusted me with two million-dollar projects. I've practically just walked in and taken off my coat. I can't walk out and leave them hanging. I'm not made that way. But I thank you for the offer."

Another two weeks went by and he called again. This time, he offered triple what I was being paid at Standard Products. I thought and thought. I said, "I don't doubt the money is good. I don't doubt that this is a wonderful opportunity, but you wouldn't want me to leave you in the lurch, and I can't leave these people."

CHAPTER 39
GETTING MY FIRST PC

When IBM brought out the model 5150 personal computer everything changed. Up to that point, IBM computers had been large, expensive mainframes. Commodore and Radio Shack had previously introduced desktop-size computers, but the IBM PC platform became a standard for microprocessor-based systems, and other manufacturers began making computers that were "IBM PC compatible."

My job as plant engineer involved more than just completing the building additions and new manufacturing lines for which I had appropriations. I also had to keep all the machines in the plant running and supervise their maintenance.

One problem was we didn't have qualified industrial electricians who could diagnose and fix a machine that went down. Their electrical experience came from wiring houses or similar jobs. If you weren't watching over their shoulders, they might tear the whole electrical panel apart, not know how to put it back together, and still not have found the problem. They'd been hired by my predecessor and had worked long enough to be in the union, so I couldn't fire them. The only solution open to me was to help them do their jobs better.

Perry Gullett was smart as a whip. I convinced him he ought to work for me as an engineer. I took him off his job on the factory floor and put him on salary. We discussed computers, and I said, "My goal is to put a computer on every machine in this plant."

He looked at me like I was crazy. But my reasoning was that by putting computer interfaces on all our machines, an electrician or maintenance man could look at a panel of LED lights and know exactly where the problem was. This would cut downtime drastically.

Shortly after Perry came to work for me, I was writing specs for a thirty-foot-long automated oven to dry and bond extruded rubber we glued on roll-formed metal to make automobile trim. I told Perry, "When we meet with the vendor, I want to specify that the oven is to be computerized. Instead of old-fashioned electromechanical relays, I want it to have an Allen-Bradley AT computer."

The Allen-Bradley didn't look as fancy as IBM's desktop computer. It had a more industrial-looking metal case, but inside it was equivalent to the IBM AT model.

We met with the oven manufacturer and when the discussion came to controllers, I said I wanted an Allen-Bradley AT with it. They said they could do that, and it would only cost a couple of thousand dollars more. That amount was trivial compared to the overall bid. I told them Perry would work with their man. I said I'd take care of having Allen-Bradley instruct us on the computer, but when they were installing the connections for the oven, Perry would be right at their side. I wanted us to know all about the computer.

While we were waiting for the vendor to ready the oven, Perry told me he had a buddy on the other side of Lexington who had an IBM AT running AutoCAD (a program for drawing industrial and building schematics). I met Perry's friend and asked him what I needed to make AutoCAD work. He said to buy the AutoCAD software, a digitizer tablet to draw with, and a plotter to print out the blueprints. The oven cost less than the amount I'd budgeted, so I spent the extra money on the items he suggested.

Once the oven was installed and running, the computer only needed to be attached if we had to diagnose a problem. So, we took the computer to my office, loaded on AutoCAD, and got everything set up for the engineering department to do drawings. We drew blueprints for the plant layout, and Perry did electrical schematics for the electricians.

The accounting department got word that we had the only computer in the entire plant. They came down to my department. "We're taking your computer up to our office."

"No, you're not. That computer is necessary to service the new oven when it goes down. Unless you're willing to be here twenty-four hours a day, all three shifts, and take it onto the factory floor whenever the oven needs to be fixed, it stays right here."

"Well, we're going to have that computer in our office."

"You better get approval from somebody higher up, because I'm telling you that you're not taking it."

Eventually, they got a computer of their own, but for a while they had fire in their eyes over mine.

I continued my plan to put computer controllers on every machine. I rewrote the electrical specification for the whole plant and gave it to purchasing. I told them a copy had to be attached to every purchase order for a machine because it spelled out exactly what the vendor had to supply for the electrical controls.

There were two vendors who had been building machinery for Standard Products for years. One was in Georgetown, Kentucky, and the other in Lexington. I personally sent each of them a copy of our new spec with a polite letter explaining that we had changed our electrical specifications for the company and the attached document contained our requirements for all future purchases.

They didn't ask any questions or respond further, but when their next machine was ready, they had put some little off-brand computer on it. Our chief engineer said, "Well, it's got a computer."

"Not the right one," I said.

"What the hell difference does that make?" he said.

"Every one of these computers is different, has a different board in them, and uses a different computer language. I'm not stocking parts for six or eight different brands of computers. We have specified two choices, the Allen-Bradley or the Omron. They can choose whichever they want, but nothing else. Our people are trained on those brands."

"Well, you can just get along with this."

"No, I can't. I've written a spec, and it was part of their purchase order. They knew what was required before they ever quoted the machine. I'll be glad to send Perry over to their plant and show them how to put in an Omron. He'll even program it for them if they want."

They shipped the machine over anyway, with the wrong computer.

"What are we going to do with it?" Perry said.

"Just let it sit in receiving," I said. "Don't move it."

"They want to put it on the line."

"Tell them to come see me."

Pretty soon, they did. I said, "No, it's got the wrong computer. I don't care who pays, but it's going to have an Omron on it before it goes in that line."

We argued it out a little more, and the chief engineer said, "Okay, put on an Omron, and let's get it in production."

I don't know if Standard Products ever got the vendor to reimburse us for the Omron. I didn't care.

About six months later, the same company sold us a cut-off press that cut rubber molding to specific lengths. It too, arrived with the wrong computer. I said, "Let it sit."

Hoot Gibson had retired, and we had a new plant manager. At the morning production meeting, he said, "Dick, I want you to put that machine in the line today."

"It's not ready," I said.

"When will it be ready?"

"I have no idea, but it's not ready right now."

I left the meeting and asked Perry if he'd heard anything about an Omron coming from the vendor. He said no.

"Well, be prepared to tear the electrical panel off. Go to the electrical department and build a new panel using an Omron computer. Then we can just take their panel off and put the new one on."

About then, the chief engineer came. "I want that machine put on the line."

"That machine is not ready," I said. "First, it hasn't got an Omron. Second, it hasn't been fully tested, and so far, it hasn't cut correct lengths. So it needs work on the tooling and the settings that cause the knife to cut the material."

"Well, put it in the line and we'll work on it there."

"No, you said it just right. We, my department, would be on the line trying to get the machine working with a bunch of people leaning over our shoulders asking when it's going to be fixed. There is no reason for that. You already have a cutting machine on the line doing a half-ass job. You don't need a second one. When we get this one making good parts, then we'll put it in production."

"Well, the manager says you've got to put it in the line." The manager was standing a little way off, watching our conversation.

"I don't give a damn who says it. I am the plant engineer here and I'm not putting it online until I see it cut a good part."

They both disappeared, and Perry worked feverishly getting the panel built. A while later, the chief engineer came back. "How long before you have that panel on there?"

I looked at Perry. "What do you think?"

"I'll finish it this afternoon," Perry said. "Second shift can install it."

"So tomorrow morning we'll be ready to start testing?" I said.

Perry nodded.

I turned to the chief engineer. "Probably another day, maybe two and we'll have it cutting good pieces."

"Well, they better be good."

"They will be," I said.

A day later, we moved the new machine into the line, and within fifteen minutes we had it cutting pieces to exact specification every time.

I had to take stands like that or they'd walk all over me.

Next, I computerized the maintenance logs of every machine in the plant. To accomplish this, the machines needed unique ID numbers. Our accounting department assigned asset numbers to capital equipment Standard Products owned. But we also had machines paid for by auto companies to make something custom for them. Since these were not owned by us, they had no asset tags. So I started a separate numbering system, distinct from the asset numbers accounting used, and tagged every machine with a maintenance tracking ID.

I had the maintenance crews check the machines at least once a month, fill out a report, and bring it to my office. I set up a spreadsheet program and my secretary entered the data. We also kept track of downtime for each machine and whether the cause was electrical, mechanical, pneumatics, or whatever the men selected from a list of fifteen reasons. She entered that data as well.

The system was effective in tracking downtime of our machines, but implementation of the formalized maintenance schedule was weak. We didn't have foremen on each shift to ensure the men utilized their time for maintenance when they weren't doing repairs.

One day, in the production meeting, I was told that Ford Motor Company was sending a man to review our preventive-maintenance program.

"I've got one," I said.

The men in the meeting said, "Wow. When did you get one?"

"I've had one for a long time."

"Yeah, but Ford wants a certain one," the plant manager said.

"Well, we'll see what the Ford man says when he gets here."

"Our Goldsberry, North Carolina, plant has one they're using."

"No, we've got our own, and it's working fine."

"Well, it better be good because Ford has already seen the one at Goldsberry."

Later that morning, the man from Ford arrived. They introduced us and I said, "Why don't you come to my office, and I'll show you what we've got?"

I showed him a card the maintenance guys turned in when they worked on a machine and explained it. I had my secretary pull the file for the machine number on the card he was holding. I showed him the preventive-maintenance slips for that machine, indicating what the electrician checked and what the mechanic checked. He looked it all over and handed it back. He didn't say anything.

"Then we go one step further," I said. I reached over on my desk and picked up a computer printout of a downtime report. I highlighted the row for the machine we'd been discussing and handed him the report. "Now, this goes beyond preventive maintenance," I said. "We can see how often and for how long a machine has been down. If it's been down more than three times in a month, we come in on a Saturday and completely take it apart to correct the problem. Then we monitor it on our preventive-maintenance sheet to make sure it runs like it is supposed to."

He handed it back and said, "Very good."

"Is there anything else you'd like me to show you?"

"No."

"Are you satisfied?"

"Yes."

We returned to the plant manager's office and the Ford man said, "You've got the best preventive-maintenance system I've seen. Better than your Goldsberry plant. We don't even have a program this good at the Ford plant."

I was glad to hear him say that. I wouldn't have to hear any more about the system at our Goldsberry plant. Although, in retrospect, I realized I'd made the maintenance checkups more complicated than necessary to meet the auto companies' expectations.

Chapter 40
Trip of a Lifetime

I stayed at Standard Products until 1989. One day, I was at work when a clutching pain gripped me. I was rushed to the hospital and told I'd had a heart attack.

Doctors didn't know then all they know now. They told me my artery was plugged just below the heart, where it branches in two. The blockage was too far down for them to reach it.

"What are my choices?" I said.

"You only have two. You can go back to work and die on the job, or you can sit home in a rocking chair and die."

I didn't like either one.

Richard sent me a book by a California doctor, Julian Whitaker, titled *Is Heart Surgery Necessary: What Your Doctor Won't Tell You.* I read it and decided to start walking.

When I began, I could barely walk from the car to the house. I built myself up to where I walked two miles a day at a thirty-minute clip.

Standard Products took good care of me. They gave me a medical retirement, which paid two-thirds of my salary until I was old enough to draw Social Security.

Richard came to visit and made Mary and me an offer. The software company he worked for had become very successful. He'd been flying the last four years on business trips and had accumulated more than enough frequent-flier miles to take all three of us to Europe. "A retirement present," he said. My grandparents on Mother's side had emigrated from Northeastern Germany. A trip to see their homeland was appealing.

We began planning a trip for October, the time of Oktoberfest. We'd visit not only Germany but also Austria and Switzerland. Mary had always wanted to see Luxembourg. We threw that in, too. We ordered our passports and Eurail passes. I studied maps, read travel books and brochures, and even tried to learn German.

Mary and I started packing Thursday for our Saturday flight. Richard, who had been practically living out of a suitcase for the last four years, kept warning us to pack light. One suitcase, one carry-on bag each, he said. But the darn garment bag wouldn't hold enough, so I cast it aside and packed our twenty-six-inch and thirty-inch suitcases plus a small satchel, a tote bag, and a camera case with a shoulder strap.

A commuter flight from Knoxville took us to Atlanta, where we rendezvoused with Richard, who was coming from Florida. Our Lufthansa flight to Frankfurt was superb. The pilot announced that our flight time would be seven hours, fifty-five minutes, and fifty-five seconds. Upon landing, the captain informed us we were precisely on time. "How does he do it?" he added, wryly.

We set our watches five hours ahead, gathered our baggage, and caught the train to Koblenz, where I learned what Richard had warned me about. Hotels in Germany are within walking distance of train stations, but it was a struggle with our numerous bags. The next day, we rearranged things and eliminated one bag.

Mary and I found a Catholic Church and determined that they held a morning Mass at seven fifteen, but all the doors were locked. We finally saw a lady enter a side door and followed her. The entire service was in German, though it followed the familiar order of our Catholic Mass, so we understood what was happening.

As we were leaving Mass, a little old lady tried to converse with us. She soon realized we didn't understand and called to another lady crossing the street. "Maria, Maria."

Maria was a retired English teacher. We had a delightful conversation. As we said goodbye, the first lady handed Mary a small bottle of perfume for her hands and a souvenir for her purse. What a great way to start a vacation.

Back at the hotel, we had a breakfast of rolls, jelly, juice, cheese, cold cuts of sausage and various lunch meats, and strong coffee. This was a standard breakfast offered everywhere we stayed.

Boat cruise down the Rhine from Koblenz to Bingen.

After a two-mile walk from the hotel, we boarded a boat to cruise down the Rhine to our next destination, Mainz. The day was misty, cool, but not cold. Our spirits soon warmed at the sight of delightful storybook castles on both sides of the river. More castles than we'd imagined. Built by powerful rulers in the eleventh and twelfth centuries to control their section of the Rhine and adjacent lands, these castle fortresses were outstanding engineering accomplishments.

Grapes grew on steep mountainsides with retaining walls to keep the vineyards in place. Workers stood on precipitous inclines harvesting grapes. Along our route, charming villages, towns, and cities comprised of neat houses, gardens, and churches enticed visitors to come ashore and sample their wines.

The boat trip lasted seven hours. We intended to get off the boat in Mainz. Then the captain informed us he had decided not to stop in Mainz. He'd let us off in Bingen. Later, he agreed to stop in Mainz, but it would take us an additional two hours to get there. By this time, we'd seen all the castles and vineyards we wanted to see for one day, so we departed the boat in Bingen.

Bingen was my day of exercise. It was only three blocks from the boat dock to the train station. There, I met my first obstacle course. I had our suitcases on a collapsible cart I could pull behind me. When we got to the station, there was a forty-step staircase that I had to negotiate. I unloaded the cart, checked the train schedule, determined our platform, picked up the suitcases (which now felt like they were a hundred pounds each), and climbed the stairs. Richard checked the train schedule and said, "Dad you must have made a mistake. Our gate is on the other side of the track."

So I lugged our bags down the steps, under the tracks, and up the steps on the other side. *Whew*. I walked over to a schedule board that was fastened to a pole. No, it said our train would leave from the other platform. I showed it to Richard. He left to check, came back, and said, "Dad, we have to return to the original gate."

Down the steps again, under the tracks, and back up the forty steps—I was getting tired.

Now, we compared schedules. Richard's said one gate, mine the other. We'd arrived at the station only 20 minutes before our train was to depart. Most of that had already been spent running back and forth, and German trains leave precisely on time. We needed help or we'd miss it. After three or four attempts to explain, a bored, confused young man made us understand that Richard's schedule was for a train stop five kilometers up the track.

Fortunately, we made the train to Mainz, found our hotel, and had good wiener schnitzel for dinner, after which I fell into bed and slept late the next morning. Mainz was a busier city than Koblenz—more traffic, people in more of a rush. We walked around Mainz until it was time to board our train to Würzburg. On our way to the station we ambled through a beautiful garden in a wide median on one of the roads. It was two blocks long, with flowers, trees, and fountains.

Würzburg was the starting point for our trip down the "Romantic Road," the first of the medieval towns we saw. Our hotel was about a mile from the train station, and as we searched for it, we discovered our map showed two different ways to get there. We were puzzled by which route to take. A German couple stopped to assist us, but they had limited English and my German lessons proved useless. We were still studying the map when a young man, Wolfgang Ellenberger, showed us the shortest route to our hotel.

Wolfgang was a concert pianist who had toured the United States. He gave us one of his brochures and said he had been treated so nicely in the United States that he would show us Würzburg. After we checked into our hotel, we met Wolfgang and walked with him about six blocks to Dom Cathedral, one of the largest Romanesque churches in Germany. Surrounding it, a large open-air market offered wares of every description, and also musicians and acrobats. We said goodbye to our new friend and walked on through the streets. We saw a prince-bishop's palace built in 1719 and four churches built between 1371 and 1789. We also walked across an ancient bridge, Alte Mainbrücke, constructed in 1473.

Onward to Munich by tour bus. Our first stop was Rothenburg, with its narrow cobblestone streets. Large cars the size of a Cadillac or Lincoln would find it impossible to maneuver the streets. As we continued to visit fourteenth-century villages along the way, it struck me how young our country is. We think a two-hundred-year-old building is really old.

We passed through many small towns, all with characteristic narrow cobblestone streets, old houses and churches, beautiful city gates (arches), shops with sculptured wrought iron signs indicating the type of business, and the little bakery cafés so numerous in Germany. We moved on through Augsburg, founded in 15 BC by the Romans. Now *that's* an old city.

Munich dates back to the ninth century. There, people referred to the "old city" and the "new city." When they spoke of the new city, they meant anything less than three hundred years old. We spent three nights in Munich. The weather was growing cooler so I went shopping for long johns in a market area that allowed no cars. We also ate lunch at a restaurant that had been in continuous operation since 1700. Like at many German restaurants, it was not unusual to share a table with strangers. That night at dinner, I had Bavarian sauerkraut and bratwurst —best-tasting sauerkraut I've ever had.

Beautiful Mirabelle gardens in Salzburg, Austria. At the top of the photo is Hohensalzburg Castle, the Prince-Archbishop's palace.

Chapter 41
Sound of Music and Matterhorn

"The next time we do this . . ." Mary said on the train ride train from Munich to Salzburg, Austria.

I had to check my hearing. Only two weeks before, she'd said, "You and Richard go alone, I'm not going." Now here she was enjoying the trip. And why not? The people in southern Germany had been friendly and helpful everywhere we'd been.

As we entered Austria, the countryside was so similar to Germany's countryside that we could scarcely tell there was a border. The train rolled along, and suddenly—the Alps. Words are inadequate to describe our first glimpse of the Bavarian Alps and the Austrian Alps. The view was stunningly magnificent.

Our excitement swelled as we detrained in Salzburg because we both loved *The Sound of Music* and we were going to tour all the places we knew from the film.

First, we toured the city of Salzburg and Hohensalzburg Castle, the Prince-Archbishop's palace, which overlooks the city and Mirabell Gardens. While touring the gardens, we learned Prince-Archbishop Wolf Dietrich von Raitenau had built a second palace just outside the city walls in 1606. There he maintained his mistress, Salome Alt. He named it Schloss (Palace) Altenau in her honor. Perhaps in his day the church did not keep such a tight rein on the clergy. We decided he must have enjoyed children, for he fathered fifteen.

A subsequent prince-archbishop renamed Schloss Altenau to Schloss Mirabell, and eighty years later, a third prince-archbishop added the splendid Mirabell Gardens, considered one of the most beautiful baroque gardens in Europe. The garden's symmetrical, swirling design is embraced by marble railings. At its center is a large fountain surrounded by statues of mythological figures and Roman gods. Mirabell Gardens contains multiple flower gardens, statuary, and a gorgeous ornamental rose bed. In *The Sound of Music*, Maria and the Von Trapp children dance around the Pegasus Fountain singing "Do-Re-Mi." They end the song on the steps with a view of the palace and gardens behind them.

Leaving Mirabell, we next visited Mozart's birthplace, then his mother's birthplace, and then on to Schloss Leopoldskron, where the scenes of the Von Trapp's outside porch were filmed. On the patio overlooking the lake, we recalled the scene where Julie Andrews and the children capsize. As we left, our bus passed the trees that the movie children climb while wearing the play clothes made from curtains.

Then we learned a bit of movie magic. Everybody remembers the opening scene where Julie Andrews is on a hill singing "The Sound of Music," hears the church bells, realizes she's late, and runs to the convent. Our bus took us to the picturesque hills where she sang, and we recognized the place immediately. Still the same, developers hadn't ruined it. The next stop, the convent, was actually twenty miles away. *Fa* is, indeed, a long, long way to run.

The last stop on the tour was the charming village of Mondsee and the church where they filmed the wedding. When we returned to Salzburg, we took another stroll through the Mirabell gardens and its lovely rose garden, before our train ride back to Munich.

There we ate a final dinner with Richard. He was still a working man and his vacation time was at an end. He would take a train to Frankfurt that night, and Mary and I would catch a morning train for Chur, Switzerland. When we finished our dinner, Richard and I decided we should not leave Germany without trying apple strudel. They served it with thick, fresh cream. I thought, *This must be heaven.*

We dropped our plans to visit the area my ancestors came from because at that time, Germany was still divided into two countries, and my grandparents' homeland was located in Soviet Union-controlled East Germany. Originally, we thought we could cross over from West Germany, but we were there just prior to the Berlin Wall coming down and the risk seemed too great that we'd get caught on the wrong side of a political turmoil.

Up early, we caught our train and crossed Germany to Füssen, over to Lake Constance, down to Buchs and St. Margareth, and then to Chur. Sharing our compartment on the train was a couple from New Jersey, the Melsons. The husband, a retired Air Force pilot, told us his fascinating story. During World War II, he was shot down over Switzerland and captured by the Nazis. While he was a prisoner of war, he escaped twice with the help of the Swiss, but when he was caught, the Swiss convinced the Germans he had robbed and threatened them. The third and final time he escaped, he made it to the French Underground, who got him out.

Chur was nestled in a valley surrounded by snowcapped mountains. Unlike in Germany, little English was spoken there. We got a room in a small, quaint inn-hotel and had soup and bread for dinner. It tasted so good. Our room, while clean and neat, lacked two amenities we'd become accustomed to—heat and down comforters. Every hotel in Germany had warm, fluffy down comforters. Whatever the comforters were filled with in Chur, it wasn't warm enough.

Double beds in Europe weren't like what we had in America; they were like two narrow beds pushed together. To keep warm, Mary and I crowded into one narrow bed under both comforters. We put sweaters on over our pajamas and still felt we were freezing.

The next morning, we boarded the Glacier Express to Zermatt, a train ride across Switzerland not to be missed for its beauty. However, the railroad was privately owned. Our Eurail pass covered only a portion of the fare, and we had to pay the difference. We decided to have lunch at about one o'clock in the afternoon, but at the dining car we learned lunch service had ended and they were taking the dining car off the train at the next stop. They did have lunch baskets made up, which we could buy. I thought, *Why not?*

What a pleasant surprise. The basket contained a small picnic cloth, a cutting board, a jackknife with a bottle opener, a glass, a bottle of red wine, a container of juice, cheese, nut bread to eat the cheese on, sausage, rolls, a tube of mustard, a candy bar, a little strawberry jelly tart, and a bag of mixed nuts and raisins. What more could we need?

We were surprised in Zermatt, too. We were met at the station and taken to our hotel in an electric-powered vehicle. No cars in Zermatt. Our room had a view of the Matterhorn.

It was Saturday evening, so we attended Mass at a beautiful church. The service was in Swiss-German, but I didn't care—the ceiling fascinated me. An exquisitely detailed painting of Noah's Ark covered three-quarters of it.

At one in the morning, I woke and went to the window. Outside, a full moon was showering the Matterhorn with light. *What a sight.*

In the morning, Mary and I rode a cable car up Klien Matterhorn. We both experienced dizziness and shortness of breath as the cable car reached its terminal. An elevator inside of the mountain would take us further up. The altitude gave Mary a headache, and she decided not to go any higher. I rode the elevator and then climbed what seemed like a hundred steps. A brochure said I was 3,820 meters (12,532 feet) high. The air was very thin—breathing was a little difficult—but the view was everything you'd expect it to be and more. Bright sun reflecting off the snow, glaciers, crevasses, skiers, mountain peaks, valleys, small villages off in the distance, and the Matterhorn. . . . Wow.

I went back down to get Mary and convinced her she wouldn't regret the climb. Even during my second viewing, the vista was not one I'd ever tire of because the sun angle and shadows were constantly changing. At the very, very top of the mountain, there was a crucifix with a sign in three languages. It read, "Be a better man."

View of the Matterhorn from outside their hotel.

When we returned to our hotel, Mary lay down to rest while I explored Zermatt at a leisurely pace. I walked for two hours in the sun, enjoying the chalets, gardens, flowers, and shops. They'd had snow, and in sheltered areas, three or four inches remained on the ground.

Mary and I found a small restaurant inn for dinner. It had two accordion players and a bass fiddle player. A waitress informed us we were too early for dinner. We could sit at a table for now, but we'd have to vacate it at 6:30 p.m. as it was reserved. I ordered wine, Mary a Coke, and we enjoyed the music.

When a table became available, we asked another waitress if it would be all right for us to move to that table for dinner. She said yes. Then 6:30 passed, but we received no service even though all the other tables were being served. Mary observed that other American couples coming in and sitting down were also being ignored. They left, but we stayed. Our waitress did not look at us, but she looked over us. We sat stubbornly for another twenty minutes and then left. So much for Swiss hospitality. Up the street, we found another restaurant and had a good meal for less money, but the rude staff at the first restaurant had created a frustrating conclusion to a fantastic day.

The straw that seemed too much for me was that the hotel had put one quarter-inch-thick sliver of soap in our bath for the two of us. We used that the first day, and they didn't replace it. At the front desk, I asked the clerk to have more soap sent up. He said, "Did you use it *all*?"

Originally, we intended to stay in Switzerland one more day, but Mary and I both had a strong urge to shake the frost of icy Swiss manners from our feet, so we left the next morning. As our train was leaving Zermatt, we took one last look at the Matterhorn and somehow our experiences with the waitress and clerk didn't seem important.

However, that day turned out to be extremely long. I'd made an error when planning our trip and thought we had to go through Zurich. We didn't. We changed trains unnecessarily several times and had to retrace our route to Basel.

Back among the friendly German people, we rode to Mannheim with a German industrialist from Köln who insisted on carrying all of our luggage to our train for Frankfurt.

It was nine-thirty at night when we reached Frankfurt. I needed to exchange currency, but Mary was tired, so I left her while I called our hotel for directions. I returned from the phone to find a very excited Mary. Two men had exited the bank holding cash in their hands and a young man had grabbed their money. He ran past Mary and up the stairs, being chased by the men he'd robbed.

"I still need to go to the bank," I said.

"Not without me," she said.

To reach our train platform, we had to descend two long escalators. At the bottom of the first, Mary fell. She insisted she was okay, but then at the bottom of the second escalator, she fell again. We were both too tired to go on, but we had to—one more train to Bad Soden, where our hotel was. When we arrived in Bad Soden, a German woman who spoke almost no English insisted on carrying our bags to the hotel.

Mary at a café in Bad Soden, Germany.

We set aside the next day for rest. The day after, we fulfilled one of

Mary's childhood dreams, visiting Luxembourg. It was a small, wealthy country without taxes. This enticed the moneyed from all over the world. Luxembourg was very busy, but clean.

Our vacation was great, and we never forgot it, but, as Mary said when we landed in Atlanta, "Dick, listen. Doesn't that sound good—people talking a language we understand?" We were home.

Chapter 42
Three Letters

December 21, 1989—first day of winter—I walked down the long drive of our farm outside Somerset, Kentucky to get the mail. In the box I found an envelope with the following return address:

White House

Washington, DC

No street address or zip code necessary. It was a response to the letter I'd written to President George H.W. Bush. This wouldn't be the last letter I'd receive from a US president, nor was it the first. I'd written President Jimmy Carter after his term as president ended:

> Dear President Carter,
>
> I am extremely proud of a man by the name of Jimmy Carter from a very small rural community of Plains, Georgia.
>
> This man is a world statesman and a former president of one of the largest and most powerful nations in the world. He donned a carpenter's apron and traveled to a ghetto where most Americans, if given a choice, would probably bypass, to help restore a home for those who have less. If Jesus was preaching to the disciples today, he might just make a parable about such a man.
>
> I can think of no other statesman or world leader, in the past or present, representing any foreign government or our own

government, living or dead, who would do such a very simple and loving deed.

May God continue to bless you and Rosalynn, and thank you for this inspiring moment.

Sincerely,

Richard A. Gartee

President Carter responded with a personally signed note, which I framed. Since that letter, he and Rosalynn send me a signed Christmas card every year.

Writing letters became important to me while I was in the Navy—my only means of keeping in touch. No email in those days, no phone calls when you're overseas, and while stationed stateside, long-distance calls were too expensive. Letter writing has remained a habit. I still write letters every week. Sometimes just to keep in touch with family and friends, other times to advise or comfort someone who is seriously ill or dying.

This time, I'd been inspired to write President George H. W. Bush about our nation's need to develop alternate modes of travel. Our recent trip abroad had opened my eyes.

I told him we had just returned from Europe, where clean, fast, punctual, affordable trains took us wherever we needed to go. Our travel companions along the way were girls, boys, retired ladies, and men all safely traveling alone. We'd shared trains with businessmen, university professors, and daily commuters. The European city streets and roads had already reached the point we were swiftly approaching in the United States—overcrowded and unsafe.

I listed my concerns (as of 1989):

(a) lack of economical public transportation.

(b) overloaded expressways and turnpikes.

(c) growth-saturated car market resulting in unemployment.

(d) reluctant reduction in defense spending, creating deficit spending.

(e) emissions to our atmosphere.

I have little patience with people who see the problems but are not willing to offer a solution. So I offered my solution to many of these problems —a good, economical, nationwide, public monorail system. I proceeded to list the advantages of a monorail system as I saw them:

(1) No purchase of additional right-of-way would be required if they were built in the existing medians of our Interstate highway system, except for parking facilities at each terminal.

(2) Since the monorail tracks run overhead, there would be no conflict or safety issues with expressway traffic.

(3) Monorail is compact, fast, efficient, and clean, and it could return economical transportation to the public. Monorails have larger passenger capacity than automobiles and fewer emissions.

(4) Construction and ongoing operation would provide a long-term economic boon. For example, steel and concrete for the track and supporting structure, aluminum, plastics, and manufacturing of the monorail cars, ticket sellers, conductors, engineers, construction personnel, the list goes on and on.

(5) Returning quality and safety to American travel, providing a solution to overcrowded airways and airports, and a viable alternative to get aged drivers off the freeway.

I suggested if he were to start such a program in 1990, it should be possible to complete the planning, engineering, and design work necessary to have a basic system built in ten years. I closed with the following:

> You and I might not be around to see its completion or reap its benefits, but what a legacy you would leave for your grandchildren and your country.

Thank you, Mr. President.

Sincerely,

Richard A. Gartee

In my hand was his response, but I didn't tear open the envelope. I waited until I reached the house so I could preserve the envelope. I slit it open with a letter opener and removed the letter. President Bush hadn't responded directly. It was from his secretary, who thanked me for sharing my thoughts and assured me that my comments had been shared with the president's advisors. Not discouraged, I wrote identical letters to my congressmen and senators.

Two decades later, Barack Obama was elected. We still had no monorail system under development. I wrote him a letter laying out the gist of the ideas I'd sent the first President Bush. This time, I received a personal response signed by President Obama.

THE WHITE HOUSE

WASHINGTON

August 5, 2010

Dear Richard:

Thank you for writing. I have heard from men and women across America who are concerned about our transportation infrastructure, and I appreciate hearing from you.

As we become more mobile and interconnected, our reliance on transportation networks has never been greater. However, too many of our Nation's railways, highways, bridges, airports, public transit systems, and neighborhood streets are slowly decaying due to lack of investment and strategic long-term planning. Poor transportation systems are risky to both our security and our economy, and we must modernize them to address our current needs.

To meet the demands of the 21st century, my Administration has made strengthening our transportation systems a top priority. The American Recovery and Reinvestment Act (ARRA) made the largest investment in our Nation's infrastructure in 50 years and dedicated key resources to high-speed rail. ARRA has already initiated thousands of restoration projects in all 50 states and created hundreds of thousands of jobs.

This new American landscape will make us safer, more energy efficient, and more competitive. Cleaner vehicles will improve fuel efficiency and reduce pollution. Intermodal centers, which link transportation hubs, will improve public transit so people can travel with greater ease and speed.

Vice President Joe Biden and I are monitoring ARRA projects closely to ensure they are being implemented quickly and transparently. To follow where your tax dollars are being spent and track projects in your state, please visit: www.Recovery.gov.

Thank you for your service and sacrifice.

Sincerely,

I have saved the original letters from the three presidents for my grandchildren and their children.

CHAPTER 43
'TIL DEATH DOES PART

Mary had high blood pressure and other health issues throughout the 1990s, but her problems turned serious the last two years of her life. By 2001 her kidneys began to act up. Then one kidney died. The doctors decided to put her on peritoneal dialysis, done through a catheter in the stomach. I took training so we could do the dialysis at home. I didn't care much for the idea, worried she'd develop an infection. But peritoneal would be the easiest for her. The other type of dialysis required her to go to a medical facility every three days to be hooked to a machine that took hours to clean her blood. We were living in Lake Waynoka, Ohio, and the drive to the facility would add two hours to the process.

The nurse who trained me said she would come to the house and watch me do it the first time to make sure I did everything right. The last day of my training, I was told the kidney doctor wanted to see me. They paged him and he took me into his office. "I'm sorry," he said. "The dialysis will do no good. Her other kidney has died, and she won't live. It would take a transplant to keep her alive, and we don't have a donor. There is no chance."

"How long has she got?"

"Maybe ten days."

Ten days turned out to be ten weeks. She was a lot like Eileen in that she never complained. When she was hurting, she never said a word. Mary died at home.

Mary surrounded by her family eight weeks before she passed away.

We had moved to Ohio when Mary's health declined so she would be close to her family in her final years, but now I was alone. Sharyl lived eight hours north and Richard sixteen hours south. Mary's kids never visited after her death.

As Christmas season approached, Richard convinced me to come to Florida for Christmas and stay through the winter. "Ohio is cold, and Florida warm," he said. "Anyhow, what are you going to do up there all winter?"

He made sense.

I stayed through the holidays and planned to return home. Then I looked around me, and thought, *What for?*

I did go home, but only to put the house on the market. It sold the first day. I returned to Florida and started house hunting. Richard kept directing me toward Gainesville, but the prices were higher than in the surrounding rural towns. He was living out of town on Lake Santa Fe anyway. I bought a little brick house in Keystone Heights, Florida, about fifteen minutes from Richard's. He rode to Ohio with me, helped me pack, and drove back to Florida in a U-Haul truck pulling a trailer. I followed in my van.

Once I settled into my Keystone Heights house, I did a little remodeling. When that was finished I built a woodworking shop in the backyard. I had been making furniture as a hobby for several years.

As a young man, I owned few electric tools, just a drill, a saber saw, and a skill saw. The rest of my tools had been manual: a handsaw, a keyhole saw, a hand plane. Before I retired, while I was still making good money, I began to acquire power tools for a complete woodworking shop. I bought a table saw, a drill press, a lathe, a planer, a router, two power sanders, a jigsaw, and a radial arm saw. Everything I needed to make furniture. Perhaps I wanted to fulfill a legacy of my dad's. He was never a professional cabinetmaker, but he was always making stuff.

When I was a kid, shipping crates were made of quality wood—almost flawless, hardly a knot in the wood. Dad brought home a six-foot-long box that held materials shipped to his work. He'd disassemble it and cut out eight boards, each six feet long and one inch thick. He made me a desk and chair that I used for a long time.

Dad did all his woodworking with a hammer, saw, hand plane, and brace and bit. And he could do a marvelous thing I never learned to do. He could take a regular (straight) handsaw and cut a perfect circle from a piece of wood. He'd saw, making slow adjustments to the angle, until he'd cut out a wheel. He made carts and hose reels and other things for his garden.

While Mary was alive, I built us a beautiful cherry four-poster bed, a baby crib for a grandchild, quilt holders, decorative wall shelves, picture frames, and clocks. Later, when I moved to Florida, I continued building large pieces of furniture, including two desks, two sewing machine cabinets, and end tables, as well as a china cabinet shown on page 253.

Then I grew older. My eyesight got dimmer, and I had difficulty seeing pencil marks on the wood while trying to cut. One day, I watched artist Bob Ross on PBS and said, "Oh, I can do that."

I took classes from local artists and started oil painting. It expressed my creativity, like the woodworking had. I sold most of my wood shop equipment, but I kept enough tools to make frames for my canvases and other small projects. I laughingly call my paintings "thirty-footers" because they look pretty good from thirty feet away.

* * *

Loneliness struck, again. Richard only lived a few miles away, and we got together almost every night, but he was working long hours and I couldn't ask him to be my sole source of entertainment. I spotted a notice that a square-dance club in Keystone Heights was having a Fourth of July dance, so I went. I didn't dance that night, but I met the caller, Lonnie Ligon, and mentioned that I wanted to get back into square dancing. He said, "We've got classes going right now. Why don't you come? Classes are at six thirty and then the dance starts at seven thirty."

The following week, I arrived too late for the class. It was already time for the dance to start. Lonnie said, "Come on, get in here. The others will help you out."

"No, I won't do that. It's been too many years since I danced. I need a refresher. I'll wait and take a class next week before the dance. I don't have a partner, though."

"Just show up," Lonnie said. "I'll have a partner for you."

He told me what her name was. I don't remember anymore what he said, but it wasn't Flo.

The next week, I made it in time for class. I joined the square nearest the caller. In my experience, the better dancers would be there, and if I had a problem, they would help me through it.

I was standing in position alone, waiting for my mystery partner to arrive, when Flo Smith walked up. I thought she was the woman Lonnie sent. Unbeknownst to me, that woman had failed to show.

"You need a partner?" Flo said.

"Yes, I do," I said.

I didn't know she was going to be my partner for life. Thirteen months later, we wed.

Chapter 44
Wedding in a Hurricane

Flo and I set the date of our wedding for Labor Day weekend. Since most of Flo's family lived in Ohio, and my daughter, Sharyl, lived in Michigan, the long Labor Day holiday would be ideal for both our families to attend. True, this date was in the middle of hurricane season, but most years, hurricanes miss Florida. They move up the Atlantic seaboard or into the Gulf of Mexico, or dissipate harmlessly. When they do hit, they rarely come as far inland as Gainesville, which is sixty miles from either coast. But 2004 would prove to be the exception. Four major Category 4 and 5 hurricanes formed that year: Charley, Frances, Ivan, and Jeanne.

Hurricane Charley had hit southwest Florida in August, weakening as it made landfall in Punta Gorda. It crossed Florida, entered into the Atlantic, regained hurricane strength, and moved toward North Carolina. But Charley was long gone by the time our families arrived.

Sharyl flew in on Friday, as did Flo's oldest son, her daughter, son-in-law, granddaughter, and Flo's twin sister. Saturday, our wedding day, Flo's other son drove down from Jacksonville, and my son, Richard, brought his two children. We heard on the news that Hurricane Frances had developed in the Atlantic and reached Category 4 with sustained winds of 145 miles per hour, but it was still in the Bahamas.

We proceeded with the wedding. I'd invested good money in the marriage license and wasn't about to waste it. This was a running joke between Flo and me that started when we bought our marriage license.

The clerk said, "That'll be $97.50."

"You've got to be kidding!" I said. I couldn't believe it. When I married Eileen, a license cost two bucks. Talk about inflation.

Dick and Flo wed on September 4, 2004, in Gainesville, Florida.

We got married at the Wesley United Methodist Church that Flo attended in Gainesville. My best man was Lonnie Ligon, the caller at the square dance where Flo and I met. Our reception was held at Richard's house in Melrose. We intended to honeymoon at a waterfront hotel on the St. John's River, but the hotel canceled our reservations as Hurricane Frances approached Florida.

Our house in Keystone Heights was too small to accommodate all of our out-of-town guests, but it wasn't far from Richard's, so we divided into two groups. Flo's relatives stayed at our house while Sharyl, Richard's children, Flo, and I stayed with him. The first night of our honeymoon was spent in my son's guest room. Not exactly what we'd planned.

In the morning, all of us at Richard's drove to my house for breakfast. Meanwhile, Hurricane Frances hit Florida 250 miles southeast of us and airlines canceled all flights. Our families wouldn't be flying home.

Frances came ashore on the Atlantic coast, aiming toward the Gulf. The storm weakened to Category 1, and then to a tropical storm with sixty-mile-per-hour winds. Soon we were among the 4.27 million Floridians without electricity. I had a freezer full of food I didn't want to thaw. Luckily, our neighbor across the street had a generator. I ran a long extension cord to his house. That kept the freezer running, but we didn't have electricity for other appliances. We had stocked up on water as we always do during hurricane season, and we had food, but it was raining too hard to stand outside and grill.

When there is a hurricane, our area rarely gets more than prolonged heavy tropical rain. This time, we had that and more. It was pouring bucketsful. We raised the garage door and set up the grill as close to the opening as we could without getting it wet, then proceeded to barbecue. It was a grand party, an extension of our reception. We had plenty of drinks, food, and even leftover wedding cake.

When it was time for Richard and Sharyl to take his children back to their mother, everyone said goodbye and they drove away. Moments later, they were back. Storm winds had taken down trees, and live power lines blocked roads in every direction.

I only had a two-bedroom house plus a pullout sofa-bed. We put Flo's daughter, son-in-law, and granddaughter in our room. Sharyl and Flo's sister shared the guest bed, and Richard's children slept on the floor of the guest room. In the living room, Flo and I took the sofa-bed and Richard slept in our La-Z-Boy recliner. Night two of our marriage.

Except for worry about when they could get flights home, everyone had a good time and made the best of it. Frances crossed Florida into the Gulf, turned, came back onto land, and headed for Georgia. But the storm's energy was spent, and mostly it rained. The utility company got the electricity back on, airlines resumed operation, and our guests left for home.

We'd long remember our wild wedding weekend, but we still hadn't had a proper honeymoon, so Flo and I packed the car and drove to New Orleans.

We stayed at the Hotel Saint Marie, a historic New Orleans hotel just off Bourbon Street in the French Quarter. They had been renovating the hotel, and a part of the parking lot was blocked off to accommodate the renovation. I worried about where I had to park my car. But our hotel location made it convenient to walk anywhere in the French Quarter. We went into a casino on the corner, wasted a couple of dollars in slot machines. A lady next to us put her credit card in the slot machine, and she was pulling the handle down as fast as she could. She never won a cent the entire time we were there. I said, "Let's get out of here. This is the wrong place for us."

We walked on and visited St. Louis Cathedral. I also showed Flo a paddle-wheel riverboat. That night, we ate dinner at a fine-dining restaurant owned by famous chef John Besh, who has a TV cooking show on PBS.

Flo and I ordered, and after our order came, a guy who'd been standing by the bar walked over. He wore a regular dress shirt open at the collar, not a suit or chef apparel.

"How is the food? Is everything okay?" he said.

"I think it is. It seems all right. Flo, is your food good?"

"Yes," she said.

"Well, if anything isn't to your liking, let me know and we'll make you something else."

"Thank you," I said, "but everything is fine."

"Okay, have a nice evening." He left us and walked into the kitchen. We didn't have a clue who he was—maybe an assistant manager.

It wasn't until we saw an advertisement for his restaurant later that we recognized him as the owner, celebrity chef John Besh.

While Hurricane Frances was messing with our wedding, Hurricane Ivan had developed into a Category 4 storm down near Grenada. As it moved north, it passed Jamaica, the Cayman Islands, and Cuba. New

Orleans TV stations announced that they expected Hurricane Ivan and might have to evacuate the area. People who planned on traveling were advised to leave right away. Flo and I looked at each other, piled everything in the car, and headed back home.

We made it to Keystone Heights before Ivan hit Gulf Shores, Alabama with winds of 120 miles per hour. Ivan was a beast that wouldn't die. It lost strength, becoming a tropical depression, and then wandered back and forth over Florida, Alabama, and Louisiana for the next five days. When Ivan returned to the Gulf of Mexico, it regenerated to tropical-storm strength. It was the most expensive storm of the season, causing $20.5 billion in damages in the US. By comparison, $97.50 for my marriage license didn't seem so bad.

* * *

In the twelve years that followed, hurricanes missed us. Then, in 2017, just days after our thirteenth wedding anniversary, the largest hurricane in recorded history crossed Cuba, turned north, and came straight for us. Hurricane Irma was massive. Larger than the entire state of Florida, the powerful Category 5 storm had already destroyed the islands of Saint Martin and Barbuda and damaged the Virgin Islands and Puerto Rico. After crossing the Florida Keys, it made landfall near Fort Myers and proceeded up the state, passing west of Gainesville. By the time it reached our area, it dropped in strength below Category 1, but that was still strong enough to bring down trees and knock out electricity for many people.

Flo, Richard, and I weathered it without any problem and suffered no damage to our houses, but southern Florida had serious flooding on both coasts. My stepdaughter Pam and her husband, who live in St. Pete, evacuated to Kentucky and weren't able to return home for over a week. I pray this is the last storm we see of this scope, but I fear not. There are people in our government who claim climate change is a hoax. Obviously, it's not. Global warming does not cause hurricanes, but higher water temperatures allow storms to grow more massive and powerful. It seems evident that if we don't reduce mankind's impact on the climate, nature will do it for us.

Oak china cabinet made by Dick in 2005.

Chapter 45
Becoming a Chaplin

Of all the things I've done in my life, becoming a chaplain at Alachua General Hospital, I feel was the best. I'd always gone to church—that's the way my mother brought me up. Mom started me out Lutheran, but I changed denominations several times.

When I was a kid in Ida, Michigan, Mom and I attended an evangelical church. Dad would only go on Christmas and Easter, and then he was usually boozed up. You could smell him halfway across the sanctuary. I don't recall if our church had Sunday school, but I have a vague memory of coloring pictures. I do remember at age six, I had to get up and sing a solo.

After we moved to South Custer Road, Mom and I switched to a Lutheran church next to Bridge School in Raisinville Township. My parents only had one car, so she and I didn't go on Sundays that Dad worked.

For the one semester I lived in Monroe, we went to the Lutheran church Uncle Hank attended. After Mom and Dad divorced, my churches were random. If Mom was in Dundee on a Sunday, we'd go to the Lutheran church there. Otherwise, I'd go to the church of whichever aunt I stayed with that week—usually Lutheran.

After Mom got us an apartment in Dundee, I continued in the Lutheran church until I got out of the Navy. Then I got into a disagreement with the Lutherans.

A Fraternal Order of Eagles opened in Dundee, and I joined. The lodge was a nice place to go. They put on a fish fry—all you could eat for a buck. They had beer, good camaraderie, and a couple of pool tables. One day, our minister stopped me on the street and told me I couldn't go there anymore.

"Why?" I said.

"They require a password," he said.

"So?"

"As a Lutheran, you can't belong to any organization that has to have a password. Church rules."

"What about Old John's Saloon?" I said. "That may not be a fraternal organization, but I see good Lutherans sitting there on Saturday night sipping whiskey and beer. How are they better than the guy who goes to the Eagles lodge?"

"You cannot belong to the Eagles, that's all there is to it."

"Then I don't want to belong to the Lutheran Church," I said. I joined the Congregational Church instead.

That's where my first wife, Eileen, and I had our wedding. She was fine with the Congregational Church. Eileen's mother, Ruth, belonged to the Church of God, but I don't know if she made her kids go regularly after their father died. Ruth was scrambling to make ends meet and working odd hours, so she was not likely home to take them. Eileen worked at the Triangle restaurant, sometimes on Sundays, so I think in her teen years, church often got skipped.

We stayed with the Congregational Church until it caught fire and burned to the ground. The building was old, dried wood. It's hard to describe how it feels to watch your church burning when you can do nothing to stop it.

After the fire, the congregation never could raise the money to rebuild it. Eileen and I had moved to Tecumseh by then, and with the church gone, it made sense for us to find something local instead of driving to Dundee every week.

Tecumseh didn't have a Congregational Church. While we were trying other churches, I got to thinking, *John King and his whole family have always gone to the Presbyterian Church. Heck, they're the kind of people I like to associate with.* So Eileen and I visited the Presbyterian Church in Tecumseh. We liked it and joined.

We hadn't been Presbyterians long when I found myself wishing I could duck under a pew and hide. Our son was misbehaving during Sunday service, and twice I'd grabbed him by the arm and told him to sit still. The third time, I raised my hand intending to smack him on the butt. From the pulpit, the minster's voice boomed across the sanctuary, "Don't strike that child!"

Embarrassed, but not deterred, I engaged fully in the activities of the church. I became a deacon, then an elder. I was on the building committee and the stewardship committee, and I represented our church in a multi-denominational organization of local churches. I was also superintendent of the Sunday-school classes. Very simply, I couldn't say no.

It started when they said to me, "Will you teach Sunday school?"

I didn't want to teach Sunday school, but I agreed, and I taught the sixth- and seventh-grade classes. When they lost the superintendent, they said, "Will you be superintendent of Sunday school?"

"Can't we get anybody else?"

"No."

"Okay, well, I'll do it."

Now not only did I have to teach sixth and seventh grade, but if a teacher didn't show up for one of the other grades, then I'd also have to find someone to cover that class.

Our church recorded Sunday services on a big reel-to-reel tape recorder, and someone took the tape and a player to the homebound. Every third or fourth week was my turn to deliver the recording.

The Tecumseh church burned me out. The year before we moved to Somerset, I realized I was giving six days a week to the church. I was there for a meeting or to teach nearly every day.

When we moved to Somerset and joined the church there, I decided I would not allow what happened in Tecumseh to repeat. But the Somerset church kept after me, and finally, I agreed to finish out someone's term as a deacon.

They also got me to join the choir because they only had one male and needed another. I'd never sung in a choir before and had no vocal training, but they needed a bass and I could sing low.

I recounted earlier that when Mary and I wed, I left the Presbyterian Church and converted to Catholicism. Again, I kept from getting drawn into too many duties. I limited it to ushering and serving communion. One year, they wanted to raise money to fix up the old school, so I helped with writing letters and so on.

I stayed in the Catholic Church after Mary died, and even after I married Flo, who was Methodist. I would go to Mass Saturday night and then to her church with her on Sunday morning. Interestingly, Flo hadn't always been a Methodist. She'd been raised Lutheran, like I was —small world. When she married her first husband, he wouldn't go to the Lutheran church, so they compromised on Methodist.

When the news reported that instead of firing bad Catholic priests, the church was spending huge sums to cover up sexual abuse scandals, I quit. I wrote a letter to the priest at the church in Keystone Heights and sent a copy to the Bishop of the Diocese. It said I couldn't support their actions or inaction and wouldn't contribute to it. I didn't want to be a Catholic anymore. I was going to the Methodist church with Flo, so joining her church was an easy choice.

I'd already become a chaplain by then. How that came about was through the Catholic priest in Gainesville, Father Julian. He'd been sending me out to give communion to parishioners in nursing homes and rehab because he couldn't get to them all. I asked if he wanted me to cover for him at the hospital as well. He said, no, he liked the experience and wanted to continue the hospital rounds himself. Once I became a chaplain myself, I understood what he meant.

Father Julian kept what I'd said in mind. One day, he brought it up. "You said you'd like to work at the hospital like a chaplain."

"Yes, or something similar."

"Well, Alachua General Hospital is looking for chaplains. They really need them. Would you consider doing it?"

"Yes, if they want me."

Father Julian gave me the name of the woman in charge of the chaplain program, Constance Keaton, and sent me for an interview. She had me start right away. I accompanied another chaplain for my first three weeks. Then I came in one day, and there was no one to go with. I was on my own.

I really learned what it meant to serve from Father Julian's example. He was a great inspiration. Often called at all hours of the night, he would stay as long as needed. It didn't matter if the patient was Catholic, Protestant, or any other religion.

Chapter 46
Serving as Chaplain

I served as chaplain for five years. I was Catholic when I started and Methodist before I stopped, but a chaplain's work is non-denominational. My job was to serve patients of every religion, or no religion. I'd talk with the patients and ask if they wanted a word of prayer. If they didn't, that was all right too. Sometimes they just needed someone to listen.

Each chaplain did hospital visitation one day a week. I told the program director, Constance, I wanted to do more. I worked Monday, Wednesday, and Friday. A lot of my day as a chaplain I worked the cardiac floor. I saw 30 to 35 patients a day.

With my three-day-a-week schedule, I often saw the same patients multiple times over the course of their stay, and again if they were readmitted. One day, this backfired. The chaplain's office got a call for a chaplain to visit someone on the cardiac floor, so they sent the first chaplain available. She entered the room and introduced herself.

"No, I want the *real* chaplain," the patient said.

"I am a real chaplain."

"No, I want the chaplain named Dick."

The chaplain said she'd see if I was in the hospital that day and returned to the chaplain's office, bothered that the patient thought we were not at the same level.

It wasn't because I was special, just that patient had seen me so often she assumed I must be the full-time chaplain and anyone else was a substitute. The other chaplain understood, but it still didn't sit well with her.

Patients frequently called me Father or Reverend, but I ignored that. I am neither. One patient said he had no trouble believing I was a chaplain because he'd had a buddy in the service who was an Army chaplain, and I talked and acted just like his buddy. When I left his room, he said, "Have a nice day, Chaplain."

During the period I served as chaplain, Flo and I lived in Keystone Heights. This involved a forty-five-minute drive to the hospital three times a week. After three years, I decided I needed to cut back to twice a week. Then I tried once a week. But that didn't seem like enough, so I resumed my three-day-a-week schedule.

Being a chaplain was a greater ministry than anything I have ever done in any church, but I reached a point where I didn't feel I was as beneficial to my patients as I should be. It had become routine, and I found myself repeating the same thing in every room. I thought, *This is wrong. I've got to change.* I stopped in my tracks and prayed on it. When I got to the next room, I didn't recognize the words coming out of my mouth. I had no idea where they came from, they just poured out like a river. Thereafter, I made a habit to pray for guidance before I met with each patient.

One day, a male nurse passed me in the hallway and we exchanged greetings. I knew all the hospital staff members. I was a fixture there. "Good morning," I said. "How are you?"

"Pray for me," he said.

I'd prayed for plenty of nurses and doctors who were patients, but I'd never had one on duty make this request. "Do you mean right now?"

"Yes."

So we stepped to the side of the aisle and had a word of prayer.

I had patients die on me, of course—it was part of the job. But one case really bothered me. A young woman about forty-years old was in a coma in intensive care. Sometimes she'd awaken briefly, but her doctors didn't expect her to live. She had a boyfriend near her age, but no husband or children. He'd quit visiting her because she was in a coma. Chaplains became her only visitors.

Each time I visited, I'd talk to her and pray with her, saying anything that might bring her to awareness. "Good Morning, this is Dick, the chaplain. Do you remember me? I came here on Monday. You and I prayed together. Would you like to pray again?"

If her eyes were open, I'd say, "If you'd like a prayer, blink to say yes." Her eyes wouldn't blink, but I'd pray, anyway. One day, I thought she really blinked. I couldn't prove it, but I took it as a good sign. I began to spend more of my time on duty with her, encouraging her to believe she could get better and someday walk out of there.

Then the boyfriend told the hospital to pull her off life support and send her to a nursing home. I never saw her again. That pained me because I felt I'd been making a little inroad.

One Saturday, the priest from St. Patrick's, Father Joe, called and asked if I would take the Eucharist to someone in the hospital. Father Joe was from India, and I sometimes had trouble understanding his accent. So Monday on my way to the hospital, I called the church and obtained the name of the patient requesting the Eucharist.

When I arrived at the chaplain's office, Constance told me there were two more patients on the cardiac floor I needed to see.

My first cardiac patient was Father Jim, a Catholic priest to whom I was taking the Eucharist. After the typical formalities of introductions, he said, "Would you please take time and pray with me this morning."

"Certainly," I said. We talked a while, shared Eucharist, and prayed.

I left his room and walked into the next. The patient was a Baptist. Sometimes Baptist patients were hard to crack and didn't want me to pray for them. It seemed they thought if someone wasn't a Baptist, their prayer wouldn't be worth anything. But this patient *did* want me to pray, not only for him but also for his wife.

I knocked on the door of the third room. A Jewish professor from the University of Florida, Samuel Proctor, said, "Come, sit down."

I sat down and we talked. We hit it off just like that.

I felt I had to pray for him, but I didn't know any Jewish prayers. I tried to think of something appropriate when an inspiration came. "Samuel, would you like me to read you a psalm this morning?"

"Yes, I would, Dick."

Now, in several psalms King David's verses start out about loving God and how wonderful He is, when suddenly the poet throws in a line like "Kill your enemies." I wanted to keep my ministry to the sick positive and uplifting, so in the pocket Bible I carried, I had crossed out lines of a negative nature.

As I read to Samuel, I automatically skipped the crossed-out lines. When I finished, I closed the Bible and put it back in my pocket.

Samuel looked up at me, smiled, and said, "Dick, you did very well. Except . . .you didn't read all the psalm."

His words hit me like a bolt of lightning. I said, "Well, Samuel, I've got to confess what I did." I showed him my little Bible, and he laughed.

When I returned to the office, I said to Constance, "You will never believe it. This morning, I've prayed with a Catholic priest, a Baptist, and a Jew, in that order."

She laughed. "How do these things happen with you?"

Samuel and I became good friends. He was hospitalized frequently over the next two years, battling a mysterious virus. I'd visit him three times a week during his stays. He'd ask me to sit down, and we'd talk.

"You need an office over at the University," he said one day.

"I don't need an office."

"Yes, you need an office over there."

After that, we went through that routine every time.

The day before he died, he was pretty sick. His room was filled with family and friends. He asked me to sit by him and made the person in the chair get up. As we talked, I sensed he was near the end, and asked if he wanted a word of prayer.

"If you would, please," he said.

That was the last time I saw him. He died at 3:29 the next morning. Professor Proctor had been the University of Florida's official historian, dean of state history, and founder of the UF Oral History program. Also, I would say, my friend.

* * *

I explained in an earlier chapter that I never had the opportunity to get to know people of other races where I grew up, but as a chaplain, about a third of my patients were African-American and we developed excellent relationships. Many of them would wait after being discharged until I got to their floor because they wanted to give me a hug before they left.

One lady was in and out of the hospital frequently, and I saw her for two years before she died. I'd enter her room, and she'd say, "Come over here and sit down, Dick."

We'd talk. I'd pray for her. Sometimes I'd read scripture to her. But it wasn't until I read her obituary in the newspaper that I learned she had been a minister over a major church plus seven branch churches in Europe. Most people would have mentioned it, I'm sure, but she'd never said a word about it.

I got my own lesson in humility, though. I finished at the hospital about five o'clock one Friday night. As I walked to my car, I encountered a large, overweight woman. She easily weighed 250 pounds or more. "Sir, I need a ride."

My rule had always been to never pick up a woman. I considered it too risky. I asked myself, "What should I do?"

Finally, I said, "I'm truly sorry, but I can't take you." Not for any reason other than I never gave rides to women I didn't know.

She hadn't even told me where she needed to go, just that she needed a ride. But I walked on to my car, got in, and started out of the parking lot.

A voice said to my mind, "Hey, I thought I created you a chaplain. What are you doing?"

I turned around, drove back, opened the door for her. "Come, get in the car. I'll take you where you want to go."

When she climbed in my compact car, she took up nearly all the space.

"I need to go to the bus terminal," she said.

"You mean the one a few blocks up the street?"

"Yes."

When we got there, she said, "I need some money."

Well, I never carry much cash. Maybe a couple of bucks. I looked in my wallet and said, "All I've got is a dollar."

"I need two dollars."

"I'm sorry, I only have one." I handed it to her and she got out.

I left her at the bus terminal and went home.

Monday morning, I started my rounds. When I got to the cardiac floor, in one room was the woman I'd given a ride on Friday. "What are you doing back in here?"

"Oh," she said, "I caught the bus and it stopped right in front of my house. As I got out, I collapsed. Somebody called the ambulance and it brought me here. I'd had a heart attack."

Another miracle, I thought. If I'd let her walk to that bus station, she might have collapsed on the side of the road and never made it.

When she was discharged, she gave me a big hug. And when she gave a big hug, you knew you were hugged.

I am thankful God permitted me this ministry and by His grace made me strong enough. Every day was an adventure, and with each new patient came a wonderful opportunity to share love, compassion, prayer, or scripture. Most times my sessions were one-to-one, but on occasion, there were couples or families as large as six or eight. Each one was special.

I once had a white male patient over one hundred years old who had an African-American young lady as his caregiver. The three of us prayed together during my many visits to him. Then one day, I came as he was in his passing. She had her arm under his pillow and around his shoulder, singing softly, "Jesus loves you. Jesus is your friend. Jesus is waiting." On and on.

She paused and whispered, "Do you want to pray?"

I bent down to her, gave her a hug, and said, "No, your prayer is better than mine. Thank you, and please continue."

Dick Gartee while chaplain at Alachua General Hospital.

Chapter 47
Answered Prayers

In 2004, at my annual physical exam, my doctor recommended that I have a cardiac stress test. I'd had a heart attack fifteen years before, in 1989, and hadn't had a stress test since. I arrived at the cardiac center and they wired me up. I stepped on the treadmill and started walking.

I was doing great.

The technician said, "Is it all right if we increase the elevation?"

"Sure."

He raised the front of the treadmill so I had to walk up an incline. No problem.

"Can I raise it higher?"

"Go ahead." I felt fine.

We finished and the cardiologist studied the results.

"How did I do?" Surely, I must have passed.

Actually, I'd flunked.

"You need a CABG, a coronary artery bypass graft," he said. "Your heart is plugged in two places."

"When can you do the operation?"

"Oh, you can wait a month or two—any reasonable length of time."

"No," I said.

"When do you want it?"

"Do it tomorrow morning. I don't want to wait."

"We can't do it that quickly. Why do you want it so soon?"

"I want you to do it while I'm healthy and strong, not wait until I'm sick and weak."

In less than a week, I was lying in surgical pre-op, ready for surgery. The heart surgeon, Dr. Ken Staples, came to me and said, "We have another patient whose case is critical. You were supposed to be first, but I really need to operate on her first."

"Of course, take her ahead of me," I said.

A while later, the door across the hall stood open. Through it, I could see the woman who was going before me. Suddenly, I felt I should go over and pray with her. My nurse wouldn't let me leave my bed. I explained I was the hospital chaplain, but the nurse was sticking to her rules.

Across the hall, I saw a young woman in street clothes talking with the patient. From the way they interacted I assumed she was the patient's daughter. I pushed the button to call my nurse. "All right, I'll stay here if you will go across the hall and tell that woman's daughter I am the chaplain and would like her to come to my room so we might pray together for her mother's surgery."

The nurse agreed.

The daughter came.

We prayed.

The woman survived. So did I. Our prayers answered.

My first day home, I walked the length of our block and back, whistling a happy tune. That was fourteen years ago.

I thank God every day.

The United States of America

honors the memory of

Richard A. Gartee

This certificate is awarded by a grateful nation in recognition of devoted and selfless consecration to the service of our country in the Armed Forces of the United States.

J. R. Biden, Jr.

President of the United States

The certificate signed by President Joe Biden presented to Dick's family.

Epilogue

On July 21, 2021, at 4:00 p.m., Dick Gartee passed away peacefully at home. His daughter, Sharyl, who was sitting with him, said, "He just stopped breathing." He would have been ninety-six that September.

About ten years earlier, he'd been diagnosed with a condition called Myelodysplastic Syndrome. His hematologist explained that his bone marrow was producing less than an optimal number of blood cells. But, the doctor said, he could probably live to be a hundred. He just needed to recognize that his immune system was sub-par and to avoid people and animals that were sick. That meant giving up his work as chaplain. The prospect saddened him, but he did it.

Then on July 8, 2021, Dick told Flo and Richard he'd been passing blood and needed to go to the ER. The hospital admitted him. Flo's daughter, Debbie, came to stay with Flo. Sharyl and Norman drove from Michigan to be with him. Gastroenterologists performed an endoscopy, found a mass of bleeding blood vessels, and cauterized them with a laser. It didn't hold. He was moved into the intensive care unit (ICU) and given transfusions. A team of surgeons studied his case and said they didn't think surgery was an option. Dick elected to go home.

His funeral service was held on Monday, July 26, 2021 at First United Methodist Church in Gainesville. The next day he was interred at the Veterans Affairs' Florida National Cemetery in Bushnell, Florida.

In Chapter 42, Dick shared copies of letters he'd exchanged with several U.S. Presidents. So, it was both fitting and serendipitous that, at the burial service, a Navy Captain presented the family with one final correspondence from President Joe Biden.

At age ninety, Dick bought a three-wheel bicycle he rode to keep fit.

Author Notes

First and foremost, I thank my father, Richard A. Gartee, for the stories of his life that he shared with my sister and me as we grew up. He remains for us a phenomenal man of widespread talents and interests.

I would also like to thank the members of Writers Alliance of Gainesville who critiqued the book as I was writing it: Susie Baxter, Joan H. Carter, Ann~Marie Magné, Wendy Thornton; my copyeditors: Signe Jorgenson and Erin Wilcox; my proofreaders: Pat Caren and Cindy Elder; and my beta readers: Lee Ann Jones, Melissa Baker, Lee Schwartz, Sharyl Beal, and, of course, Dad, who read the manuscript numerous times.

About the Author

Richard W. Gartee is an award-winning novelist who, in addition to eight novels, has also authored seven college textbooks, six collections of poetry, and four nonfiction books. A complete list of his available titles, upcoming events, and forthcoming books is available at www.gartee.com.

If you enjoyed this book, please take a moment to leave a short review on Amazon and/or other booksellers' websites. Reviews help to sell books, and sales help an author to keep writing. You can readily find links to post reviews by visiting www.gartee.com and clicking on the book cover image. You can also sign up to receive updates on new publications by this author.

A Note from Dick Gartee

No one but my son, the author, could take my rambling conversations, poorly written notes, and sometimes mistaken memories and compile a coordinated biography that both makes sense and is written so my grandchildren, great-grandchildren, and all who follow might know a little about my life, the times to which I was a witness, and in which I participated.

My son, Richard, is a good man who is compassionate, loving, and intelligent with an abundance of patience. I was also blessed with a loving daughter, Sharyl, who lost her mother at a young age but knew her father loved her and was never further away than a phone call.

I would be remiss if I failed to acknowledge that I was also blessed with amazing stepchildren. I came not to replace their father but to be a loving and caring friend.

My prayer:

> Dear Lord, by your love, you blessed me when I was weak and unthoughtful and when I sinned against you and my fellow man. With your Grace, you have blessed each step of my life, not by my achievements, but only by your Grace and steady hand. Thank you, Lord.
>
> Your Servant,
> Dick Gartee

Poems of Dick Gartee

It is said that those who excel in mathematics and engineering are left-brained, while poets and artists are right-brained. I believe this book has shown that my dad uses both the analytical and artistic sides of his brain. In addition to his long industrial career in various engineering positions, he has crafted furniture, created oil paintings, and written songs and poems.

An avid reader, he also kept journals of his travels and wrote papers on his spiritual beliefs and thoughts on other religions. He told me, "My life has been full, positive, and joyful because of the written word, sheets of music, thought-provoking articles, and the Bible."

He expressed to me his desire that readers see his many varied interests and specifically asked me to include fourteen of his poems, which start on the following page.

FIFTY YEARS

Fifty years have come and went
A half of century I have spent
Trying to achieve those many dreams
Including those beyond my means
If age brings forth wisdom in man
I'll need another century on this land.
For the many mistakes, I have made
And each were end to end laid,
They surely would make a long, long line
For fifty years is a very long time.

Fifty years have come and went
God has many blessings sent
Not just the material things of life,
health, and children – and a good wife.
But life is like a marriage, a little give and a little bend
And because I am fifty will not end
So I'll just continue on my way,
enjoying life – day by day.

VALENTINE

Across your path, wings of a dove,
A sign of peace or a sign of love
God created you a special kind
A woman, a man would pray to find
To me you are that little dove
For you have given me both peace and love
A man could search his entire life
And never find a better wife.
My love, wife and special friend too,
All of this I am asking of you
For there can never be a better time
I pray you will be my valentine.

My Son, My Daughter

My son, my daughter is a wonderful phrase,
one I'll cherish all of my days.
A gift entrusted to my care,
more precious than diamonds and
twice as rare.
I thank you for each of the many years,
of joy, laughter, and yes, even the tears.
Thank you for the patience of
my foolish way,
you are my thought. of each and
every day.
So with the advent and the New
Year to come,
I am very proud to say,
this is my daughter and son,
a precious one.

Day Dreams

There sat a lad without a care
with wind ruffling thru his hair
Daydreaming adventures that might be
when he is at least one score and three.
Will he be an enforcer of law
with equal justice for one and all
or a kind of doctor to heal the sick
with a bag of medicine to do the trick?
Perhaps the pilot of a jet
flying faster than anything invented yet.
Maybe a truck driving man
wheeling the big ones across the land.
Son, stop that daydreaming, and come to eat.
How many times must this I repeat!
Oh, there go the dreams slipping away,
But – tomorrow will bring new ones to play.

Shrove Tuesday

By the flickering candle light,
in this holy place tonight.
All hidden by our mask,
of sins committed in the past.

What a sorry lot we are,
We confess, we've slipped so far.
Selfishness and greed, our daily fare
we rush through these without a care.

As we hasten on our way,
we just haven't time to pray.
Or worry about our fellow man,
He doesn't fit into our plan.

But, tonight we gather in thy name,
a prayer from all, the very same.
Forgive us Father of our sin,
Have mercy on us once again.

Bee or People

It seems to me,
that some people are like a bee.
Some that work,
and others that are the drone.
Some who travel,
and others who stay at home.
Some who are easily aroused,
and become very mean.
Others who are loving,
and protect their queen.
Who are you – the worker or the drone?
The foot loose and the traveler,
or the stay at home!
Is the lesson we learned from the bee,
that we are not all the same to be?

Rain

Mud and rain, mud and rain,
every day seems the same
Won't the sun ever shine?
Surely it will, if given time.
If'n it don't, with rain and mud
there'll sure be a hell of a flood.

TRAILER CAMPING

A nickel in my pocket, my trailer hitched behind,
A place to eat and sleep, no worry about the time.

Don't know where I am going, but I can tell you where I've been
I'm not sure if the Lord will let me, that I will pass this way again.

Coffee on the stove and bacon in the pan,
The morning smells of a campground, that stirs the appetite of man

Clean up. Let's get on our way.
So many things to do, not enough hours in the day.

So long, take care, be careful when you drive,
perhaps we'll see each other in another campground when we arrive.

Christmas In The South

Where has the snow gone?
It has gone away.
How will Santa get here with his sleigh?
My child you must worry not.
Santa seldom misses adult or tot.
Always looks after girls and boys,
with fruit, candy, or toys.
Where has the snow gone?
It has melted away.
But Santa with his magic
will be here Christmas day.

Do Not Weep

Why for me, do you weep?
I have gone, my appointment to keep.
No suffering here, so rejoice.
Let there be happiness in your voice.
Tell a joke, sing a song
Do not waste your years
mourning long.
So live, laugh and this promise keep,
Remember me, but do not weep.

Ninety-two Today

Today, I'm ninety-two,
I could just sit and go boo hoo,
Another option is not to sit and be a fool.
Shout with joy in a loud voice,
There is a much better choice.
Thank you God for another day,
By your Grace ninety-three is on the way.
I pledge to use each day,
to be more caring and kinder in every way.
My prayer, give me strength, a loving heart too,
That I might find a better way to serve you.

HAIR

When I was four and had some hair,
my Dad would say, sit on the chair.
Then out came the shears,
clip, clip, clip.
Then those feared hand clippers.
Snip, snip, snip.
Ouch as the clippers pulled my hair,
a little slap, sit still, when in the chair.

A little later in my young life,
the barber said get in the chair,
for two bits, I will cut your hair.
electric clippers buzz, buzz, buzz,
and hair falling everywhere.

As years passed, the barbers would taper my hair,
on sides and neck,
It felt great, for a couple of bucks,
what the heck.

But then one fateful day, I came home and said,
something is wrong, my hair feels long.
She laughed and said, it is o.k. on the side,
but in back on the neck, it is blocked instead.

I went to get a hand mirror,
so I could see.
My eyes must be failing me.
A round spot on the top of my head;
the hair was no longer there.
I'm bald with amazement I cried,
and she laughed at me.
No man ever looks at the back to see.
With your comb and hand a gentle pat,
Leave it alone, just like that.

What has happened to my hair?
As years have come, passing by,
No reason for me to worry why,
the lines in my face deeper too,
my hair is thinner with time,
but it is still all mine.

But, I smile at that old mirror as I look at my hair,
still has a curl or two there.

Thanksgiving

Off on I-75 we did go,
going to St. Pete's Beach you know.
We drove in rain,
but no sleet or snow.

An answer to Pam and Larry's prayers,
in sun shine when arriving there.

Larry was up 4:30 that Thanksgiving morn,
checking the turkey properly cooked,
checking each item, nothing overlooked.

With bowed heads, a feast to be thankful for,
we stuffed ourselves, we could hold no more.

We took a walk for exercise and fresh air,
but received a St. Pete's benefit of exercise, rain shower,
but not a time to linger there.

Can you believe, back to the house for three kinds of pie,
then a nice visit, and good bye.

Our day ended the same,
we arrived home tired and in the rain.
with many memories to share and keep,
until some future date we meet.

The Path We Choose

The path of life has twist, turns, ups and downs,
but we are never alone on the path we seek,
God is with us, his love abounds.
Endless blue and fluffy clouds fill the sky,
limited by the range of the human eye.
God has traveled this path before,
but never has he closed a door.
If Salvation and Eternal life was your choice,
let your heart say I believe with your voice.
Just put your trust and faith in him,
he will be with you always,
from beginning to end.

www.ingramcontent.com/pod-product-compliance
Lightning Source LLC
Chambersburg PA
CBHW051943090426
42741CB00008B/1245

* 9 7 8 0 9 9 0 6 7 6 8 2 9 *